Sectarianism and Renewal in 1920s Romania

Sectarianism and Renewal in 1920s Romania

The Limits of Orthodoxy and Nation-Building

Roland Clark

BLOOMSBURY ACADEMIC
LONDON • NEW YORK • OXFORD • NEW DELHI • SYDNEY

BLOOMSBURY ACADEMIC
Bloomsbury Publishing Plc
50 Bedford Square, London, WC1B 3DP, UK
1385 Broadway, New York, NY 10018, USA
29 Earlsfort Terrace, Dublin 2, Ireland

BLOOMSBURY, BLOOMSBURY ACADEMIC and the Diana logo
are trademarks of Bloomsbury Publishing Plc

First published in Great Britain 2021
This paperback edition published in 2022

Copyright © Roland Clark, 2021

Roland Clark has asserted his right under the Copyright, Designs
and Patents Act, 1988, to be identified as Author of this work.

Cover image: Curtea de Arges Monastery the interior view. Inside attention is
drawn especially by the group of 12 columns representing the 12 Apostles.
The monastery was founded in the reign of Neagoe Basarab between 1512–1517.
(© ralucahphotography.ro/Getty Images)

(CC) 2021 by Roland Clark. This work is licensed under the Creative
Commons CC-BY License.

This work is published open access subject to a Creative Commons Attribution-NonCommercial
3.0 licence (CC BY-NC 3.0, https://creativecommons.org/licenses/by-nc/3.0/). You may re-use,
distribute, reproduce, and adapt this work in any medium for non-commercial purposes,
provided you give attribution to the copyright holder and the publisher and provide a link to
the Creative Commons licence.

Bloomsbury Publishing Plc does not have any control over, or responsibility for, any
third-party websites referred to or in this book. All internet addresses given in this book were correct at
the time of going to press. The author and publisher regret
any inconvenience caused if addresses have changed or sites have ceased
to exist, but can accept no responsibility for any such changes.

Every effort has been made to trace copyright holders and to obtain their permissions
for the use of copyright material. The publisher apologizes for any errors or
omissions and would be grateful if notified of any corrections that should
be incorporated in future reprints or editions of this book.

A catalogue record for this book is available from the British Library.

Library of Congress Cataloging-in-Publication Data
Names: Clark, Roland, author.
Title: Sectarianism and renewal in 1920s Romania : the limits of
Orthodoxy and nation building / Roland Clark.
Description: London ; New York : Bloomsbury Academic, 2021. |
Includes bibliographical references and index.
Identifiers: LCCN 2020035988 (print) | LCCN 2020035989 (ebook) |
ISBN 9781350100954 (hardback) | ISBN 9781350197039 (paperback) |
ISBN 9781350100961 (ebook) | ISBN 9781350100978 (epub)
Subjects: LCSH: Biserica Ortodoxa? Roma^na?–History–20th century. |
Church renewal–Romania–History–20th century. |
Secularism–Romania–History–20th century. | Nationalism–Religious
aspects–Orthodox Eastern Church. | Romania–Religion–20th century.
Classification: LCC BX693 .C59 2021 (print) | LCC BX693 (ebook) |
DDC 281.9/49809042–dc23
LC record available at https://lccn.loc.gov/2020035988
LC ebook record available at https://lccn.loc.gov/2020035989

ISBN:	HB:	978-1-3501-0095-4
	PB:	978-1-3501-9703-9
	ePDF:	978-1-3501-0096-1
	eBook:	978-1-3501-0097-8

Typeset by Integra Software Services Pvt. Ltd.

To find out more about our authors and books visit www.bloomsbury.com
and sign up for our newsletters.

For the peacemakers, for they shall be called children of God.

Contents

Acknowledgements   viii

Introduction   1

Part One   A Modern, National Church

1. Romanian Orthodox Christianity   19
2. Renewal   35
3. A Contested Patriarchate   51

Part Two   Orthodoxy's Others

4. Reaction   77
5. Catholics   87
6. Repenters   101
7. Missionaries   125

Part Three   Renewal Movements

8. The Lord's Army   143
9. The Stork's Nest   169

Conclusion   193

Bibliography   198
Index   219

Acknowledgements

I am deeply indebted to many outstanding people whose generosity, insights and hard work have enriched both the project and myself personally. A number of exceptional studies on church history and religion in inter-war Romania have appeared in recent years, finally making a book of this nature possible. This project has developed in conversation with the members of two scholarly organizations in particular – the Society for Romanian Studies and the Association for the Study of Eastern Christian History and Culture. I have presented this material at conferences run by both organizations over the years, receiving valuable feedback from Scott Kenworthy, Jennifer Spock, Matthew Miller, James Kapaló, Aleksandra Djuri Milovanović, Ryan Voogt, Iemima Ploșcariu, Iuliana Cindrea and Dumitru Lisnic, among others. Ionuț Biliuța, Anca Șincan and Martin Heale read drafts of the entire manuscript and made invaluable suggestions for its improvement.

Emanuel Conțac has generously shared documents with me and commented on earlier versions of Chapter 9, which was originally published in a different form in *Plērōma* under his editorship. Philippe Blasen and James Kapaló have also shared some fascinating resources and discoveries in Romanian archives that I would otherwise never have come across. Thanks also goes to Dumitru Lăcătușu for assisting with the archival research, and to Catherine McManamon, Mary Dixon, Helen Hall and Kathryn Barnes at the University of Liverpool Library, who have spent a great deal of their institution's money locating hard-to-find books for me. In Bucharest, I am grateful to the staff at the Library of the Holy Synod, the Central University Library, the Library of the Romanian Academy, the Romanian National Archives and the Archives at the National Council for the Study of the Securitate Archives. They have tirelessly helped track down materials and generously opened their collections to me. Archives are no longer only held in hard copy these days, and my task would have been much harder without the digitized collections at Moldavica, Publicații Baptiste, OasteaDomnului.info, the digital library of the Alexandru D. Xenopol Arad County Library and the digital library of the 'Lucian Blaga' Central University Library in Cluj.

Finally, an ocean of thanks goes to my wife Laura, my daughter Linda and our parents Geoff, Yvonne and Daniela, for their support, encouragement and patience while this book was being written.

All Biblical quotations are taken from the New Revised Standard Version.

***

Open Access was made possible by the support of the University of Liverpool, UK, and for this both the author and Bloomsbury Academic are deeply grateful.

Introduction

Ruth Rouse, a former Anglican missionary, spent eight days in Bucharest as part of a fact-finding journey through Europe for the World Christian Student Federation at the end of January 1911. She found Romanian attitudes to religion completely foreign and inexplicable according to the criteria of British Protestantism. Rouse noted down some of her observations in a report to the Federation.

> Irreligion prevails amongst the educated. I will not say Agnosticism or Atheism: their irreligion is far too unreasoned and a matter of atmosphere to be classified under one form of unbelief or another. They have simply no interest in religion, no idea that it could possibly have significance for any educated person. Religion is for them dead and gone. Never in any country have I suffered so from the impression that spiritual ideas, however simply expressed, were simply not understood. The church of the country is Orthodox, but can do nothing for educated people. They openly mock at their priests, who are for the most part low-class men, uneducated, sometimes unable to read, often with no form of training for their work except ability to read the services, unpaid, venal, because dependent for their livelihood on fees for religious services, and too often of bad life.
>
> Yet, with all their contempt for their church, the Roumanians have a Chauvinistic dread of foreign influence, and do all they can to make missionary work among them impossible. They are exceedingly suspicious of Roman Catholicism, which has made some progress. They are suspicious also of Protestant effort, though in a less degree. Protestant missions are represented by the Seventh-Day Adventists and Plymouth Brethren. Both have made some progress, though their missionaries are put over the border as soon as they are found at work.
>
> Reform movements within the church scarcely exist. There are, however, some signs of hope. The Roumanian Church possesses one great advantage over all other Orthodox Churches. The services and the Scriptures are read in

the language of the people, not in an incomprehensible Archaic tongue. Some priests are striving after better things ... Some earnest laymen are issuing a little magazine giving very simply religious instruction of a decidedly evangelical kind. It is rather closely modelled on the magazine issued by the Plymouth Brethren, and even reproduces its articles, but it is an Orthodox effort.[1]

Rouse's reports about her visits to Balkan countries were consistently derogatory and her language more than a little racist. She wrote about Serbians, for example, that they had a

fanatical attachment to [the Orthodox Church] as a national institution, combined with open avowed scepticism [sic] and utter contempt for the priests as uneducated and corrupt. But whether from a kind of superstition or a primitive sort of hypocrisy, (the Servians are very primitive in lots of ways) many of them still seem to go through a certain amount of church attendance.[2]

The idea that Serbians went to church when Romanians did not gives us an insight into the reliability of Rouse and other commentators who bemoaned the lack of Romanian religiosity. Serbians were famous in the Balkans for failing to attend church services, and Romania had roughly one parish priest for every 900 people, compared to Serbia's one per 3,000 people.[3] Commentaries about how 'religious' a society is are always in the eye of the observer. Knowing what is going on in someone else's heart and mind when they close their eyes in prayer is impossible when you are standing next to them, let alone when we are talking about entire countries of people who lived a hundred years ago.

Regardless of how accurate Rouse's negative views about Romanian religiosity were, such opinions were consistently reiterated by Romanian writers for the next twenty years. During the late nineteenth century British and American ideas about what constituted 'good' religion came to dominate Romanian public opinion. According to Western criteria, churches were judged based on how many people attended weekly worship services, how much they respected their clergy, how well lay people were able to articulate their beliefs, how fervently people embraced these beliefs (as expressed through their emotional states)

---

[1] Ruth Rouse, Report to the World Student Christian Federation, 'Roumania, 25 January to 2 February 1911', Lambeth Palace Archives, R. T. Davidson Papers, Student Christian Movement, 1905–25, vol. 491, ff. 50–1.

[2] Rouse, 'Serbia, 3–7 February 1911', in ibid., ff. 53–4. On Ruth Rouse, see Ruth Franzén, *Ruth Rouse Among Students: Global, Missiological and Ecumenical Perspectives* (Uppsala: Uppsala University, 2008).

[3] Bojan Aleksov, *Religious Dissent between the Modern and the National: Nazarenes in Hungary and Serbia 1850–1914* (Wiesbaden: Harrassowitz Verlag, 2006), 42 n. 50.

and how strongly religion shaped believers' everyday lives. Grigorie Comșa, a dedicated anti-Protestant evangelist, complained in 1921 that 'in church life we see indifference about indifference. We acknowledge painfully that even some priests are addicted to commerce. No one goes to church anymore; the laws and commandments of the church are ignored. Adultery is becoming widespread; the name of God is mocked, the holy mysteries are trodden underfoot, and sectarianism ravages the land.'[4] The editors of the church magazine *Crucea* (*The Cross*) introduced their first issue in 1923 by stating that 'almost everyone now believes that the Romanian Orthodox Church is incapable of doing its job'.[5] Nicolae Iorga, a well-known atheist, committed nationalist and erudite historian, concluded the second edition of his two-volume *History of the Romanian Churches* (1928) by observing that, at the beginning of the First World War, 'following the destruction of its spirit and purpose by the constant intrusions of the state as [political] parties vied for its control, the Church of the Romanian Kingdom no longer represents that moral force which once constituted its glory'.[6] Rouse and other commentators point to a general dissatisfaction with the Romanian Orthodox Church (ROC) as a social and spiritual institution, coupled with a deep hostility toward foreigners – and towards foreign missionaries in particular. At the same time, they noted that there were efforts by both priests and laypeople to spread 'evangelical' ideas through magazines and newspapers.

Rouse writes that young women in Bucharest welcomed her and were eager to spend time with her. A chance to speak English and to learn about the West was worth the time spent answering the questions of this interesting English woman. Orthodox writers frequently compared themselves to the British when discussing the merits of their own church.[7] An anonymous priest commented in 1909 that 'the [religious] questions that are now being discussed in Romania, the civilized peoples of the West have been discussing for a long time. We have opened our eyes quite late. But at the end of the day it is a good thing that we have opened them at all.'[8] Prominent Orthodox leaders in Bucharest welcomed the increasing dialogue between the Anglican and Romanian Orthodox

---

[4] Gheorghe Comșa, *Istoria predicei la români* (Bucharest: Tipografia Cărtilor Bisericești, 1921), 3.
[5] 'Starea de plâns a Bisericei Ortodocse', *Crucea*, 1 March 1923, 6.
[6] Nicolae Iorga, *Istoria Bisericii Românești și a vieții religioase a românilor*, vol. 2, 2nd edn (Bucharest: Saeculum, 2011), 319.
[7] 'Congresul preoților', *Biserica Ortodoxă Română*, December 1923, 1125.
[8] Un preot de mir, *Chestiuni de discutat* (Pitești: Tipografia Transilvania, 1909), 1.

Churches that began in the early 1920s.⁹ Rouse's interest in 'reform movements', her position at the intersections between Orthodox and Western Christianity, her discussions of lay spirituality and her observations about the Orthodox use of Protestant literature all lie at the heart of this book.

Rouse was not imagining the productive relationship between these religious currents. She visited Archimandrite Iuliu Scriban while she was in Bucharest, who was the director of the Central Theological Seminary in Bucharest. 'He is a remarkable man', Rouse wrote, 'full of both spiritual and intellectual power'.

> He is, perhaps, the only priest in Roumania who has entered the priesthood from a sense of vocation. He is a man of good family and independent means. He studied theology for five years in Germany (1904 to 1907), at Strasbourg and Heidelberg, has a library full of theological books and magazines in five languages, and has travelled in France and Switzerland. He corresponds with friends of his abroad, both Protestant and Catholic. He was a member of the German Student Christian Union all the time he was in Germany, and is now an 'Altfreund der DCSV'. He reads *Die Furche* [*The Furrow*], *Le Semeur* [*The Sower*], *Fide e Vita* [*Faith and Life*] regularly (all Student Movement magazines), cheerfully greeted me by saying he knew all about me, and was just contemplating an article on the Constantinople Conference in a Roumanian newspaper! One felt at once in the completest sympathy with him. He is a man of deep spiritual life and evangelical fervour, and it is glorious that he has the training of young priests in his hands. He longs to see the Federation at work in Roumania. 'Our young people don't understand that the Gospel is the basis for practical life', he said again and again.¹⁰

During the early twentieth century Scriban and a small but influential group of Orthodox leaders set out to 'rejuvenate' the Romanian Orthodox Church. Their efforts coincided with an increased interest in religion and spirituality in both cities and villages.¹¹ Miron (Ilie) Cristea became the Metropolitan-Primate of Greater Romania in December 1919. As metropolitan-primate and then as patriarch, he reorganized the Church, placing it on a new constitutional

---

⁹ Irineu Mihălcescu, 'Relaţiunile dintre Biserică Ortodoxă şi cea Anglicană', *Biserica Ortodoxă Română*, November 1923, 1053. On Anglican attempts at building relationships with Eastern Orthodoxy in the early 1920s, see J. A. Douglas, 'Prospects of Union between the Eastern and Anglican Churches', *The Christian East* 1, no. 1 (1920): 36–46; Bryn Geffert, *Eastern Orthodox and Anglicans: Diplomacy, Theology, and the Politics of Interwar Ecumenism* (Notre Dame: University of Notre Dame Press, 2009), 71–85; and Romanian National Archives (henceforth ANIC), Fond Ministerul de Cultelor şi Artelor (henceforth MCA), Dosar 109/1925, ff. 91–105.

¹⁰ Rouse, 'Roumania', f. 52.

¹¹ George Enache, 'Biserică – societate – naţiune – stat în România interbelică: I. Explorări în orizont liberal', *Revista teologică* 2 (2010): 169–70.

setting, expanding its jurisdiction and presiding over the establishment of new seminaries, libraries, theological faculties, printing presses and newspapers across the country. In the process, he fought to marginalize the Roman and Greek Catholic Churches and oversaw a reform of the liturgical calendar that gave rise to the Old Calendarist (*Stilist*) movement.

Strong regional tensions dominated 1920s Romanian Orthodoxy. Each region approached the challenges of expansion, modernization and spiritual renewal in different ways. The Transylvanian wing of the Church was led by Nicolae Bălan, elected Metropolitan of Transylvania in February 1920. Almost immediately Bălan established *Lumina satelor* (*The Light of the Villages*), a church newspaper dedicated to spreading the Gospel in rural areas, appointing a young priest by the name of Iosif Trifa as its editor. The newspaper soon gave rise to a grassroots lay movement known as the Lord's Army (Oastea Domnului), which brought an evangelical flavour into Orthodox lay practices and was eventually suppressed by Bălan himself. In Oltenia, Vartolomeu Stănescu became Bishop of Râmnicul Noului Severin in March 1920. As bishop he launched his own renewal movement, Rebirth (*Renașterea*), aimed at parish priests, and the magazine *Solidaritatea* (*Solidarity*) to bring theological ideas into the public sphere.[12] His colleagues from Moldavia, such as Gurie Grosu, the Archbishop of Chișinău și Hotin, and Visarion Puiu, the Bishop of Hotin, pursued similar agendas in their preaching and writing while encouraging a specifically Moldavian approach to church governance.

In Bucharest the prolific writer and teacher Irineu Mihălcescu shaped a generation of priests and theologians through his all-encompassing vision of dogmatic theology.[13] One of his colleagues at the University of Bucharest, the Old Testament scholar Ioan Popescu-Mălăești, established a reading circle entitled 'Take and Read' (*Ia și citește*) to encourage both priests and lay people to read Christian literature. Parish priests who had trained under Scriban, Mihălcescu and Popescu-Mălăești began publishing newspapers and preaching fiery sermons encouraging their listeners to repent and to take the spiritual life seriously. Two of them, Teodor Popescu and Dumitru Cornilescu, drew crowds to St Ștefan's Church, colloquially referred to as the Stork's Nest. Their success attracted unwelcome attention from other reforming priests and the two men were driven out of the Church on charges of heresy. Popescu and Cornilescu, their colleagues decided, had gone too far and had somehow become Protestants.

---

[12] Petre Sperlea, *Vartolomeu Stănescu: Episcop al Râmnicului Noului Severin (1921–1938)* (Bucharest: Basilica, 2014).
[13] Ion Vicovan, *Ion Irineu Mihălcescu: 'Apostol al teologiei românești'* (Iași: Trinitas, 2006).

Protestantism has deep historical roots in Transylvania, but less elsewhere in the country. The 1930 census listed 15.5 per cent of the population of Transylvania as Reformed Calvinists and 7.6 per cent as Evangelical Lutherans.[14] Predominately made up of ethnic Hungarians, the Reformed Church dates back to the sixteenth century, when Calvinism spread through the region encouraged by the Edict of Turda (1568) granting freedom of conscience and religion in Transylvania.[15] The Evangelical Lutheran Church emerged among Transylvanian Saxons following Johannes Honterus's publication of a 1542 edition of Martin Luther's writings in Brașov. It adopted the Augsburg Confession in 1572, and remained a predominately Saxon church until 1918, when a separate Evangelical Lutheran Church was established for non-Saxon Lutherans.[16] The majority of Transylvanian Lutherans were liberal Protestants who valued their church as much as a bastion of Saxon culture as for its spirituality, but the incorporation of Lutherans from Bessarabia and Dobruja after the First World War brought Swabian Pietist currents into the church as well. Many Saxons became disillusioned with their church during the inter-war period, just as they were with the Romanian state. Some turned to National Socialism in the early 1930s, much to the chagrin of church leaders who were then placed under significant pressure to ally themselves with German Nazism, which they did by the end of the decade.[17] Neither of these 'historical' churches particularly worried the Orthodox leadership so long as they remained predominantly Hungarian and Saxon and did not try to convert ethnic Romanians.

Protestant 'Repenter' churches, on the other hand, encountered staunch opposition from the Orthodox. Baptists represented the largest of the Repenter denominations. Although they only made up 0.001 per cent of Romania's population in 1920, almost all Orthodox newspapers and magazines mentioned Baptists, Repenters and sectarianism in every issue.[18] Of the roughly 18 million people living in Romania at the time of the 1930 census, 0.3 per cent were

---

[14] Sabin Manuilă, *Recensământul general al populației României din decemvrie 1930*, vol. 2 (Bucharest: Institutul Central de Statistică, 1938), xxiv, xxvii.

[15] Robert Kann, *A History of the Habsburg Empire 1526–1918* (Berkeley: University of California Press, 1977), 104–17.

[16] Oskar Wittstock, *Johannes Honterus, der Siebenbürger Humanist und Reformator: der Mann, das Werk, die Zeit* (Göttingen: Vandenhoeck und Ruprecht, 1970); Ludwig Binder, *Die Kirche der Siebenbürger Sachsen* (Erlangen: Martin Luther Verlag, 1982).

[17] Ulrich Andreas Wien, 'Biserica Evanghelică C.A. din România începând cu anul 1918', in *Un veac frământat. Germanii din România după 1918*, ed. Ottmar Trașcă and Remus Gabriel Anghel (Cluj-Napoca: Institutul pentru Studierea Problemelor Minorităților Naționale, 2018), 201–2, 214–16.

[18] Direcția Generală a Statistice, *Anuarul statistic al României 1922* (Bucharest: Tipografia Curții Regale, 1923), 20.

Baptists, 0.08 per cent were Seventh-Day Adventists and 0.04 per cent were classified as belonging to 'other religions and sects'.[19] Fears about Repenters dominated Orthodox discussions about the meaning and character of Orthodoxy throughout the inter-war period. Baptist churches were established among ethnic Germans in Bucharest and Tulcea during the 1850s and 1860s, respectively, spreading among Saxons and Hungarians in Transylvania during the 1870s. These communities began attracting ethnic Romanians during the 1890s and a flourishing, albeit small, communion of Romanian Baptist churches existed by the turn of the century.[20] Nazarenes, a Protestant group that emphasized adult baptism, pacifism and rejected oath-taking, spread in the Banat from the 1870s onward and in Greater Romania once the Banat was split between Romania and Serbia in 1918.[21] Seventh-Day Adventist missionaries from Poland and Germany arrived in Romania soon after the Baptists, and scores of Adventist communities were well established by the early 1920s.[22] Swiss missionaries established the first Brethren churches (*Creștini după Evanghelie*) in Bucharest in 1901. By the time of the First World War, Brethren communities could be found in Ploiești, Brașov, Sibiu and Bârlad. New churches sprung up in Iași and the surrounding region during the war, and disillusioned Baptists in Maramureș and Bihor formed their own independent churches along Brethren lines.[23] Pentecostal believers could be found in Moldavia from 1908 and spread through the rest of the country during the 1920s, supported by missionaries sent by the Romanian émigré community in Detroit.[24] Bible Students, or Jehovah's Witnesses as they later became known, began preaching in Cluj in 1911 and spread throughout Romania during the inter-war period.[25]

Despite the very real doctrinal and practical differences between Baptists, Brethren, Nazarenes, Pentecostals, Adventists and Bible Students, all became known as 'Repenters' (*Pocăiți*). A pejorative term, Repenter was used to

---

[19] Manuila, *Recensământul*, vol. 2, xxiv.
[20] Alexa Popovici, *Istoria baptiștilor din România* (Oradea: Făclia, 2007), 17–28, 279–82; Dorin Dobrincu, 'Sub puterea Cezarului. O istorie politică a evanghelicilor din România (a doua jumătate a secolului al XIX-lea–1989)', in *Omul evanghelic: O explorare a comunităților protestante românești*, ed. Dorin Dobrincu and Dănuț Mănăstireanu (Iași: Polirom, 2018), 42–64.
[21] Aleksov, *Religious Dissent*, 133–64.
[22] Iemima Ploscariu, 'Pieties of the Nation: Romanian Neo-Protestants in the Interwar Struggle for Religious and National Identity' (MA diss., Central European University, Budapest, 2015), 16–17.
[23] Dobrincu, 'Sub puterea Cezarului', 64–70; Bogdan Emanuel Răduț, 'Comunitatea creștinilor după Evanghelie: 100 ani în Oltenia și 90 ani la Craiova', *Oltenia: Studii, documente, cercetări* 4, no. 2 (2014): 111.
[24] Ciprian Bălăban, *Istoria bisericii penticostale din România (1922-1989): Instituție și harisme* (Oradea: Editura Scriptum: 2016), 15–23.
[25] ANIC, Fond MCA, Dosar 137/1922, f. 64.

differentiate these groups from the 'historical' churches by highlighting their emphasis on repentance from sin, personal conversion, devotion to prayer and personal Bible reading, and rigorous abstinence from things of 'the world' including alcohol, swearing, ostentatious displays of wealth or gluttony and sex outside of marriage. Though they remained committed to their denominational labels first and foremost, most Repenters in the inter-war period embraced the term despite its negative social connotations. As uncomfortable as I am about using a term of abuse as a category of analysis, other labels used are equally problematic. Scholars frequently use 'Evangelical' as a blanket category for Baptists, Brethren or Pentecostals, and, although this has the advantage of accurately defining those groups on their own terms, it excludes Adventists and Jehovah's Witnesses for doctrinal reasons even though they were sociologically quite similar to other Repenters and were all lumped together by Orthodox pundits.[26] Repenters are often called 'neo-Protestants' in contemporary Romania to distinguish them from Reformed and Lutheran Protestants. But this term only became popular after the Second World War and it would be anachronistic to project it back into the inter-war period. Finally, the standard term used by both Orthodox clergy and police was 'Sectarians' (*sectanți*), which implied schism, heresy and intent to destroy the Church. Anyone who was not a member of one of the 'historical' churches was a sectarian in the eyes of the state, but I avoid the word here because of its strong pejorative connotations.[27] The actual number of Repenter churches was small relative to the size of the population, but Orthodox commentators spoke constantly about their sudden appearance and apparent success, making their impact on Orthodox Christianity disproportionate to their numbers. Opposition to Repenters took different forms from one region to another. In Transylvania, groups like the Lord's Army argued explicitly that they were needed to blunt the appeal of Repenters, while Church leaders in Crișana and Bessarabia appointed 'anti-sectarian missionaries' to fight Repenters at a village level. Regional differences sometimes mirrored the actual strength of Repenter movements – Repenter communities were more common in Crișana and Bessarabia than elsewhere in the country, for example – but also reflected the resources and agendas of Orthodox leaders in those areas.

---

[26] Paul E. Michelson, 'The History of Romanian Evangelicals 1918–1989: A Bibliographical Excursus', *Arhiva Moladviae* 9 (2017): 191–234.

[27] Lucian Ionel Mercea, 'The Concept of Sect in the Interwar Period', in *The Holistic Society: Multi-Disciplinary Perspectives*, ed. Ioan-Gheorghe Rotaru and Denise Elaine Burrill (Beltsville, MD: Scientia Moralitas Research Institute, 2017), 192–205.

The institutional reforms of Cristea, Bălan, Stănescu and their colleagues are well documented, as is their militant nationalism, antisemitism and their associations with fascist and right-wing movements such as the National Christian Defense League (Liga Apărării Național Creștine, LANC) and the Legion of the Archangel Michael (Legiunea Arhanghelului Mihail).[28] A growing literature has also emerged in recent years on the history of evangelical groups such as the Baptists, Brethren and Pentecostals. Evangelical historians frequently demonize the Orthodox Church because of its role in suppressing their churches. This book brings histories of Romanian Orthodoxy into conversation with histories of Repenter Christianity, showing how both stories were catalysed by rising literacy rates, new religious practices, new ways of engaging with Scripture, a newly empowered laity inspired by universal male suffrage, a growing civil society that was taking control of community organizing and the sudden expansion of the Romanian nation-state.

Most histories of both Orthodox and Repenter churches focus primarily on the legal and institutional changes that shaped them as organizations. Although I too discuss these questions, this book draws on the sermons, pamphlets, newspapers and magazines they left behind to reveal that behind the mutual hostility and competition lay different approaches to reading the Bible and different ways of developing doctrine. Juxtaposing the thought-worlds of educated Orthodox bishops and self-taught Repenter preachers shows how Christians practised their faith in different social contexts, and gives us a clue to how and why movements like the Lord's Army and the Stork's Nest evolved out of solidly Orthodox settings into communities that looked remarkably like the Repenter movements they had set out to oppose. The picture that emerges is of 1920s Romania as a dynamic and polyphonic religious sphere. Behind the 'us against them' rhetoric lay a collection of diverse religious communities responding to rapid social change in different ways.

The Romanian story has parallels in other Orthodox countries, most notably in late imperial Russia and the Serbian regions of Austria-Hungary. Sergei Zhuk has described the clash between Repenters (he calls them 'peasant evangelicals') and Orthodox Christians as a 'culture war'. 'The paradox of this

---

[28] Hans-Christian Maner, *Multikonfessionalität und neue Staatlichkeit: Orthodoxe, griechisch-katholische und römisch-katholische Kirche in Siebenbürgen und Altrumänien zwischen den Weltkriegen (1918–1940)* (Stuttgart: Franz Steiner Verlag, 2008); Florian Kührer-Wielach, *Siebenbürgen ohne Siebenbürger?: Zentralstaatliche Integration und politischer Regionalismus nach dem Ersten Weltkrieg* (Munich: De Gruyter Oldenbourg, 2014).

confrontation', he writes, 'was that the roots of the peasants' radical religion were in popular Orthodoxy itself. To some extent, the peasant evangelicals tried to be more rigorous and pious Orthodox believers than their less religious and more cynical neighbors. They constructed their religion by appropriating the available and well-known elements of Orthodoxy'.[29] Rather than one borrowing from the other, other historians have suggested that both Repenter and Orthodox groups were responding to a complex nexus of historical changes. Heather Coleman emphasizes that the rise of Repenter Christianity was a symptom as well as a cause of a broad sea change in how previously marginalized people engaged with civil society and the state. 'Contemporary observers from all across the political spectrum', she says, 'regarded the Baptists' presence and activities as emblematic of the penetration of Western ideas beyond the educated elite, the challenge of the emergence of a culture outside the boundaries of the society promoted by the state and its church, and the increasingly articulate demands of lower-class people for a voice and a role in shaping that culture'.[30] The unique historical context that catalysed the spread of the Baptists also impacted the Orthodox Church, which is why combating Protestantism was as much about negotiating the limits of Orthodoxy as it was about stopping 'foreign influences' spreading through the country. As Vera Shevzov has argued, when the Orthodox spoke about other Christians they did so in an attempt to clarify tensions within their own church.[31] Moreover, the process of limiting Repenter evangelism involved 'radical innovations' such as appointing anti-Sectarian missionaries, as well as bringing some characteristically Protestant spiritual practices into the Orthodox Church.[32] Whereas most historians of Russian religion have focused on the Orthodox versus Repenter struggle, the reform movements of 1920s Romania such as the Lord's Army and the Stork's Nest provide an opportunity to see the same social tensions that threw the Orthodox Church into conflict with Repenters at work inside the Orthodox Church itself. Such movements are examples of what James Kapaló calls 'liminal Orthodoxy' – forms of Orthodox Christianity

---

[29] Sergei I. Zhuk, *Russia's Lost Reformation: Peasants, Millenialism, and Radical Sects in Southern Russia and Ukraine, 1830–1917* (Washington, DC: Woodrow Wilson Center Press, 2004), 3.

[30] Heather J. Coleman, *Russian Baptists and Spiritual Revolution, 1905–1929* (Bloomington: Indiana University Press, 2005), 3.

[31] Vera Shevzov, *Russian Orthodoxy on the Eve of Revolution* (Oxford: Oxford University Press, 2004), 14.

[32] J. Eugene Clay, 'Orthodox Missionaries and "Orthodox Heretics" in Russia, 1886–1917', in *Of Religion and Empire: Missions, Conversion, and Tolerance in Tsarist Russia*, ed. Robert P. Geraci and Michael Khodarkovsky (Ithaca: Cornell University Press, 2001), 40.

suspended between Orthodoxy and other religious traditions; bitterly critical of the established Church while still tenaciously clinging to it.[33]

The leaders of both of the Lord's Army and the Stork's Nest were eventually driven out of their ministries by the ROC hierarchy, and their fate reflects a deep mistrust of innovation as well as shedding light on the development of Orthodoxy in the twentieth century. Orthodoxy teaches that the full truth was revealed in Jesus Christ and that the fundamental structures of church organization were created by the Apostles, but that the truth also resides in the whole Church as the body of Christ, including all believers, living and dead. Tradition, or *parádosis* in Greek, is encapsulated in the actions and teachings of the Church in the past and the present. It acts as a guide for believers.[34] In his 1922 *Manual for Biblical Hermeneutics*, Iuliu Scriban explained that 'the Church has the duty to use the entire store of faith and piety produced by Christians hearts, and to preserve it for the future. We therefore need to listen to the Church when it comes to explaining or to guiding our faith and piety.'[35] Antonie Plămădeală, who served as Metropolitan of Ardeal between 1982 and 2005, writes that Tradition 'has a certain elasticity' and must be 'constantly adapted to the environment, mentality, and culture of the times, and even to each individual, with a great deal of consideration and generosity'.[36] It is the prerogative of one's spiritual elder to interpret Tradition, however, whether they be a priest, an abbot, a bishop or a patriarch. One cannot simply decide for oneself how to apply Tradition to one's own circumstances.

The fear that well-meaning reformers may have gone beyond Tradition has resulted in a deep-seated wariness of renewal movements within Eastern Orthodoxy. In Russia, the Holy Synod initially forbade the Grand Duchess Elizabeth Feodorovna's attempt to establish a semi-monastic community known as the Martha and Mary House of Mercy in 1909. They were concerned about the fact that the sisters' vows were only for set periods, that they were known as deaconesses, their uniforms, the fact that they ate meat and that the women could work outside of the community. Feodorovna was only able to put

---

[33] James A. Kapaló, *Inochentism and Orthodox Christianity: Religious Dissent in the Russian and Romanian Borderlands* (London: Routledge, 2019), x.

[34] John Meyendorff, *Byzantine Theology: Historical Trends and Doctrinal Themes*, 2nd edn (New York: Fordham University Press, 1983), 8–11; Theodore G. Stylianopoulos, 'Scripture and Tradition in the Church', in *The Cambridge Companion to Orthodox Christian Theology*, ed. Mary B. Cunningham and Elizabeth Theokritoff (Cambridge: Cambridge University Press, 2008), 21–34.

[35] Iuliu Scriban, *Manual de ermeneutică biblică pentru învățătura clasei VII a seminariilor teologice*. 2nd edn (Bucharest: Editura Cassei Școalelor, 1922), 109.

[36] Antonie Plămădeală, *Tradiție și libertate în spiritualitatea ortodoxă* (Bucharest: Sophia, 2010), 59–60.

her movement on its feet thanks to the direct intervention of the tsar.[37] At the same time that Feodorovna was wrestling with the Holy Synod, the Russian Orthodox Church was taking steps to suppress the Teetotaller (*trezvenniki*) movement led by a lay preacher known as 'Brother Ioann' Churikov. Page Herrlinger writes that, in addition to condemning alcohol, Brother Ioann taught 'the importance of actively embracing Scripture, living a clean lifestyle (free from swearing, drinking, stealing, and causing physical harm to others), and committing oneself to the pursuit of honest labour'.[38] His detractors complained that the joy his followers found after repenting of their sins was 'un-Orthodox', that healthy living was too 'mundane' a goal for Christian spirituality and that Teetotallers revered Brother Ioann while being openly critical of the Orthodox Church. Conflicts such as these show how quickly tensions could develop when individuals or groups developed new spiritual practices independent of those who had the institutional authority to interpret Tradition.

In Serbia, a movement known as the God Worshippers emerged at the end of the nineteenth century. In the words of one priest in 1922,

> They said they wanted to improve and be better, to go along the right path, as they could not watch and listen to the disorder and talking in church. They wanted to improve themselves in terms of order and devotion, to wash away sins, to move in the right direction, to stand still in the church and to listen to God's service with understanding, and to serve others as a beautiful example and become like their ancestors, once true and devout Christians.[39]

Despised by other Orthodox Christians, treated with suspicion by the police and persecuted when they joined the military, God Worshippers were nonetheless not cast out of the Church. Instead, Patriarch Dimitrije attempted to bring them under church control and advised his priests to 'refrain from throwing stones at them because you could hit Christ'.[40]

In Greece, the Holy Synod investigated the parachurch organization Zoe for heresy twice, in 1914 and 1923, only to acquit it both times. The origins of

---

[37] Paul Ladouceur, '"In My Father's House There are Many Mansions" (Jn 14:2): New Institutions in Modern Orthodox Spirituality', *St Vladimir's Theological Quarterly* 55, no. 4 (2011): 447–56.

[38] Page Herrlinger, 'Orthodoxy and the Politics of Emotion in the Case of "Brother Ioann" Churikov and His Followers, 1910–1914', in *Orthodox Paradoxes: Heterogeneities and Complexities in Contemporary Russian Orthodoxy*, ed. Katya Tolstaya (Leiden: Brill, 2014), 196.

[39] Quoted in Radmila Radić and Aleksandra Djurić Milovanović, 'The God Worshipper Movement in Serbian Society in the Twentieth Century: Emergence, Development, and Structures', in *Orthodox Christian Renewal Movements in Eastern Europe*, ed. Aleksandra Djurić Milovanović and Radmila Radić (Cham: Palgrave Macmillan, 2017), 138–9.

[40] Quoted in ibid., 146.

Zoe lay in a community established by Apostolos Makrakis in 1876, which ran Sunday schools for children, philosophical lectures and sermons for adults and published its own magazine, *Logos*. The 'Logos School' was closed down by the Greek government in 1878 after Makrakis attacked the Holy Synod for failing to defrock and excommunicate bishops who had obtained their offices through bribery; a practice known as simony. In 1907 one of Makrakis's collaborators, the Archimandrite Eusebios Matthopoulos, created Zoe. Matthopoulos and his followers took vows of chastity, poverty and obedience, but not as monks, and carried out an extensive programme of preaching aimed at educating lay people about Orthodoxy. The first issue of their newspaper declared that 'with the help of divine grace, our goal is to contribute to the revival of religious feeling and to bring people back to the original form of the Christian life'.[41] The organization expanded dramatically after 1927, when Archimandrite Seraphim Papakostas took over as leader and began opening hundreds of catechetical schools for young people across the country. Under his leadership Zoe formed specific branches dedicated specifically to students, women, scientists, workers, teachers and nurses. Despite, or perhaps because of, its popular success, the Church's hierarchy remained aloof and hesitant of embracing an organization that they did not have direct control over.[42]

The one exception to ecclesiastical mistrust of parachurch organizations during this period occurred in Bulgaria, where the Holy Synod established the White Cross fraternity in 1923, followed by the Union of the Christian Orthodox Fraternities a year later. The *Christiyanka* magazine provided a mouthpiece for both women's movements, which flourished during the 1920s and then came to an end with the rise of the Bulgarian Communist Party after the Second World War. The White Cross defined its goal as being 'to support the mission of the people's Orthodox Church by contributing to and developing the expression of Christian mercy and religious and moral education through the service of its sisters'.[43] *Christiyanka* elaborated on the role of these groups, stating that its members

---

[41] Quoted in Pandora Dimanopoulou, 'L'oeuvre de la propagation de la foi et de la morale chrétienne dans la société grecque: L'action de la Confrérie Zôè en Grèce, 1907-1938', *Revue d'Histoire Ecclésiastique* 105, no. 1 (2010): 121–46.

[42] Ibid., 121–46; Ladouceur, 'In My Father's House', 441–7; Christos Yannaras, *Orthodoxy and the West* (Brookline, MA: Holy Cross Orthodox Press, 2006), 217–350; Amaryllis Logotheti, 'The Brotherhood of Theologians: Zoe and Its Influence on Twentieth-Century Greece', in *Orthodox Christian Renewal Movements in Eastern Europe*, ed. Aleksandra Djurić Milovanović and Radmila Radić (Cham: Palgrave Macmillan, 2017), 285–302.

[43] Galina Goncharova, 'The Bulgarian Orthodox Charity Network and the Movement for Practical Christianity After World War I', in *Orthodox Christian Renewal Movements in Eastern Europe*, ed. Aleksandra Djurić Milovanović and Radmila Radić (Cham: Palgrave Macmillan, 2017), 309–10.

'should be bearers of its ideas, workers of the White Cross, missionaries for the restoration of harmony between faith and life, Samaritans relieving the sadness and pain of neighbours ... builders of a living vigorous Christianity, deaconesses in the renovated and regenerated native church'.[44] Newspapers and magazines played a central role in almost all of the early twentieth-century Orthodox renewal movements. Most also emerged out of complaints that the Church was not doing its job properly, was not sufficiently 'alive', and the conviction that the solution lay in dedicated, voluntary social engagement outside of existing church structures, whether that be through preaching, charity or education.

Western Christianity – especially Anglicanism – frequently served as the standard by which reformers and leaders of parachurch movements judged Orthodoxy. As George Demacopoloulos and Aristotle Papanikolaou point out, during the twentieth century the concept of the West 'functioned as an absolute marker of difference from what is considered to be the essence of Orthodoxy, and, thus, ironically, has become a constitutive aspect of the modern Orthodox self'.[45] The logical starting point for grasping twentieth-century Orthodoxy, therefore, is to examine how it engaged with Protestantism and renewal movements on its own soil. Doing so promises to facilitate a more authentic encounter of I and Thou, as well as helping generate more fruitful reflection on where the limits of Orthodoxy really lie. A historical approach, moreover, avoids beginning with an interrogation of whether the Other is a wolf in sheep's clothing. Instead, it observes how the various strands of Christianity became entangled with one another in a time of complex social change.

Part One explores the historical context of the 1920s in which new ecclesial structures, Repenter Chrisitanities, and liminal Orthodoxies developed. Chapter 1 traces changes in preaching and catechal practices at grassroots levels, showing what lived religion looked like in Romanian villages and flagging the quiet sea changes produced by attempts to explain the Church's teachings to its followers. Turning to the cities, Chapter 2 looks at the influence of Western Christianities on renewal movements such as Vartolomeu Stănescu's Social Christianity and the Christian student movement associated with the YMCA. The stakes were more obvious and Western influences more explicit in places like Bucharest. Here Church leaders were quick to intervene whenever they believed that something was amiss. Chapter 3 unpacks the regional tensions produced by the unification

---

[44] Ibid., 309.
[45] George E. Demacopoulos and Aristotle Papanikolaou, 'Orthodox Naming of the Other: A Postcolonial Approach', in *Orthodox Constructions of the West*, ed. George E. Demacopoulos and Aristotle Papanikolaou (New York: Fordham University Press, 2013), 2.

of separate Orthodox Churches into a single Romanian Orthodox Church. Those regions that came under the authority of the Romanian patriarchate during the 1920s had been ruled by different empires, nation-states and church bodies in the years before the First World War. Each approached the new church with its own ambitions and past experiences, making the process of church-building one that was fraught with difficulties. Dissatisfaction with the new patriarchate becomes apparent in Chapter 4, which focuses on two liminal movements in Moldavia and Bessarabia: Inochentism and Old Calendarism. The appearance, character and fates of these movements shows how disaffected many Orthodox believers were with the state of their church and the decisions being made by their leaders. Both movements were harshly suppressed by the Church and the state, a campaign which revealed how deeply intertwined the interests of the Church and the nation-state actually were.

Part Two focuses on Romanian Orthodoxy's relationship with its Others. Chapter 5 looks at Orthodox hostility towards Roman and Greek Catholics during the 1920s. Focusing specifically on the Concordat of 1927, it reveals the political and economic stakes in this conflict and the impact that the conflict had on the character of Orthodoxy. Chapter 6 discusses the major Repenter denominations – Baptists, Brethren, Nazarenes, Pentecostals, Seventh-Day Adventists and Bible Students, or Jehovah's Witnesses. It explores their origins inside and outside Romania, as well as showing how both believers and critics understood their beliefs and practices. Chapter 7 focuses on the fiercest opponents of Repenter Christianity, anti-Sectarian missionaries. Through a close reading of missionary books and pamphlets, it discusses how missionaries cultivated a modern, rigorous and clearly articulated approach to Orthodoxy in their attempts to combat Repenters.

Finally, Part Three explores two parachurch movements: the Lord's Army in Transylvania and the Stork's Nest in Bucharest. As exemplars of liminal Orthodoxy, the doctrinal and practical disagreements that dominated these movements' histories shed light on what had actually changed in the religious landscape of 1920s Romania and why Orthodox leaders opposed it so bitterly. Renewed lay interest in holy living, new approaches to the Bible, regional power struggles, dissatisfaction with the institutional Church, fears about Repenters and Western influences all lay at the heart of the conflicts over the Lord's Army and the Stork's Nest. How these conflicts were resolved and what their consequences were for the future of Romanian Christianity are questions that this book seeks to shed some light on.

Part One

A Modern, National Church

1

Romanian Orthodox Christianity

Romania was a predominantly rural country during the inter-war period. Peasants both made up the majority of the population and personified the Romanian national ideal for secular and church intellectuals. Engaging with peasant beliefs and practices thus became a priority for ethnographers and church leaders in the early twentieth century. In a book on *The Culture of our Villages*, Bishop Grigorie Comșa reflected a confident belief that Orthodoxy was inextricably bound up with a pure and unchanging rural existence. He wrote:

> The belief that there is a God who directs the world is rooted deep in the soul of our peasant, and nothing can take this belief away from him. For centuries the peasant has been used to his Christian church being at the centre of his life. The village church was the fountain of goodness from which the whole village drank. The church was the embodiment of faith, and in the church the peasant felt that he was in the house of God. Everything changed and passed away in time, but the church remained. And here in the church the peasants gathered, calling to the Saviour just as the Apostles did: 'Lord, have mercy for we are perishing'.
>
> It is well known that for many ages reading and writing have been taught in the modest Romanian schools next to monasteries and churches. Children took turns reading from the Psalms, the Horologion,[1] the Octoechos,[2] and the Apostol.[3] The Gospel was thoughtfully listened to. The contents of the holy books became cultural artefacts in the soul of the people. And thus our people in the villages placed the fear of God above the fear of evil. Our people fears God's punishment more than the laws of men. For centuries, this fear of God has preserved out people's proverbial nobility and goodness.[4]

---

[1] The Book of Hours.
[2] A liturgical book.
[3] A collection of readings from the New Testament.
[4] Grigorie Gh. Comșa, *Cultura satelor noastre* (Arad: Tiparul Tipografiei Diecezane, 1935), 80–1.

Romanian peasants apparently knew God intuitively, and if they lived sinful lives it was because of Western modernity, with its many temptations and impious ideas.[5] But ethnographic fieldwork conducted by students in inter-war Romania suggested that even if they loved the church, not everyone knew a great deal about theology. Elderly peasants interviewed by students from their own villages demonstrated a remarkable ignorance about even apparently well-known Bible stories. When asked how the world was created, for example, Anca Fieraru, a 68-year-old woman from Pieleşti in Dolj county, recalled that

> The land was created by God following the water. In the beginning there was only water everywhere, and the land was under the water. To build it he had to push the water back; a very difficult task. To see how much the water went down each time, God sent out different animals which, finding various objects, did not return. Then God sent out a hedgehog which [was the] only [animal who] brought back an answer. As a reward God gave it spikes so that no-one would eat it and so that it too could have a holiday, which is on Tuesday, when you shouldn't begin something new.[6]

Other sociologists and ethnographers of the early twentieth century recorded similar accounts. Few of them combined as many discordant elements as Fieraru's version of creation but all surprised their collectors by how significantly they diverged from the cosmologies of the educated elites.[7] Inter-war ethnographers sought out the most elderly informants and recorded only the most remarkable beliefs they could find, but their reports should nonetheless have raised concerns about how orthodox most of the population was.

Young people had more chances to learn what the Church wanted them to thanks to the expanding school system. School textbooks from before the First World War presented fables such as 'the boy who cried wolf' alongside Bible stories and lessons for students to memorize on topics such as 'who should perform a baptism?', 'what should godparents be like?' and 'what should Christians do before receiving the Eucharist?'.[8] They used a question and

---

[5] Irineu Mihălcescu, *Cauzele necredinţei contimporane şi mijloacele de a-o combate* (Bucharest: Tipografia cărţilor bisericeşti, 1915).

[6] 'Folklor in Dolj' (unpublished MS, Biblioteca Centrală Universitară – Litere), A60.238.

[7] G. F. Ciauşanu, G. Fira and C. M. Popescu, *Culegere de folclor din jud. Vâlcea şi împrejurimi* (Bucharest: Cultură Naţională, 1928); Aurel Cosma, *Cosmogonia poporului român* (Bucharest: Tipografia Ziarului Universul, 1942); Ion I. Ionică, *Drăguş: Un sat din ţara Oltului (Făgăraş)* (Bucharest: Institutul de Ştiinţe Sociale al României, 1944); Ion Cherciu, *Spiritualitate tradiţională românească în epoca interbelică* (Bucharest: Muzeul Naţional al Satului 'Dimitrie Gusti', 2010).

[8] Al. Popescu-Cernica, *Catechismul religiunei creştine ortodoxe conform cu programa analitică în us şi însoţit de povestiri şi istorióre morale şi evangelice pentru usul clasei IV urbană şi V rurală* (Bucharest: Lito-Tipografia Motzatzeanu şi Lambru, 1896).

answer format, often supporting each lesson with a Bible verse. Moise Toma's catechism, for example, taught:

> *How can one gain a good reputation?*
> Someone earns *a good reputation* with good behaviour and good deeds. Solomon the wise spoke about a good reputation: 'A *good name is to be chosen rather than great riches and favour is better than silver or gold.*' (Proverbs 22:1)
>
> *How should we seek happiness?*
> We should look for *happiness* in spiritual riches and pleasures and in good deeds. The Saviour says: *'Blessed are those who hear the word of God and obey it!'* (Luke 11:28).[9]

By the inter-war period lessons for primary school students were bookended by prayers when entering or leaving the classroom, and textbooks were illustrated with icons and snippets of poetry. Students were told Bible stories in simple language, then had their significance explained in more detail.[10] The curriculum for secondary schools stated that, during their two hours of religious education per week, in their first year students should learn basic Old Testament stories such as the creation of the world, the Flood, the Tower of Babel, the kings David and Solomon and the Babylonian captivity. In the second year they studied Jesus's life and parables as presented in the gospels. They learned about Orthodox liturgy in the third year, including the history of the liturgy, ritual books, priestly garments, church music and the liturgical calendar. The fourth year was dedicated to theological concepts such as the existence of God, the Trinity, life after death, the Virgin Mary and sacraments such as baptisms or weddings. Church history occupied the fifth and sixth years, dogmatics the seventh year and Christian morality the eighth.[11]

Teachers struggled with how to transfer these lessons into everyday life. It was at moments of loss such as funerals, they said, or when priests were able to *practice* the faith together with students, that effective education happened.[12] As the future patriarch Nicodim Munteanu argued, once Christians learned *what* to believe they had to change the way they lived. His advice was 'to love the Lord your God with all your soul and all your thoughts, desires, and actions, living

---

[9] Moise Toma, *Catehism pentru învățământul religiunei dreptcredincioase-răsăritene în școalele primare* (Nagyszeben: Tiparul Tipografiei Arhidecezane, 1912), 10.
[10] Irineu Mihălcescu and Petru Barbu, *Carte de religie pentru clasa III-a primară* (n.p.: Editura Librăriei Pavel Suru, n.d.); Aristide C. Cucu, *Carte de religie pentru clasa IV-a primară* (n.p.: Editura Autorului, 1938).
[11] ANIC, Fond Ministerul Instrucțiunii, Fond 310/1923, ff. 238–42.
[12] Dumitru Călugăr, 'Treptele formale și învățământul religios', *Revista teologică* 28, no. 4 (April 1938): 140–9.

in a way that pleases him.'[13] Munteanu suggested believers try to remember that everything they had came from God, that God saw all their thoughts and actions, that God sends both blessings and trials to help them grow, and that they must remain submitted to the Church in all things. Practices he recommended included frequent prayer, regular confession, Bible reading, disciplining one's thoughts and avoiding luxury or lethargy.

School was not the only, or even the most important, place that people learned about religion. As the anthropologist Vlad Naumescu notes, most believers experience Eastern Orthodoxy first and foremost as 'ritual participation … through authorized practice and collective worship'. One 'masters' Orthodoxy by growing into the faith from childhood, and taking part in the sacraments over a long period of time has a transformative impact on the self.[14] Naumescu sees this as an organic process that takes place within the family and is guided by the parish priest. In this vein, the majority of early twentieth-century catechisms focused on very practical issues such as how to visit a monastery and what to do when one goes to church.[15]

One of the most accessible of these books was a dialogue written by the priest and teacher Ștefan Călinescu in 1904. The hero is Moș Dragne, a wise peasant over a hundred years old who constantly asks his priests and cantors to explain his religion to him. Over the course of the book Moș Dragne learns that every aspect of Orthodox practice is significant. 'Why do all churches face east?' asks Moș Dragne. 'Churches are built that way so that we will look east, towards the place where Jesus Christ was born', his priest answers. 'Towards the light, just as the grass does when it bends towards the rising sun.'[16] 'Why does the cloth on the altar look like it does?' asks Moș Dragne. 'The shine of the cloth reflects the shining throne of Jesus Christ in heaven', his priest replies. 'Everything is covered, even the leg, so that no one who is not ordained touches it. For not only the *holy relics* and *incenses* are placed there, but so is the *great and holy myrrh* which no-one should touch unless they are being anointed with it.'[17] 'Truly the mysteries of

---

[13] Nicodim Munteanu, *Ce să crezi și cum să trăești? Adică schema credinței și moralei creștine* (Bucharest: Albert Baer, 1905), 17.

[14] Vlad Naumescu, 'Becoming Orthodox: The Mystery and Mastery of a Christian Tradition', in *Praying with the Senses: Contemporary Orthodox Christian Spirituality in Practice*, ed. Sonja Luehrmann (Bloomington, IN: Indiana University Press, 2018), 31–2.

[15] Ioan Mihălcescu, *Explicarea Sfintei Liturghii* (Bucharest: Institutul de Arte Grafice Carol Göbl, 1917); Damian Stănoiu, *Cum se vizitează o mănăstire* (Bucharest: Tipografiile Convorbiri Literare, 1923); Al. Săndulescu, *Mergerea la biserică* (Buzău: Tipografia M. Mracek, 1941); Florea Codreanu, *Cunoștiințe liturgice* (Arad: Editura Diecezană, 1945).

[16] Ștefan Călinescu, *Dialog între Moș Dragne și Logofătul Stoica Călinénu explicând întregul organism liturgic* (Bucharest: Tipografia Gutenberg, 1904), 11.

[17] Ibid., 15.

God are great and wonderful!' exclaims Moş Dragne once everything has been explained. 'May God teach these divine truths to everyone; that every soul might lift itself up towards divine things and understand the power of God and the *gift of the anointed [priests]*.'[18]

Symbolism is particularly strong in Orthodox worship. Trying to explain 'mysticism in the Eastern Church' to Western readers, the Serbian theologian Nikolaj Velimirović commented that everything in the natural world can be a symbol or a sign of spiritual realities. In the words of Symeon the New Theologian, 'the man who is enlightened by the Holy Spirit ... contemplates spiritually visible things and bodies as the symbols of the things invisible'.[19] Thus someone who washes themselves in baptism 'becomes clean, just like they had been born again', and a chandelier (*policandrul*) hanging in the centre of the church directly under an icon of Jesus holding everything in his hands (the *Pantocrator* icon) can symbolize the fact that God cares for and sustains all light in the world.[20]

Icons adorn every Orthodox church in the world and are 'a way of exteriorizing an external feeling'.[21] Apologists for icons argued that they have existed since the time of Christ, citing the tradition that a woman wiped Jesus's face on his way to be crucified, leaving an image of his face on the cloth. Icons portray stories from the Bible as well as moments from the lives of saints, who mediate between believers and God just as one might ask a holy person to pray for them. Particularly important churches also housed the relics of saints, which were venerated in the same way as icons. These were primarily medieval Romanian saints associated with particular cities such as Parascheva of Iaşi, Filofteia of Argeş, John the New of Suceava and Dimitrie the New (Basarabov), the patron saint of Bucharest.[22]

Protestants claimed that Orthodox Christians worshipped icons as idols, but Orthodox writers reminded them that there is a significant difference between 'worship' – which is due to God alone – and 'veneration' – which should be given to icons and holy people. Moreover, they insisted, 'when we venerate and bow to the icons we are not bowing before the paint or the wood, but to the saints

---

[18] Ibid., 145.
[19] Quoted in Nicholai D. Velimirovich, *The Universe as Symbols and Signs: As Essay on Mysticism in the Eastern Church* (Libertyville, IL: St Sava Monastery, 1950), 2.
[20] Călinescu, *Dialog între Moş Dragne*, 20, 26. See also Laurenţiu Streza, 'Liturgical Space', in *Orthodox Theology in the 20th Century and Early 21st Century: A Romanian Orthodox Perspective*, ed. Viorel Ioniţă (Bucharest: Basilica, 2013), 591–603.
[21] Const P. Beldie, *Cultul sfintelor icoane* (Bârlad: Tipografia N. Chiriac, 1937), 3.
[22] Ioanichie Bălan, *Sfintele moaşte din România* (Roman: Editura Episcopiei Romanului, 1999), 5–6.

who are portrayed in the icons'.[23] The veneration of icons followed a particular pattern which constituted polite behaviour in church. The priest Alexandru Săndulescu explained that

> One bows twice, kisses the icon, bows a third time, then moves on. The believer goes first to the icon of the Saviour, then to the icon of the Mother of God, to the icon on the left of the Saviour, to the icon on the right of the Mother of God, to the icon on the iconostasis and then goes to their place. If the Holy Gospel has been placed on the tetrapod in the middle of the church, the believer kisses the Holy Gospel after they have kissed the icon on the iconostasis then goes to their place.[24]

Antonie Luțcan reflected that by 'viewing the face of the saint we are praying to, even our physical eyes take part in the prayer, making it, in the words of Scripture, "face to face" (Exodus 33:11)'.[25]

The Bible also plays an important role in Orthodox worship. The Gospel is placed at the centre of the room during church services, sections of the Bible are read out loud as part of the liturgy, Biblical scenes are represented on icons and the prayers incorporate many Bible verses and references. But the idea that lay believers would read the Bible for themselves was a relatively new one as rising literacy rates prompted a growing desire for Bible reading across the country.[26] Priests taught that explaining Scripture puts believers 'in connection with the divine spirit itself' and encouraged lay Bible reading because 'God revealed his teachings and his holy will to all people, regardless of nation, sex, social standing, or age'.[27] At the same time, however, they warned that interpreting the Bible is not easy. Iuliu Scriban wrote that only someone with adequate moral and intellectual abilities and training was able to properly understand the Bible. Even then, it could not be done by an individual but only in accordance with the teachings of the whole church.[28] Biblical interpretation, insisted inter-war textbooks, was a *scientific* endeavour that required a deep knowledge of historical context, archaeology, philology and spiritual insight.[29]

---

[23] Ibid., 12.
[24] Săndulescu, *Mergerea la biserică*, 10.
[25] Antonie Luțcan, *Cuvinte de îndrumare* (Jud. Soroca: Editura Monăstirei Dobrușa, 1926), 16.
[26] Vasile Vasilache, *Biblia în ortodoxie* (Neamț: Tipografia Sfintei Mănăstiri Neamțu, 1939), 6–11.
[27] Ibid., 95, 115.
[28] Scriban, *Manual de ermeneutică biblică*, 18–22, 151–3.
[29] Ibid.; Iustin Suciu, *Ermeneutica biblică sau știința interpretării Sfintei Scripturi* (Arad: Editura Autorului, 1933).

Worship was and is a particularly sensory experience in Eastern Orthodoxy. Antonie Luțcan wrote that 'seeing the holy icons, illuminated by candles, the candlesticks full of light, the ceiling of the church reflecting the vault of the heavens, we are easily overcome by the humble thought that God is near and easily our lips mouth the words of the prayer'.[30] In addition to the visual stimulation of the icon, the aroma of incense and the physical sensations of crossing oneself and of standing still for long periods of time, choral singing became common at large religious gatherings from the late nineteenth century onwards, combining polyphonic Western harmonies with traditional Orthodox chant.[31] Musicians such as Gavril Muzicescu, Nicolae Lungu and Ioan Chirescu created new harmonies that brought religious music back to the attention of the Romanian public.[32] In the preface to a songbook assembled by the director of the patriarchal choir, Eugen Bărbulescu wrote that 'when it rises in the careful harmony of talented voices, religious music transforms the entire prayer time, joining it with the *supreme being*, to whom you give yourself completely'.[33]

Prayer in Eastern Orthodoxy can be chanted or recited, out loud or silent. Believers are encouraged to pray in their own words but most make use of prayer books. Books with prayers to be prayed together during worship services usually contained musical notation alongside the words. Like corporate singing, praying together allowed believers to express particularly strong emotions, knowing that their feelings were echoed by others. Quoting Teophan the Monk, for example, Bishop Andrei Magieru pointed out that 'the Paraklesis of the Mother of the God is a call for help to the Virgin Mary "which is sung with complete disgust at oneself and at times of need"'.[34] Repentance and contrition feature heavily in Orthodox prayers. Most of the prayers collected by the monk Nicodim in 1799 and used throughout Romania contrasted the absolute holiness of God – 'He who is unknowable in being, incomprehensible in greatness, and whose goodness is immeasurable; the deep and untold fount of power and wisdom' – with the abject sinfulness of man, who is 'not worthy to speak, for I am very sinful'.[35] This

---

[30] Luțcan, *Cuvinte de îndrumare*, 9.
[31] Stelian Ionașcu, 'Chanting in the Romanian Orthodox Church in a Pan-Orthodox Context', in *Orthodox Theology in the 20th Century and Early 21st Century: A Romanian Orthodox Perspective*, ed. Viorel Ioniță (Bucharest: Basilica, 2013), 859–67.
[32] Jim Samson, *Music in the Balkans* (Leiden: Brill, 2013), 150.
[33] Eugen Bărbulescu, 'Prefață', in *Zece cântece religioase*, ed. G. Cucu (Bucharest: Editura Proprie, 1928), 3.
[34] Andrei Magieru, *Acatistul Domnului nostru Iisus Hristos și Paraclisul Preasfintei Născătoarei de Dumnezeu* (Arad: Diecezana, 1940), 3.
[35] *Rugăciunile Sfinților Părinți sau Apanthisma* (Bucharest: Cartea Orthodoxă, 2007), 129–30.

contrast allowed believers to reflect on the amazing mercy that God shows by not destroying them but instead giving them salvation and eternal life.

It was the parish priest who mediated God's mercies to believers, and his role expanded significantly during the early twentieth century. In the mid-nineteenth century priests were expected to do four things: (i) to teach the people; (ii) to live holy lives; (iii) to administer the sacraments; and (iv) to pray for the people.[36] As the population increased and levels of education rose, the expectations placed on priests rose with them. Ștefan Călinescu reflected in 1908 that 'things which were tolerated and passed over in the past can no longer be tolerated today. Everything is changing in the world, and we change with it'.[37] In addition to administering the sacraments and running church services, Călinescu said that

> The priest should actively direct all activity for the better. He should encourage the inhabitants of rural areas to build good, healthy houses, to manage their businesses well so that their lives might be made easier and they might preserve their energy for things that must be done. He must be a guide in economic matters so that no one lacks anything or is forced to rely on the charity of others. He should instruct people to send their children to school so that foreigners no longer think of us as a country of blind people. He should be a devoted supporter of the popular banks so that the people might escape from usurers who wring out even the marrow from the bones of those who are suffering. He should set a wise example in improving the cultivation of the soil so that everyone's productivity might increase.[38]

Priests argued that they played an irreplaceable role in ensuring social progress. They called for people to support their efforts because, working together with parents and teachers, they were the ones responsible for guiding the next generation to maturity.[39]

The number of monks and nuns, on the other hand, decreased significantly during the second half of the nineteenth century in part because the secularization of monastic estates deprived them of important financial resources.[40] The spiritual life of the monasteries also suffered to the extent that Epicaria Moiescu complained that 'today's monasteries do not reflect their calling in any way'.[41]

---

[36] *Datoriile preoților*, trans. C. Mavrula [1852] (Bucharest: Editura Bizantină, 2011), 27.
[37] St Călinescu, *Povățuitor în activitatea pastorală a preotului* (Bucharest: Tipografia Gutenberg, 1908), 3.
[38] Ibid., 7.
[39] Florea Codreanu, *Sămânța de lângă cale* (Arad: Tiparul Tipografiei Diecezane, 1929).
[40] Mihai Săsăujan, 'Țara românească și Moldova', in *Monahismul ortodox românesc: Istorie, contribuții și repertorizare* (Bucharest: Editura Basilica, 2014), 615.
[41] Epiharia Moisescu, *O chestie de interes moral* (Bucharest: Minerva, 1910), 4.

Monastic properties from the new territories were nationalized during the land reforms of 1921 just as those in the Old Kingdom had been sixty years earlier, although monasteries in Bessarabia remained more active than those in the Old Kingdom thanks to the patronage of Metropolitan Gurie Grosu.[42] Nonetheless, his successor, Metropolitan Visarion Puiu, argued that inter-war monasticism 'is in the most concerning stages of decomposition. Totally lacking in spiritual models, writings that show its necessity and the need for its reorganization, and leaders who can put these things into practice, the trunk of monasticism is drying out, the leaves wither, the roots weaken, and its entire appearance is pitiful.'[43]

Preaching became an increasingly common practice during the early twentieth century as priests began writing their own sermons instead of reading from published collections of homilies. Romanian Orthodox writers connected to the magazine *Predicatorul* (*The Preacher*) had vigorously promoted preaching during the late 1850s, but the enthusiasm surrounding preaching and the number of publications on the topic that appeared after 1900 was unprecedented.[44] Scores of books appeared exhorting priests to preach regular sermons on Sunday mornings and it became common for individuals to publish collections of sermons for particular audiences.[45] Prominent preachers began delivering sermons on the radio, taking their message directly into people's homes.[46] Sermons were not always high quality, as many priests were discovering the sermon as a genre for the first time. As Dumitru Buzatu noted in 1933, preaching is easier said than done and empty churches were a sign that priests needed time and training if they were going to become better preachers.[47]

---

[42] Eugen Onicov, 'Viața monastică din Basarabia îni cadrul României Mare (1918–1940)', in *Monahismul ortodox românesc: Istorie, contribuții și repertorizare* (Bucharest: Editura Basilica, 2014), 867–71.

[43] Visarion Puiu, *Monahismul ortodox din România de astazi* (Chișinău: Tipografia Uniunii Clericilor Ortodocși din Basarabia, 1936), 1. See also Visarion Puiu, *Glas în pustie: Îmbunătățiri bisericești întârziate* (Chișinău: Tipografia Eparhiala 'Cartea Românească', 1931), 123.

[44] Comșa, *Istoria predicei la români*, 171ff.; Teleanu Bogdan Aurel, *Metaforă și misiune: Valorificarea literaturii laice în predica românească* (Iași: Doxologia, 2007).

[45] On the importance of preaching, see Coman Vasilescu, *Datoria preotului de a predica învățătura creștină* (Bucharest,: Tipografia Cărților Bisericești, 1900); Constantin Nazarie, *Călăuza predicatorului* (Bucharest: Tipografia Cărților Bisericești, 1902); Alexandru Popescu-Cernica, *Predica și foloasele ei* (Bucharest: Institutul de Arte Grafice Universala, I. Ionescu, 1911). For examples of collected sermons, see Grofșoreanu, *Scrieri pentru popor*; A. Cristea, *Colecțiune de predici populare* (Bucharest: Tipografia 'Speranța', 1907); Luțcan, *Cuvinte de îndrumare*.

[46] Toma Chiricuță, Gh. Comana, Marin C. Ionescu and Manea S. Popescu, *Chemări de departe: predici la radio* (Bucharest: Editura Librariei Pavel Suru, 1929); 'Faptele proaspete din viață bisericească', *Luminătorul*, February 1937, 117–18.

[47] D. Buzatu, 'Predicatorii', *Calendarul*, 2 October 1933, 3.

The sermons of the future patriarch, Miron Cristea, reveal a strong emphasis on morality and good deeds. The image that comes through in Cristea's sermons is of a jealous and vengeful God who punishes wrongdoers but rewards the righteous. When floods devastated the Banat in 1910, he distributed a circular saying that

> I have arrived at the conclusion that the warnings of the prophet Ezekiel have come upon the inhabitants of this region: '*I ... bring up the deep over you, and the great waters cover you*'. (26:19) Considering this unhappy event in cold blood brought to mind the thought that our Heavenly Father has disciplined us for our sins and errors. He had to, for in this way he revealed his anger at those who have forgotten and ignored his stories, as Jesus the son of Sirah tells us: '*And the Lord will show his mighty voice, so as to let his anger be seen in his outstretched arm ... with thunder, hail, and heavy rain*'.
>
> (30:30)[48]

At the same time, Cristea consistently portrayed Romanians as an oppressed people suffering at the hands of foreign rulers. He compared them to 'a flower, a noble plant, or a useful vegetable planted in uncared for and uncultivated ground, choked by hidden weeds that are killing it'.[49] Only Jesus's commandments could save them from their condition: 'Without [God's teachings] life is a trial and the future is a riddle (enigma) that we cannot unravel; a mystery that we cannot penetrate. But the law of Christ brings us light and shows us the way to happiness in this world and eternal joy in the next.'[50]

Ștefan Călinescu, a respected teacher and priest in Bucharest, wrote that parish priests should 'find time to speak, in particular, to the lost, showing them the evil they do to themselves, to their families and to the society they live in'. He gave a long list of topics that preachers should focus on which provides an insight into Orthodox preaching of the period. Călinescu said that sermons should ensure that lay people might not only know how to recite:

1) The symbol of the faith, but to understand it properly;
2) To explain the ten commandments;
3) The commandments of the church;

---

[48] Episcopal circular, 1910, ANIC, Fond Miron Cristea, Dosar 1902/1, f. 25. The quote from Sirah 30:30 is entirely fictitious. No such verse exists in the Bible.

[49] Elie Cristea, 'Cuvântare la Asociațiuni pentru literature română și cultura poporului roman la 12/25 Mai 1902', in ANIC, Fond Miron Cristea, Dosar 1902/1, f. 3.

[50] Miron Cristea, 'Circulară', 6 December 1910, in ANIC, Fond Miron Cristea, Dosar 1902/1, f. 92.

4) An understanding of the *Our Father* prayer, which every Christian should be able to recite piously;
5) To explain the parables in the gospels, which contain the most beautiful examples of those morals necessary for life;
6) To explain the church service and the mysteries of Orthodoxy;
7) To explain the Gospel and the Apostle and the holy days of the year;
8) To speak about the duties of husbands and wives in a family or a marriage;
9) About raising children;
10) About the duty of care that every citizen has to educate and guide their children towards the right occupation;
11) About the ties of goodness and brotherly love between citizens;
12) About love of country, or patriotism;
13) About the duty to respect the laws of the country and to submit ourselves to the authorities of the country and the church for the good public ordering of the state;
14) About the health of the body, which can be injured by poor housing, bad food or illnesses that come from dirtiness or are transmitted from person to person;
15) About the health of the soul, which is darkened by bad habits, cravings and drunkenness;
16) About helping poor widows and orphans who have nowhere to lay their heads, no help in sickness and loneliness or who beg on the streets;
17) About decorating the town with useful plants;
18) About respecting your neighbour's life and property, for this is why we come together in communities;
19) About the duty to avoid strangers and foreigners who spread unsettling ideas among the children of the Romanian people;
20) About forming community groups for helping homeless orphans and the sick.[51]

In the 1921 *History of Preaching in Romania*, Grigore Comşa critically assessed the best published collections of sermons available. Many of the sermons he discussed were translations from the Church Fathers, but a number were by talented preachers experimenting with the sermon as a new genre. Comşa was not always impressed. Describing Coman Vasilescu's collection of sermons from 1902, he commented that 'in some sermons he talks about a topic without going

---

[51] Călinescu, *Povăţuitor în activitatea pastorala*, 14–16.

into it in any depth … Some sermons lack life; they are missing any practical and unifying aspect'. He noted that Visarion Puiu's sermons were written 'in urban church language' even though they had originally been published in a magazine for peasants. Puiu rarely quoted Scripture, Comșa said, and focused on topics such as 'love of the church, education, submission to authorities, theft, drunkenness, slander, Christian love, fasting, prayer, etc.'. Ilie Teodorescu's sermons, on the other hand, were mostly exercises in explaining church doctrine. Teodorescu quoted frequently from the Bible but lacked any stories to help his listeners connect what he was saying to real life. Comșa consistently praised Iuliu Scriban's preaching, noting that 'we find a clear analysis of different virtues in every sermon' and showing that Scriban always chose his topics based on the appropriate dates on the church calendar.[52]

Other manuals on preaching developed the sermon from different angles. In *Heart and Soul: Homiletics of our Times* (1927), Marin Ionescu argued that priests should master secular knowledge so that they could be convincing from the pulpit. In another book he suggested that preaching served the same function as the liturgy, which is to say that it should elevate the mind.[53] Grigore Cristescu argued that the preacher must be a psychologist and establish a spiritual connection with his audience if he wanted to win them over.[54] Cristescu's sermons focused on relating the Bible to problems of modern life. In a book from 1927 he promised to

> Present the Saviour in various social positions so that we understand how to become his disciples according to our function in life. Like in a movie, we will see him as a worksite supervisor, a businessman, a bank director, a theatre director, a teacher, a judge, a military general, a lawyer, a doctor, a politician, a journalist, a prison director, a university student, a society president, an editor and a librarian.[55]

Similarly, the Old Testament scholar Ion V. Georgescu wondered

> what chaos would the words of the prophet [Isaiah] produce today if he spoke to the priests of Christ's church in our country? If today's life required

---

[52] Comșa, *Istoria predicei la români*, 193–201.
[53] Marin Ionescu, *Inimă și suflet: Omiletica vremurilor noastre* (Bucharest, 1927) and Marin Ionescu, *Altarul și amvonul* (Bucharest, 1942), quoted in Vasile Gordon and Silviu Tudose, 'The Development of Pastoral Studies: Homiletics, Catechetics and Pastoral Theology', in *Orthodox Theology in the 20th Century and Early 21st Century: A Romanian Orthodox Perspective*, ed. Viorel Ioniță (Bucharest: Basilica, 2013), 781.
[54] Grigore Cristescu, *Predică și cateheză* (Sibiu, 1929), quoted in ibid., 781–2.
[55] Grigore Cristescu, *Isus în viață modernă* (Sibiu: Tiparul Tipografiei Arhidiecezane, 1927), 5.

sacrifice and a spirit of sacrifice from everyone; if the priests were called to transform society? 'Depart from the world and sacrifice everything; by descending into the world some of you *might* change some of what you have destroyed!'[56]

Successful preaching required a sound knowledge of the Bible, which not all priests had. Romanian dogmatic theology of the early twentieth century relied heavily on translated lectures by Russian and Greek theologians with a strong scholastic bent, and no Romanian moral theology to speak of had yet been written.[57] In 1924 the New Testament professor and future metropolitan Nicolae Colan commented that 'the West continually asks us for doctrinal books of our orthodoxy. We do not have them and we do not miss them. The faith of the first seven Ecumenical Councils is enough for us.'[58] The attitude of Colan's colleagues was already changing before the ink was cold on his article. The most positive thing Iuliu Scriban could find to say about Romanian theological publishing was that students now had access to some textbooks of questionable quality and a commentary that covered most of the New Testament.[59] According to Gala Galaction, the state of learning was so dismal that 'in all of Romania there are probably only ten or fifteen theologians who know Orthodox doctrine'.[60] Teodor Păcescu agreed, noting that, because of the poor state of education, 'the seminarian and the theology student learns the religious sciences for his exams, not for himself (*nu pentru conștiința sa*)', and consequently few priests really knew much about their own religion.[61] Such complaints were not unique to Orthodoxy. Greek Catholic writers similarly bemoaned 'the almost complete lack of textbooks for our theological seminaries' in the early 1920s.[62]

---

[56] Georgescu was referring specifically to Isaiah 52:11. Ion V. Georgescu, *Actualitatea profeților* (Bucharest: Tiparul Academic, 1934), 28.

[57] Ștefan Buchiu and Cristinel Ioja, 'The Development of Dogmatic Studies', in *Orthodox Theology in the 20th Century and Early 21st Century: A Romanian Orthodox Perspective*, ed. Viorel Ioniță (Bucharest: Basilica, 2013), 396; Nichifor Crainic, *Zile albe - zile negre: memorii* (Bucharest: Casa Editorială Gândirea, 1991), 93.

[58] Nicolae Colan, 'Ortodoxie și esența ei', *Revista Teologică*, 14, no. 2-3 (1924): 61, quoted in Ionuț Biliuță, 'Periphery as Center? The Fate of the Transylvanian Orthodox Church in the Romanian Patriarchy', in *Discourse and Counter-Discourse in Cultural and Intellectual History*, ed. Carmen Andraș and Cornel Sigmirean (Sibiu: Astra Museum, 2014), 386.

[59] Iuliu Scriban, *Studiul pastoralei în biserica românească* (Sibiu: Tiparul Tipografiei Arhidiecezane, 1924), 6.

[60] Gala Galaction, *Jurnal*, vol. 3 (Bucharest: Editura Albatros, 1999), 164.

[61] Teodor P. Păcescu, 'Propaganda neo-protestantă', *Noua revistă bisericească*, 1 January 1924, 244.

[62] I. Volbură, 'Chestiunea manualelor teologice', *Cultura creștină* 9, no. 1-2 (1920): 52.

Orthodox Biblical Studies in the nineteenth century was heavily reliant on Catholic writings, but this began to change after the First World War.[63] Only two of the twelve works Iuliu Scriban listed in the bibliography to his 1922 textbook on Biblical hermeneutics were by Orthodox writers. One was by an American Methodist, another by a Reformed theologian from Germany and the other eight were Roman Catholic scholars from continental Europe. All reflected the latest developments in the field.[64] A new generation of Romanian Orthodox Biblical scholars came into its own in the 1920s, including Vasile Tarnavschi (OT) and Vasile Gheorghiu (NT) at Cernowitz, Nicolae Colan (NT) at Sibiu and Haralambie Rovența (OT) and Ion Popescu-Mălăiești (NT) at Bucharest.[65] The 'neo-Patristic turn' to the Church Fathers took place during the 1930s through the work of theologians such as Dumitru Stăniloae and Vladimir Lossky, but Romanian theologians had already begun to appreciate the value of the Church Fathers as they found them presented in Russian textbooks of the late nineteenth century.[66] Not everyone was happy with the new direction Romanian theological education was taking. Once again critics accused the reformers of introducing Western ideas. The priest, archivist and politician Ștefan Meteș wrote that theological education was now being

> Delivered in the seminaries by lay professors who learned their culture from Protestant universities in Germany. The professors and students from the German and English Protestant theological faculties are a true catastrophe for our church. Their souls and minds are disorderly, anarchic; they understand nothing about how it is here and instead of consolidating the church, they destroy and undermine it. The teaching in Catholic seminaries, where they learn fanaticism and religious discipline loses us students who pass over to the law of Rome.[67]

---

[63] Vasile Mihoc, 'The Development of the Biblical Studies', in *Orthodox Theology in the 20th Century and Early 21st Century: A Romanian Orthodox Perspective*, ed. Viorel Ioniță (Bucharest: Basilica, 2013), 189.

[64] Scriban, *Manual de ermeneutică biblică*, 4–5.

[65] Mihoc, 'Development of the Biblical Studies', 190–3.

[66] Adrian Marinescu, 'Patrology and Related Studies in Orthodoxy in the 20th Century and Early 21st Century: Schools and Research Directions', in *Orthodox Theology in the 20th Century and Early 21st Century: A Romanian Orthodox Perspective*, ed. Viorel Ioniță (Bucharest: Basilica, 2013), 333–8.

[67] Ștefan Meteș, 'Câteva observații critice asupra Bisericii Românești în cei din urmă zece ani', *Societatea de mâine* 5, no. 22–4 (1928): 406, quoted in Florian Kührer-Wielach, 'Orthodoxer Jesuitismus, katholischer Mystizismus: Konfessionalismus in Rumänien nach dem Ersten Weltkrieg', in *Orthodoxa Confessio?: Konfessionsbildung, Konfessionalisierung und ihre Folgen in der östlichen Christenheit*, ed. Mihai-D. Grigore and Florian Kührer-Wielach (Göttingen: Vandenhoeck & Ruprecht, 2018), 321.

Ironically, most of the leading Orthodox voices in inter-war Romania had all been schooled in Western theological faculties abroad. Miron Cristea earned his doctorate in Budapest, Nicolae Bălan and Gala Galaction studied at the Franz-Josephs-University in Czernowitz, Vartolomeu Stănescu learned Catholic and Protestant theology alongside law and sociology at the Sorbonne in Paris, Irineu Mihălcescu studied in Berlin and Leipzig, Iuliu Scriban in Strasbourg and Heidelberg, and Ioan Popescu-Mălăești in Strasbourg. Among the prominent reforming hierarchs of the inter-war period, only Gurie Grosu and Visarion Puiu had studied in an Orthodox country, which was to say, in Kiev. No matter how often Orthodox leaders complained that Repenters were bringing Western ideas into their Church, *they* were the ones whose theology had been profoundly shaped by Western learning. Not only had they personally studied in Western universities, they also quoted Protestant and Catholic writers in their own works and encouraged the translation of Western Christian texts into Romanian. At the same time, Orthodox priests and bishops alike cherished an Orthodox, Romanian spirituality centred on the liturgy, the eucharist and the sacraments of the Church.

2

Renewal

Responding to repeated complaints about apathy and irreligion of Romanian Orthodox believers, a number of Church leaders engaged in concerted campaigns to renew the interest of parish priests and lay Christians alike in attending church services, reading the Bible and cultivating holy living. One of the most outspoken pro-revival church publications of the early 1920s was *Noua revistă bisericească* (*The New Church Magazine*). Established in Bucharest during March 1919, *Noua revistă bisericească* was owned and edited by Teodor P. Păcescu, a priest who had earned his diploma with a study on whether or not the Bible was divinely inspired.[1] Its editorial board included several distinguished theologians and church leaders. 'Our Orthodoxy is passing through a deep crisis of understanding, method, and action', Păcescu wrote in one issue. 'Everything in our Orthodox church needs to be reestablished on the ancient foundations of Orthodoxy and rejuvenated in today's struggle to shape and govern Orthodox Christian identity (*conștiința creștină ortodoxă*)'.[2] Păcescu and the other contributors to *Noua revistă bisericească* wanted a revived Orthodoxy characterized by piety, good works, a passion for the study of the Bible and an enthusiasm for spreading the gospel.[3] Revival was a Protestant concept, however, and had been the standard Protestant solution to religious indifference since the Great Awakening of the eighteenth century. At first preachers had thought of revivals as spontaneous, divine movements of the Holy Spirit, but by the nineteenth century churchmen had begun organizing them and scheduling them into the liturgical calendar.[4] Orthodox leaders were aware of the Protestant

---

[1] Teodor P. Păcescu, *Inspirația cărților sfintei scripturi: Teză pentru licență* (Bucharest: Tipografia Speranța, 1907).
[2] T. P. Păcescu, 'Noui noștri episcopi', *Noua revistă bisericească*, 1 May 1923, 33.
[3] P., 'Cum înțelege biserica unită intensificarea apostolatului în parohii?' *Noua revistă bisericească*, 1 May 1923, 61.
[4] Janice Holmes, *Religious Revivals in Britain and Ireland, 1859–1905* (Dublin: Irish Academic Press, 2000), 168–9.

connotations that talk about revival had, and Păcescu counselled that 'all these efforts need to be directed, guided and defined lest we pass beyond Orthodox dogma in our desire to evangelize and unexpectedly find ourselves in the camp of the sectarians'.[5]

Despite their small numbers, Repenters featured heavily in discussions about Romanian religiosity. The priest Gheorghe Sălcescu wondered why he saw 'a breathtaking fanaticism' among 'heretics' such as Baptists, Brethren and Seventh-Day Adventists, who are willing 'to suffer beatings, (military) prison, insults' and who take their Bibles to church 'to follow the sermon with interest', while among the Orthodox there was only 'indifference'. The average Orthodox believer, Sălescu wrote, 'swears about his own faith, fights with his brothers from the village and lives a life devoid of holiness, almost without faith'.[6] Păcescu and his colleagues attributed the rapid spread of Repenter Christianity to the Romanian Orthodox Church's (ROC's) failure to satisfy the widespread desire for a renewed spiritual life. He wrote, 'the need for repentance and spiritual rebirth, for religious activism, for an interiorization of the Christian faith, for consistency between words and actions, cannot be satisfied by mechanically carrying out church rituals. The sectarians profited from this spiritual moment and attacked'.[7] If it was to survive, they said, the ROC needed to begin evangelizing more heavily. In the words of Petre Chirică, 'it is a painful fact, but we have to admit that so far the Church has remained silent. The Gospel has not been preached with zeal that it might serve the will of Jesus Christ. Its servants have focused on other domains, they have served zealously, but they have done no evangelistic work'.[8] Orthodox leaders decided that if they wished to remain competitive in the twentieth century they would have to begin preaching, distributing literature, expounding Scripture and developing intentional communities of pious believers whose holiness and commitment rivalled that of the Repenters.

Attempts at renewing the Church began shortly before the First World War. Regular congresses for priests and deacons in the Old Kingdom began in 1910, which included discussions on how to run church services, how to confront social problems and how to minister to young people. One writer recommended that 'the giving of blessed icons to school children is a powerful way of attracting

---

[5] Teodor P. Păcescu, *Noua revistă bisericească*, 1 January 1922, 1.
[6] Gh. Sălescu, 'Fanatism şi indiferentism', *Noua revistă bisericească*, 1 May 1923, 36–7.
[7] Teodor P. Păcescu, *Noua revistă bisericească*, July 1930, 1.
[8] Petru Chirică, 'Diferite soiuri de evanghelizare', *Noua revistă bisericească*, 1 April 1922, 6–7.

their attention to sacred history. Coloured icons are preferred to uncoloured ones because they stimulate much more the imagination and the happiest feelings.'⁹ The Church threw itself into printing church newspapers and establishing parish libraries, and George Ursul writes that

> By 1909, 3,032 village parishes [in the Old Kingdom] had libraries, mostly with 150 volumes or less; the 398 city parishes surveyed in 1919 revealed holdings of 500–2,000 volumes, some of them housed in their own buildings and providing facilities for lectures and conferences. By 1920 as the result of an active church press and the parish library movement, 123 societies of a religious and cultural nature had been established and were conducted by priests.¹⁰

There was a general consensus in the early 1920s that renewal was coming. The poet Dimitrie Nanu wrote that 'the breeze of a spiritual springtime has begun to blow here and there: Father Gala Galaction, speaking from various pulpits with his skill and vast erudition, Father Nicolai Popescu at the Măgureanu Hermitage church, Father [Toma] Chiricuță in Botoșani, Father Ion Petrescu at the St. Visarion church, Simion Mehedinți in pamphlets, Mihail Sadoveanu through his most recent writings …'.¹¹ Galaction, Popescu, Chiricuță and Petrescu were all dynamic preachers at prominent churches with exceptional clerical careers ahead of them, while Mehedinți and Sadoveanu were, among other things, leading figures in the literary world. Toma Chiricuță moved to Bucharest later in the decade, where he began popular prayer evenings.¹² As Grigore Cristescu argued, prayer was central to religious renewal. 'Orthodox contemplation is not sterile and static', he wrote. 'It is essentially an infinitely creative dynamism. The contemplative Christian is the most active Christian. The most heroic. He is, completely, an earthly angel and a heavenly man.'¹³ Hesychast prayer had been central to the monastic revivals of the eighteenth century. It was cultivated in the Burning Bush movement of the 1940s but was largely missing from efforts at reform during the 1920s.¹⁴

---

⁹ Quoted in George R. Ursul, 'From Political Freedom to Religious Independence: The Romanian Orthodox Church, 1877–1925', in *Romania Between East and West: Historical Essays in Memory of Constantin C. Giurescu*, ed. Stephen Fischer-Galati, Radu Florescu and George Ursul (Boulder: East European Monographs, 1982), 232.
¹⁰ Ibid., 233.
¹¹ D. Nanu, *Iisus vă cheamă* (Bucharest: Atelierele Adeverul, 1923), 8.
¹² Grigorie Comșa, *Ființa și necesitatea misionarismului* (Arad: Tiparul Tipografiei Diecezane, 1932), 21.
¹³ Grigorie Cristescu, 'Înapoi la Molitfelnic', *Predania*, 15 February 1937, 7.
¹⁴ Serafim, *Isihasmul: Tradiție și cultură românească* (Bucharest: Editura Anastasia, 1994).

Social Christianity

In addition to seeking to inspire greater lay participation in the church, clerical writers began arguing that the ROC should engage more deeply with contemporary social problems. 'The Kingdom of God', that is, 'must start to reign on the earth as it does in heaven'.[15] The leading exponent of Social Christianity was Vartolomeu Stănescu, Bishop of Râmnicului Noului Severin. Stănescu was a passionate advocate of religious reform, arguing that 'to keep [the church] as we have it now, for old women, for people about to be married and for a few sick people who still believe in the power of faith, would mean to replace the Gospel with the Horologion, that is, with the sort of strict ritualism that was around in pagan times as well'.[16] Stănescu's vision involved changing what clergy did day to day. He said that the church 'must start to come down from the abstract heights that it had to climb in the days when it formed its dogmas and, without giving up its teachings, spend its energies more in social work to pull the simple multitudes out of the moral and material misery in which they suffer in our individualistic times'.[17] As a reaction against secular liberalism and the separation of church and state, Social Christianity taught that the church must engage with society in new ways that took secular modernity into account. This was an ideology that treated not just individuals but society as a whole as a being 'with its own body, soul, and rules of life'; insisting that morality was social as well as individual and that Christianity must move beyond teaching dogma into practical action.[18] Initially a reactionary theocratic movement led by French Catholics, it was enriched by the influence of Christian Socialists such as Charles Kingsley and Frederick Denison Maurice and expressed most powerfully in documents such as Pope Leo XIII's encyclical 'On Capital and Labor', *Rerum Novarum*.[19] Gala Galaction championed the idea of Christian Socialism in Romania through his journalism and stories such as *Roxana*, in which a socialist priest uses the resources of his

---

[15] Varolomeu Stănescu, *Scurte încercări de creștinism social*, reproduced in Vartolomeu Stănescu, *Puterile sociale ale creștinismului: Opere alese* (Cluj-Napoca: Eikon, 2014), 173.

[16] C., 'În jurul alegerii mitropolitului primat. Convorbire cu P. S. Arhiereul Vartolomeiu Băcăoanul', *Dacia* 2, no. 27 (1920): 1, quoted in Cătălin Raiu, *Democrație și statolatrie: Creștinismul social la Bartolomeu Stănescu, Episcopul Râmnicului Noului Severin (1875-1954)* (Bucharest: Editura Universității din București, 2014), 101.

[17] Stănescu, *Scurte încercări*, in Stănescu, *Puterile sociale*, 179-80.

[18] Ibid., 178.

[19] Cătălin Raiu, *Democrație și statolatrie: Creștinismul social la Bartolomeu Stănescu, Episcopul Râmnicului Noului Severin (1875-1954)* (Bucharest: Editura Universității din București, 2014), 29-70.

parish to help the poor.[20] Galaction's Christian Socialism did not gain many followers but Stănescu's position as bishop meant that he could enshrine Social Christianity in a number of his episcopal initiatives.

Stănescu argued that

> Social Christianity is simply about introducing an equitable regime into the social body of the state, and of all human collectivities and institutions, which guarantees people of all classes an impetus to work, payment for their efforts, personal independence and moral prestige. Public offices and their corresponding salaries are organic elements of the social body and they should be organized equitably within this body; not in an arbitrary manner, but in line with the gospel morality of Christ the Saviour in a just system that dignifies.[21]

Stănescu's Social Christianity aimed at social reform through religious regeneration. It resonated strongly with clerical calls for renewal while also being able to frame itself as both anti-communist and anti-capitalist.[22]

In 1920 Stănescu established the Solidarity Social Christian Study Circle, together with prominent Orthodox thinkers such as Vasile Ispir and Ștefan Ionescu. In an attempt to articulate the problem that the circle set out to solve, Ispir wrote in their magazine *Solidaritatea* (*Solidarity*) that 'I have not seen and I still don't see any social activities in the church that reduce the misery of many poor people, widows and orphans through offerings or by other means. I don't see an organized clergy fighting with all its might for social reforms, for charity, for social assistance.'[23] The Solidarity Study Circle only lasted until 1926, but in 1923 Stănescu also created a clerical society called Rebirth (Renașterea). He strongly encouraged all priests in his episcopate to join and published a regular magazine as well as holding frequent meetings for them to attend. The goals of the society included providing further study for priests, educating the people through the clergy, combating sectarianism, defending the prestige of the Church and cultivating a spirit of solidarity between priests and their parishioners.[24] In the society's inaugural manifesto, Stănescu explained that he wanted to

> Bring together our church culture with secular culture, from which for the time being we should appropriate only that knowledge which is absolutely necessary

---

[20] Gala Galaction, *O lume nouă* (Bucharest: Editura Cugetarea, 1919); Gala Galaction, *Roxana* (Bucharest: Editura Naționala S. Ciornei, 1930).

[21] 'O nouă orientare pentru plata funcționarilor publici și a clerului', *Solidaritatea*, 1, no. 9–10 (1920–1): 330, quoted in Raiu, *Democrație și statologie*, 199.

[22] Raiu, *Democrație și statologie*, 202.

[23] Ibid., 111–12.

[24] Sperlea, *Vartolomeu Stănescu*, 46–7.

for the *health* and the *quality of life* of our people. We will *unite morality with hygiene* as the Old Testament does, and endeavour to help the people in their labour and in managing their households and society as a whole. We contribute not as specialists, but as moral guides and defenders of day to day needs of any and every variety.[25]

Rebirth hosted lectures for priests on topics such as 'Biblical interpretation', 'The impact of the Gospel on the family, society, and the state' and 'What can the results of a Christian conscience be?'.[26] Priests were then expected to form their own 'Christian centres' and 'Moral Councils' (*Sfaturi moralizători*) in villages, where they would teach people about the relationship between religion and science, the dangers of pornography and sectarianism, angels and the relationship between priests and laypeople.[27] In a circular from 1924, Stănescu instructed that

> Every priest, as president of the moral council, will make a list of sins and virtues based on Holy Scripture and human habits and will study them together with the members of his moral council. Study will be according to Holy Scripture, from which members of the council – not the priest – will read indicated sections. The priest will elaborate with real cases and examples from the history of the church, national history, from anywhere in the world and from everyday life so that people will understand the text of Holy Scripture.[28]

In line with official church policy Stănescu insisted that his priests avoid becoming involved in politics, but he and other leading Church figures struggled to follow this advice. Antisemitism was already deeply embedded in theological seminaries. From the economic antisemitism found in the writings of Pomponiu Moruşca during the mid-1920s, by the mid-1930s even renowned Biblical scholars such as Nicolae Neaga and Ioan Popescu-Mălăeşti were arguing that the Jews were a cursed people; enemies of God.[29] The theology student Valeriu Beleuţă led a 'nest' of the fascist Legion of the Archangel Michael at the Andriene Theological Academy in Sibiu as early as 1932, and a few years later a solid group of young legionary theologians were employed in the Academy at Sibiu under

---

[25] Vartolomeu Stănescu, 'Ce urmărim cu Societatea Clerului Oltean "Renaşterea" şi cu organele de propagandă', *Renaşterea* 1, no. 1 (1922), reproduced in Stănescu, *Puterile sociale*, 341.

[26] ANIC – Craiova, Fond Societatea Preoţească Renaşterea, Dosar 49/1930, ff. 1–2.

[27] Ibid., f. 95.

[28] Quoted in Sperlea, *Vartolomeu Stănescu*, 52.

[29] Ionuţ Biliuţă, 'Sowing the Seeds of Hate: The Antisemitism of the Orthodox Church in the Interwar Period', *S:I.M.O.N.* 3 (2016): 26–7; Ionuţ Biliuţă, 'Arianizarea studiilor biblice în perioada interbelică: O polemică în studiile biblice româneşti', in *Interpretarea Biblică între Biserică şi Universitate: perspective interconfesionale*, ed. Alexandru Ioniţă (Sibiu: Andreiană, 2016), 28–30.

the patronage of Nicolae Bălan, including Liviu Stan, Nicolae Mladin, Spiridon Cândea and Teodor Bodogae.[30] Theologians such as Grigore Cristescu, Ion V. Georgescu and Gheorghe Racoveanu joined the Legion during 1933 and 1934, dedicating themselves to fascist activism until the movement was suppressed in 1941.[31] In Bessarabia Gurie Grosu, Visarion Puiu and Veniamin Pocitan actively patronized legionary gatherings.[32] Other reforming priests, including Ioan Gheorghe Savin, Irineu Mihălcescu and Ion Popescu-Mozăceni, supported A. C. Cuza's antisemitic National Christian Defense League and encouraged their students to do likewise.[33]

Stănescu began patronizing legionary gatherings in 1932. He performed liturgies at their meetings, encouraged legionaries to do building projects on churches in his episcope and priests spoke in his name when doing legionary propaganda.[34] In the process, Stănescu alienated local officials associated with the National Liberal or Peasantist parties as well as coming into conflict with other Church leaders he accused of corruption.[35] A perfect storm of scandals broke out around Stănescu in 1936. One of his cooks accused him of rape, others accused him of promoting only people with legionary politics and still others accused him of misappropriating church funds.[36] On trial for corruption, Stănescu resigned his post and withdrew to a monastery in 1938. It is tempting to see a connection between Stănescu's commitment to Christian social reform and his involvement in fascist politics. His talk about reform, corruption and self-sacrifice resonated perfectly with legionary discourses on the same topics. At the same time, support for the Legion was widespread within the upper echelons of the ROC and it is quite possible that anyone in Stănescu's position would have affiliated themselves with fascism for political gain regardless of their theological convictions.

---

[30] Ionuț Biliuță, 'Un fascism regional? Cazul Academiei Teologice Andreiene din Sibiu (1930–1941)', in *Cler, Biserică și Societate în Transilvania, sec. XVIII–XX*, ed. Cornel Sigmirean and Corina Teodor (Cluj-Napoca: Argonaut, 2016), 404–24.
[31] ACNSAS, Fond Informativ, Dosar 258626, f. 23, Dosar 233835, vol. 2, ff. 224–30, and Dosar 234303, vol. 2, ff. 324–34.
[32] Viorica Nicolencu, *Extrema dreaptă în Basarabia (1923–1940)* (Chișinău: Civitas, 1999), 84; Zosim Oancea, 'Ion Moța și Vasile Marin', *Lumina satelor*, 24 January 1937, 1–2.
[33] ANIC, Fond DGP, Dosar 1/1938, ff. 17–18; ACNSAS, Fond Penal, Dosar 011784, vol. 8, f. 202; I. G. Popescu-Mozăceni, 'Înviere și trădare', *Apărarea națională*, 24 April 1927, 1.
[34] Raiu, *Democrație și statolagie*, 173–81; ACNSAS, Fond Informativ, Dosar 236684, ff. 26–107.
[35] ANIC, Fond DGP, Dosar 45/1937, ff. 4–10; C. Cernăianu, *Răspuns adversarilor mei spre eterna lor osândă* (Bucharest: Tipografia Capitalei, 1934); Vartolomeu Stănescu, *O lămurire în legătură cu eparhia locală* (Râmnicul Vâlcea: Tipografia Episcopul Vartolomei, 1938).
[36] ACNSAS, Fond Informativ, Dosar 236684, ff. 26–30.

Christian students and the YMCA

Orthodox currents of renewal also appeared among university students in Bucharest thanks the to efforts of the Young Men's Christian Association (YMCA). A Congregationalist by the name of George Williams founded the YMCA in London in 1844. With a strong focus on sport and recreation, the organization flourished in an age of muscular Christianity and eugenic thinking.[37] Based primarily in Britain and the United States, the YMCA first appeared in Russia in 1868 and opened an office in Vienna in 1873, but had more success in Bulgaria, where it began in 1899. It earned the respect of Romanians for its work alongside the Red Cross during the First World War and began a concerted effort to establish itself in Eastern Europe as a bulwark against communism once the war was over.[38]

The American John Swift expressed the YMCA's attitude towards work in countries where the majority of the population was not Protestant succinctly in 1889, arguing that 'we are simply inviting our fellow Christian young men in these distant lands to join us in systematic work for other young men. The workers must be the native young men. From them will soon come the leaders needed.'[39] The YMCA opened in Romania in 1919 at the invitation of Queen Maria.[40] Staffed by two Americans and receiving money from British diplomats, it nonetheless immediately began cultivating local students as future leaders of the organization.[41] The organization received the blessing of the metropolitans Miron Cristea and Pimen Georgescu, the support of the government and invited prominent public intellectuals such as Nicolae Iorga, Marin Ștefănescu, Vasile Pârvan, Simion Mehedinți and Isabella Sadoveanu to give lectures.[42]

The YMCA was legally incorporated as the Christian Youth Association (Asociația Creștină a Tinerilor, ACT). Its statutes specified that 'the Association's

---

[37] Clifford Putney, *Muscular Christianity: Manhood and Sports in Protestant America, 1880–1920* (Cambridge, MA: Harvard University Press, 2001).

[38] Kenneth Steuer, *Pursuit of an 'Unparalleled Opportunity': American YMCA and Prisoner of War Diplomacy among the Central Power Nations during World War I, 1914–1923* (New York: Columbia University Press, 2009).

[39] John Swift, quoted in Matthew Lee Miller, *The American YMCA and Russian Culture: The Preservation and Expansion of Orthodox Christianity, 1900–1940* (Lanham, MD: Lexington Books, 2012), 13.

[40] 'Police report, 23 March 1943', in ANIC, Fond DGP, Dosar 55/1937, ff. 25–27.

[41] 'Referat, 7 June 1921' and 'Notă informativa, 27 Nov 1945'; reproduced in Carmen Ciornea, *Sandu Tudor și asociațiile studențești creștine din România interbelică* (Bucharest: Eikon, 2017), 153–6, 350–4.

[42] 'Buletinul Asociației Creștine a Femeilor și Asociației Creștine a Tinerilor, Nov 1920' and 'Referat, 7 June 1921'; reproduced in ibid., 145–56.

principle focus is the education of young people in a Christian spirit, occupying itself with their religious, social, national, intellectual and physical education as well as with their protection and physical needs'. It also claimed

> to help young people to establish a life worthy of the teachings of our Lord Jesus Christ in accordance with the teachings of the Christian Orthodox Churches, respecting and being in complete harmony with the other Christian confessions; to develop true character, cultivating the spiritual virtues and enriching their lives through the study and practice of Christian truths by serving their neighbours; to continue unmoved in love for the Church, the country, and the king and to resist all opposing currents.[43]

The YMCA expanded rapidly on university campuses after the turn of the twentieth century and began outreach to Russian university students in 1909.[44] With most YMCA workers being middle or upper class and university educated, it was natural that the organization would turn to the universities when it entered Romania. Romanian students established the Romanian Christian Students' Association (Asociația Studenților Creștinilor din România, ASCR) in 1921, which became the Federation of Christian Students' Associations in Romania (Federația Asociației Studenților Creștini din România, FASCR) in 1923 with the goal of 'realizing the Christian ideal in individual and social life by shaping Christian personalities within the student body and making the Christian religion into an active ideal through the work of its members, capable of influencing the world in fundamental ways'.[45] The organization held annual congresses, which until 1928 included the active involvement of YMCA leaders in the country.

Student politics during the 1920s frequently used the label 'Christian', but rarely in a spiritual sense. The largest and most vocal student organizations were ultra-nationalist and antisemitic. From their roots on individual campuses they came together to create the National Union of Christian Students in Romania (Uniunea Națională a Studenților Creștini din România, UNSCR) in 1925. Known for their violence, hooliganism and rabid antisemitism, organized Romanian students terrorized minority students, especially Jewish students, and frequently came into conflict with the police and the military.[46] FASCR thus

---

[43] Statutul Asociației Creștine a Tinerilor, in ANIC, Fond DGP, Dosar 55/1937, ff. 13–19.
[44] Miller, *The American YMCA and Russian Culture*, 17; David P. Setran, *The College Y: Student Religion in the Era of Secularization* (New York: Palgrave Macmillan, 2007).
[45] Quoted in Ionuț Butoi, *Mircea Vulcănescu: O microistorie a interbelicului românesc* (Bucharest: Editura Eikon, 2015), 99.
[46] Roland Clark, *Holy Legionary Youth: Fascist Activism in Interwar Romania* (Ithaca: Cornell University Press, 2015), 28–62.

presented a puzzle to the authorities. One policeman commented on the 1924 FASCR congress that 'although the members of the association are Christians, and therefore antisemites, their propaganda is nonetheless based on conviction, not on violence as the propaganda of the Student Centres is'.[47] Whereas the antisemitic students worked hard to exclude non-Romanian students and promoted a misogynistic, male-dominated culture, FASCR actively included Jewish and Hungarian students in its ranks and elevated women to important leadership positions.[48]

As Ionuț Butoi notes, FASCR's language about a 'rebirth' of Christianity in the face of a mechanized modernity and the need for 'courage' to provide spiritual solutions for 'a petrified humanity, a nation suddenly without direction or orientation, a university student population without ideals but desperate to have one' echoed phrases found in the writings of the 'Young Generation'.[49] A group of intellectuals led by Mircea Eliade and including several people who were also involved in FASCR, the Young Generation claimed to be pioneering a new spirituality that would renew Romanian culture, by which they meant first and foremost art, theatre, literature, music and philosophy.[50] Open to a diverse range of influences, members of FASCR celebrated French Catholic writers and poets such as Leon Bloy and Charles Péguy, and Mircea Vulcănescu adopted a variety of neo-medievalism after spending time in Paris with theologians such as Jacques Maritain and Nikolai Berdiaev.[51]

While the Young Generation was heavily influenced by the philosopher Nae Ionescu, members of FASCR also embraced the ideas of the sociologist Dumitru Gusti, seeing them as a means for realizing the sort of Social Christianity preached by Vartolomeu Stănescu by improving the living conditions of other students. One FASCR leader, Ștefan Georgescu, wrote in 1923 that

> When our student body raised the alarm that it was suffering in poorly maintained dormitories, that it ate at inadequate and poorly run canteens, that it does not have the books and living conditions necessary for study, this cry found an echo in our souls ... A handful of ASCR students formed an action committee and took up the difficult but lovely instruction of Christ to work at supporting students.[52]

---

[47] Quoted in Butoi, *Mircea Vulcănescu*, 103.
[48] Ibid., 104, 107; 'Referat, 7 June 1921', reproduced in Ciornea, *Sandu Tudor*, 153–6.
[49] Butoi, *Mircea Vulcănescu*, 109.
[50] Cristina A. Bejan, *Intellectuals and Fascism in Interwar Romania: The Criterion Association* (New York: Palgrave Macmillan, 2019), 25–57.
[51] Philip Vanhaelemeersch, *A Generation 'Without Beliefs' and the Idea of Experience in Romania (1927–1934)* (Boulder, CO: East European Monographs, 2006), 139–40.
[52] Quoted in Butoi, *Mircea Vulcănescu*, 111.

They organized a market for second-hand clothes, gave out food vouchers, provided information about exams and university life and even ran their own clinic staffed by university doctors.[53] Sports also played a major role in the life of the organization, including gymnastics, volleyball, boxing and table tennis.[54]

The YMCA claimed not to be a missionary organization but there was a close association between its work and Protestant missions. Matthew Lee Miller writes that 'by 1900 more than 50 percent of the active American Protestant foreign missionaries were former "student volunteers," participants in the Student Volunteer Movement, the international outreach of the YMCA and the YWCA'.[55] It nonetheless worked hard to develop close ties with the Orthodox Church. The organization held a congress in Bucharest in 1923 to which it invited representatives of the Romanian, Bulgarian, Greek and Yugoslav Orthodox Churches, who participated 'on the condition that the Orthodox Christian members of the Association confess the Orthodox faith, remaining practicing children of the church and using it for the purpose of educating Christian priests within ACT'.[56]

The blending of evangelical Protestantism with Orthodoxy in the FASCR is evident from the titles of the talks given by students at the 1924 congress. British students attending the conference spoke about 'The Bible and Scripture' and 'Contemporary missions', and a Hungarian student discussed 'Luther and Calvin', whereas Romanian students gave talks on 'What Jesus thinks about holiness and submission to the will of God', 'The Virgin Mary' and 'Patriotism'. Imre Lajos, a Professor of Protestant Theology from Cluj attended some sessions, as did Vasile Ispir, the General Secretary at the Ministry of Religious Denominations and Professor of Orthodox Missiology at the University of Bucharest.[57] The YMCA also worked closely with Russian émigrés at the St Serge Theological Academy in Paris.[58] Some of these theologians attended the FASCR conference in 1925, contributing new and fecund Orthodox perspectives that inspired the Romanian students.[59]

As a student movement, FASCR existed in permanent tension with the antisemitic UNSCR. The UNSCR also enjoyed the patronage of senior Church

---

[53] Butoi, *Mircea Vulcănescu*, 113.
[54] Ciornea, *Sandu Tudor*, 74, n. 88.
[55] Miller, *The American YMCA and Russian Culture*, 15.
[56] Ciornea, *Sandu Tudor*, 67.
[57] 'Raport, 11 Sept 1924', reproduced in Ciornea, *Sandu Tudor*, 164–8.
[58] Miller, *The American YMCA and Russian Culture*, 207–25.
[59] Butoi, *Mircea Vulcănescu*, 120–1.

figures including Metropolitan Pimen Georgescu, Archbishop Gurie Grosu and the future patriarch Nicodim Munteanu.[60] At first the antisemitic students noticed few differences between them. In one article from *Ogorul nostru* (*Our Pride*) in July 1924, the author praised the American YMCA, noting that 'the movement of moral and religious renewal and the fight against the Yids is not just happening in Romania', as if antisemitism was a core programme of the YMCA.[61] This state of affairs did not last long and that September antisemitic students attended the FASCR conference in order to disrupt it by attacking Jews.[62] Two years later the UNSCR congress at Iași passed a resolution about

> The YMCA: Recognizing the upsetting activities of the international Yid associations – under cover of different charities of which the above-named society is one – we request that the appropriate ministries place the above-named society under surveillance and curtail its activities so that it would not influence the Christian student associations and thus inhibit their nationalist activities. In the case that its international humanitarian (communist) character be proven the students ask that it be abolished.[63]

The UNSCR claimed that the YMCA was bringing foreign missionaries into the country who then worked to support Repenter groups. They also blamed the YMCA for the fact that the International Student Confederation had expelled them for being too antisemitic.[64]

The popularity of FASCR dropped markedly in the face of opposition from the antisemitic students and its leadership began to question their affiliation with the YMCA from August 1927 onwards, when the right-wing philosopher Nae Ionescu and the celebrated writer and New Testament scholar Grigorie Pișculescu, better known by his pen name of Gala Galaction, both attended the FASCR congress in Bran. Although he was well known as a philo-Semite, Galaction had attended the UNSCR congress in Chișinău in March and was a dedicated opponent of Miron Cristea's attempts to form ties with the Anglican Church.[65] Ionescu spoke about the difference between religions that are or are

---

[60] 'Raport informativ, Dec 1926', 'Raport informativ, 16 March 1927' and 'Dare de seamă asupra congresului studențesc de la Mânăstirea Neamțu, 8 August 1927'; reproduced in Ciornea, *Sandu Tudor*, 191–210, 216–25, 235–67.
[61] 'Asociațiile creștine', *Ogorul nostru*, 30 July 1924, 3.
[62] 'Telegrama cifrată, Sept 1924'; reproduced in Ciornea, *Sandu Tudor*, 162.
[63] Quoted in Butoi, *Mircea Vulcănescu*, 117.
[64] Ciornea, *Sandu Tudor*, 89, 109.
[65] 'Dare de seamă asupra congresului studențesc de la Mânăstirea Neamțu, 8 August 1927'; reproduced in Ciornea, *Sandu Tudor*, 216–25. On Galaction's opposition to ecumenicism, see Galaction, *Jurnal*, vol. 3, 213, 227, 241–2.

not based on Tradition, and the following day he published an article in *Cuvântul* attacking theologians who claimed to be both Anglican and Orthodox. Two weeks later he wrote another piece accusing the YMCA of trying to 'modernize Orthodoxy'.[66] The student Mircea Vulcănescu, who became a great admirer of Ionescu, wrote that at this congress

> We in ASCR had discovered, together, by ourselves, the call of 'Social Christianity' from books by [Walter] Rauschenbusch and [Harry Emerson] Fosdik[67] and we were waiting for salvation to come this century through the realization of the Gospel in souls and in society; immediately, within a generation, with a sort of lavish jubilation in which religious values would blend with a whole garden of less pure and less religious emotions which would come from somewhere, though we weren't quite sure where ... Nae Ionescu said firmly to those of us who wanted to hear ... that Christianity with its heavenly and earthly purposes is one thing and that intellectual promiscuity and that vague spirituality which claimed to be Christian in some circles of our young people was quite another.[68]

For his part, Galaction turned to Sandu Tudor, another student associated with FASCR, and recruited his help converting theology students in Chișinău, who he described as 'mostly completely illiterate in terms of the Gospel', into 'citizens of the Kingdom of Jesus Christ'.[69] Galaction had little patience with the UNSCR's violence and antisemitism and lobbied the government to shut down future UNSCR congresses later that year.[70] Like Vulcănescu, Tudor turned his back on the YMCA at this time. The president of the YMCA's Romanian patronage committee, I. D. Protopopescu, responded to Ionescu's attack by specifying that 'the Association's goal is to form young people's character according to the norms of Christian morality. It does not involve itself in religious matters, leaving this to the churches of the different countries it works in'.[71] Tudor was horrified at these claims. He wrote back, again in *Cuvântul*, asking Protopoescu

> What do you call the so-called 'Bible circles' that I took part in, in which we explained Scripture according to Protestant methods? What do you have to say about the completely lay communal prayers that that I took part in at 17 Sălciilor

---

[66] Nae Ionescu 'Dumineca', *Cuvântul*, 29 August 1927, 1 and Nae Ionescu 'Y.M.C.A.', *Cuvântul*, 15 September 1927, 1; reproduced in Ciornea, *Sandu Tudor*, 272–5.
[67] Both Rauschenbusch and Fosdik were Baptist pastors from the New York area known as leading exponents of Social Christianity.
[68] Quoted in Butoi, *Mircea Vulcănescu*, 126.
[69] Galaction, *Jurnal*, vol. 3, 208.
[70] Ibid., vol. 3, 208–10.
[71] I. D. Protopopescu, 'În chestiunea Y.M.C.A.', *Cuvântul*, 17 September 1927, 3; reproduced in Ciornea, *Sandu Tudor*, 276–7.

Street? Do you know what the *Week of Prayer* is, when all [YMCA] branches around the world have moments of silence? What do you have to say about the religious library I know on Sălciilor Street, which has books of pure Protestant guidance? What do you say about the fact that the Association of Christian Students was housed at the headquarters of the YMCA society with hidden aspirations before it was moved? What about the missionaries and foreign propagandists who come regularly every year? What are the public lectures on religious topics? The YMCA does no religious activity? Then why does one of the current American directors have a theological education and, it seems to me, was even a pastor?[72]

The FASCR definitively broke with the YMCA in April 1928 on the grounds that 'the current leadership of the YMCA does not respect the so-called state church, which is to say that it does not apply Orthodoxism'.[73] Its congress that month was attended by both Ionescu and Galaction, and the organization came under the watchful leadership of Archimandrite Tit Simedrea, who encouraged the students to develop closer ties with other Balkan Orthodox Churches.[74] As Ionuţ Butoi argues, the character FASCR had had during the early 1920s under the leadership of individuals such as Mircea Vulcănescu and Sandu Tudor changed significantly after 1928. Now shaped by what Butoi calls 'a second generation' of students led by Paul Costin Deleanu, FASCR embraced the Orthodoxism of Nichifor Crainic and Nae Ionescu alongside the increasingly right-wing politics of the ROC.[75] As an ultra-nationalist journalist and newspaper editor, Deleanu associated himself closely with Ionescu's fascist politics during the 1930s.[76]

What had threatened to become a schismatic movement with Protestant overtones was brought back into the fold of Romanian Orthodoxy by the direct involvement of prestigious Orthodoxist figures such as Nae Ionescu, Gala Galaction and Tit Simedrea, who personally mentored the most promising of these students and guided them into a more socially and politically acceptable form of Christianity. The fate of Social Christianity, the YMCA and FASCR suggests that the stakes involved in renewing Orthodoxy were as much political as they were

---

[72] Sandu Tudor, 'Urmare la Y.M.C.A.', *Cuvântul*, 27 September 1927, 2; reproduced in ibid., 278–80.
[73] 'Referat, 18 April 1928', reproduced in ibid., 329–30.
[74] 'Referat, April 1928', reproduced in ibid, 325–8.
[75] Butoi, *Mircea Vulcănescu*, 129–36.
[76] ACSNAS, Fond Informativ, Dosar 234303, vol. 2, ff. 324–34. See also Deleanu's newspaper, *Ideea românească*, from 1935.

spiritual. Church leaders recognized that socially engaged Christianities were politically potent, and they insisted that the efforts of Christian laypeople serve the political interests of the Church lest they unknowingly benefited foreign powers.

Social Christianity, the YMCA and FASCR show that attempts to combine lay Orthodoxy with political nationalism were already underway in the early 1920s, emerging in the wake of a new openness to Western Christianity that flourished in the immediate post-war years.

3

A Contested Patriarchate

Establishing an autocephalous patriarchate in Greater Romania was far from a straightforward process. It involved five years of heated debate and negotiation to bring four churches with their own theological and political cultures together under a single umbrella. The Orthodox Church in the Old Kingdom had been firmly subordinated to the Romanian state before the war, while Orthodox believers in Bessarabia were members of the Russian Orthodox Church and Orthodox Christians had their separate metropolitanates in Bukovina and in Transylvania, each with its own history and approaches to church governance. Led by ambitious metropolitans and bishops, each region hoped to shape the new patriarchate in its own image. When Miron Cristea allied the Romanian Orthodox Church (ROC) with the policies of the Liberal dynasty from the Old Kingdom after the First World War, he cemented nation-building as the language which Church leaders had to speak if they wanted to see their plans succeed, but without placating the strong regional rivalries that festered within the Holy Synod.

Orthodoxy in Old Kingdom Romania

After being dominated by Greek bishops and theologians for several hundred years, the churches in Wallachia and Moldavia had slowly come under Romanian control from the beginning of the nineteenth century, along with politics and cultural life.[1] Enlightenment ideas about national independence and the importance of education penetrated the Romanian churches both through

---

[1] Constantin Iordachi, 'From Imperial Entanglements to National Disentanglement: The "Greek Question" in Moldavia and Wallachia, 1611–1863', in *Entangled Histories of the Balkans. Vol. 1: National Ideologies and Language Policies*, ed. Roumen Dontchev Daskalov and Tchavdar Marinov (Leiden: Brill, 2013), 67–148.

Greek scholars in Bucharest and Iași and through Moldavian church leaders educated in Kiev.² As metropolitan of Ungro-Wallachia between 1819 and 1821, Dionisie Lupu encouraged young Romanians to study in the West. He worked with Gheorghe Lazăr and other Romanians from Transylvania to transform the Greek-dominated Princely Academy in Bucharest into Saint Sava College, an institute of higher education specifically for Romanians, as well as publishing a Romanian-language church newspaper and choosing Romanians instead of Greeks as church officials. In Moldavia, Metropolitan Veniamin Costachi led his own efforts to 'Romanianize' the Church, establishing the Socola seminary at Iași, publishing liturgical books in Romanian and electing only Romanian bishops.³ Church leaders believed that a strong church was the key to a strong Romanian society. Hieromonk Eufrosin Poteca wrote to the metropolitan in Bucharest from Paris in 1824, asking

> Do you really want to raise the Romanian people out of ignorant darkness? Reward the clergy. Without asking a cent from the priests, give a stable position and an honest living to all priests who are able to teach children in the villages, provoking those without education into making themselves worthy of such an income. For so long as the priests remain in their current situation the people have no chance to become enlightened. The priests are the salt and light of the people; if they have lost their saltiness and live in darkness, what will the people be like?⁴

Romanian culture did not mean independence, though. Facing the restrictions placed on them by the Organic Regulation, Moldavian bishops struggled against the attempts of Prince Mihail Sturza to control the Church throughout the 1830s and 1840s.⁵ Romanian priests threw their support behind the revolutionary movements of 1848, praying

> Holy liberty,
> Who art in Heaven come down to earth,
> Hallowed be your name,

---

² Ionuț Biliuță, '"Agenții schimbării": Clerul ortodox din Principatele Române de la regimul feudal la statul național', in *"Ne trebuie oameni!": Elite intelectuale și transformări istorice în România modernă și contemporană*, ed. Cristian Vasile (Târgoviște: Editura Cetatea de Scaun, 2017), 45–7.

³ Lucian N. Leustean, 'The Romanian Orthodox Church', in *Orthodox Christianity and Nationalism in Nineteenth-Century Southeastern Europe*, ed. Lucian N. Leustean (New York: Fordham University Press, 2014), 104–6.

⁴ Letter, Eufrosin Poteca to Metropolitan Grigorie III, Paris, 15 September 1824. Reproduced in Nicolae Isar, *Biserică-stat-societate în România modernă (1821–1914): Sinteză și culegere de documente* (Bucharest: Editura Universitară, 2014), 82.

⁵ Leustean, 'The Romanian Orthodox Church', 106–11.

Your Kingdom come,
Your will be done,
In Romania as it is in France.
Give us this day the brotherhood we desire,
Together with justice and unity,
And break our chains of slavery,
As we also break the chains of our own slaves,
And lead us not into quarrels,
But rescue us from the Barbarian.[6]

The Moldavian Church turned decisively against Istanbul in the two years leading up to the unification of the Romanian principalities in 1859. Whereas the Greek clergy opposed unification and urged the Romanian metropolitans to submit themselves to the leadership of the ecumenical patriarch in Istanbul, Romanian bishops, priests and monks led by Metropolitan Sofronie Miclescu encouraged popular gatherings in support of a Romanian nation-state and argued that the new state deserved its own autocephalous church.[7]

Things did not always go the Church's way after the two principalities united in 1859 into a single Romanian nation-state under the rule of Alexandru Ion Cuza. The government passed a 'Law for the Secularization of the Monasteries' in 1863, declaring that 'all the property of the monasteries of Romania are and remain the property of the state'. It limited salaries of the monks and insisted that the Church could not administer its own funds without going through state officials.[8] Cuza further marginalized the Greek clergy by making Romanian the official language of the Church and united the metropolitanates of Ungro-Wallachia and Moldavia into one church under a single synod. As Lucian Leustean points out, one implication of making the ROC independent of the ecumenical patriarch was that it was now under Cuza's control.[9] Cuza decreed that 'the metropolitans and bishops of Romania will be appointed by the ruler following their presentation at the Ministry of Denominations [Ministerul Cultelor], [and] after deliberations by the Council of Ministers'.[10] A handful of bishops protested

---

[6] 'Rugăciunea românilor', *Pruncul român* (1848). Reproduced in Isar, *Biserică-stat-societate*, 104.
[7] Biliuță, 'Agenții schimbării', 49–59; Leustean, 'The Romanian Orthodox Church', 113–15; Isar, *Biserică-stat-societate*, 107–77.
[8] 'Lege pentru secularizarea averilor mănăstirești (15 Sept 1863)'. Reproduced in Paul Brusanowski, *Stat și Biserică în Vechea Românie între 1821–1925* (Cluj-Napoca: Presa Universitară Clujeană, 2010), 249.
[9] Lucian N. Leustean, 'The Political Control of Orthodoxy in the Construction of the Romanian State, 1869–1914', *European History Quarterly* 37, no. 1 (2007): 64–5.
[10] 'Lege pentru numirea de mitropoliți și episcopi eparhioți în România (1865)'. Reproduced in Brusanowski, *Stat și Biserică*, 252.

strongly against Cuza's control of the synod. In one pamphlet Neofit Scriban attacked Cuza's supporters 'who all shout: *we have no other emperor than Caesar* and he must be the President of our Church Synod'. 'Not true', Scriban wrote, 'we have another Emperor – Christ our Lord, the one who brought true liberty and brotherhood'.[11] Accused of promoting 'foreign propaganda', Scriban refused his appointment to the synod and retired to a monastery. With a few exceptions, most other Church leaders accepted the changes.[12]

The ROC also supported Cuza's successor, Prince Carol I, who declared in the Constitution of 1866 that 'the Eastern Orthodox religion is the dominant religion of the Romanian state'. Carol's constitution kept Cuza's synod, and the metropolitan-primate was still appointed by the monarch.[13] Further legislative reforms continued to reduce the autonomy of the ROC during Carol's reign. In 1872 the government limited the number of people eligible to become bishops and metropolitans and decreed that they would now be appointed by an Electoral College that included members of parliament.[14] The result, Leustean notes, was the creation of 'a small circle of people who could be controlled more easily by the regime'.[15] More regulations followed in 1873, reminding priests that they were subject to the civil legal system, introducing new administrative requirements, including an insistence that priests keep a record of their parishioners, preventing lay people from speaking in church and requiring bishops to ensure that 'the clergy preach the word of God in church and teach the people the Orthodox faith, piety, and Christian morals at every appropriate opportunity'.[16] The journal *Biserica Ortodoxa Română* (*The Romanian Orthodox Church*) established by this law became the authoritative voice of the Church in matters of doctrine and politics throughout the twentieth century.[17]

Orthodox military chaplains were first introduced by Cuza in 1860, and by 1870 every regiment had its own priest. In 1877 priests were replaced by chaplains permanently attached to specific garrisons and required to accompany soldiers during their campaigns.[18] The ROC threw its support behind the

---

[11] Neofit Scriban, *Apologia Prea Sfinţitului Arhiereŭ D. D. Neofit Scriban, faţă cu clevetitori Sěĭ din Iaşĭ şi Bucureşti: Saŭ respunsŭ acelora ce fac Apoteosa nenorocituluĭ de dînşiĭ Cuza-vodă, pentru falşa independinţă a Bisericeĭ Române* (Bucharest: Theodorescu, 1867), 9.

[12] Leustean, 'Political Control of Orthodoxy', 65–7.

[13] 'Constituţie din 1 iunie 1866', *Monitorul* oficial, 1 June 1866, Article 21.

[14] 'Legea sinodală (December 1872)'. Reproduced in Brusanowski, *Stat şi Biserică*, 257–60.

[15] Leustean, 'Political Control of Orthodoxy', 70.

[16] 'Regulament pentru disciplina bisericească (1873)'. Reproduced in Brusanowski, *Stat şi Biserică*, 267–72.

[17] Alexandru Stănciulescu-Bârda, *Bibliografia revistei 'Biserica Ortodoxă Română' (1874–1994)* (Bârda: Editura Cuget Românesc, 2000).

[18] Ursul, 'From Political Freedom to Religious Independence', 222.

Romanian campaign in the Russo-Turkish War of 1877 and was rewarded when the ecumenical patriarch recognized it as an autocephalous church in 1885.[19] The declaration of autocephaly represented international acknowledgement of the country's new status as a kingdom (rather than a principality) and followed the Romanians's own symbolic declaration of independence three years earlier when they celebrated the Holy Chrism themselves rather than receiving it from the ecumenical patriarch.[20] Autocephaly did little to improve the Church's finances, though, and parish priests struggled to survive only on voluntary contributions from their parishioners. According to a report drawn up by Partenic, the Bishop of Dunării de Jos, 'the Church and our clergy have been left to fate and forced to live off offerings and Christian pity. Poverty and destitution have overwhelmed the Church and hit the family of the priest most heavily, impacting their religion and Christian morals as well as their prestige and honour'.[21] In 1893 a new law addressed the ROC's financial crisis while bringing it further under state control. Priests now received a monthly state salary of between 50 and 200 lei, depending on their education and whether the parish was urban or rural. The same law restricted the number of urban parishes to 368 and the number of rural parishes to 3,326. New parishes could only be established by royal decree. Priests had to be ethnic Romanians with advanced degrees from Orthodox institutions.[22] When the metropolitan-primate objected to the level of state control introduced by this law, he was dismissed.[23] The decision to make parish priests into state employees reflected a firm conviction among politicians that church and state were now inseparable and that the church deserved state funding.[24] Another law in 1902 placed the administration of church property under the control of newly formed 'Church Houses' which reported directly to the Minister of Denominations.[25] This was followed in 1909 by a law which further regulated how bishops were elected, once again ensuring secular control over church appointments.[26]

---

[19] Isar, *Biserică-stat-societate*, 226–41.
[20] Leustean, 'Political Control of Orthodoxy', 71.
[21] Petru Gârboviceanu, *Biserica Ortodoxă și cultele străine din regatul român* (Bucharest: Institutul de Arte Grafice, 1904), l.
[22] 'Legii clerului mirean și a Seminariilor (1893)'. Reproduced in Brusanowski, *Stat și Biserică*, 273–9.
[23] Leustean, 'Political Control of Orthodoxy', 74.
[24] Miron Cristea, 'Biserica Ortodoxă din România și anteproiectul Domnului Ministru S. Haret referitor la reforma sinodală', *Țara noastră*, 15–28 February 1909, 1.
[25] 'Lege pentru înființarea și organizarea Casei Sfintei Biserici Autocefale Ortodoxe Române (1902)'. Brusanowski, *Stat și Biserică*, 294–6.
[26] Isar, *Biserică-stat-societate*, 271–328.

With the exception of Greece, no other Orthodox church experienced the level of subordination to the state that existed in Romania.[27] Contemporary observers such as Nicolae Iorga argued that the Church had entered a period of 'decadence' from the moment it was subordinated to the new nation-state. 'From 1860 until the turn of the century', he claimed, 'our church has been in a period of continual decline because it was not left to fulfil its ecclesiastic functions but was interfered with by the state'.[28] Church leaders felt that they had been short-changed by the government despite having done everything possible to accommodate the state and to support the cause of Romanian nationalism. A parish priest by the name of Sebastian Pârvulescu typified this feeling when he argued that 'the Church cannot be accused of any wrong-doing in our national past. … The representatives of the Church have been permanently submitted and obedient to the rulers of this world whenever those rulers served the popular good'. Nonetheless, Pârvulescu was proud of Orthodoxy's position as the 'state church'. It was, he said, 'a just recognition' of Orthodoxy's role in 'raising and nourishing our people like a small child' until Romania was ready to become a nation-state.[29]

The problems facing the Church at the beginning of the twentieth century can be seen by counting its priests. Whereas there were 9,702 priests in the Old Kingdom in 1859, by 1904 this number had dropped to 4,998.[30] Nor were all of them particularly capable, with many too old to do their jobs but lacking pensions that would allow them to retire. More than ten years after the law required all new priests to have completed higher education, still only 8 per cent of parish priests were properly qualified.[31] Older priests further complained that introducing diplomas as the primary requirement for the priesthood meant that the Church was attracting individuals who were spiritually unprepared for their role and had only joined the Church for material gain.[32] The declining number of priests was particularly obvious because churches were now standing empty. Of the 6,766 church buildings in Romania in 1913, only 56.3 per cent had a priest to hold services in them.[33] Hopeful that things would change after the

---

[27] Brusanowski, *Stat și Biserică*, 99–108.
[28] Nicolae Iorga, 'Discursul rostit în Adunarea Deputaților la 23 martie 1909', quoted in ibid., 142.
[29] Sebastian Pârvulescu, *Biserica noastră națională în raport cu celelalte confesiuni* (Vălenii de Munte: Tipografia Neamul Românesc, 1911), 34, 39.
[30] Lucian N. Leustean, *Orthodoxy in the Cold War: Religion and Political Power in Romania, 1947–65* (Houndmills: Palgrave Macmillan, 2009), 34.
[31] Gârboviceanu, *Biserica ortodoxa și cultele straine*, li.
[32] Un preot de mir, *Chestiuni de discutat* (Pitești: Tipografia Transilvania, 1909).
[33] Brusanowski, *Stat și Biserică*, 244.

First World War, in 1919 the Church asked that the state support its mission, guarantee that the ROC could keep its property and autonomy, provide material and moral support for the education of priests, establish it as a core cultural institution, protect it from political interference and support Orthodox confessional schools.³⁴ In the words of Bishop Ghenadie Niculescu of Buzău, the vision of the Church in the Old Kingdom was of a 'Romanian people', living in a 'standardized state' with '*one* church'.³⁵

The Orthodox Church in Transylvania, Bukovina, Bessarabia and the Banat

Other Orthodox churches ministering to Romanian speakers had quite different histories. Transylvania was incorporated into the Habsburg Empire in 1683 following the Ottoman defeat at the Battle of Vienna, profiting from internal squabbles among the nobility and a strategy of compromises designed to win over the Hungarian nobility.³⁶ Although Transylvanians were predominantly Calvinist or Orthodox, the Habsburgs relied on Catholicism to unite their empire. Following several years of negotiations, in 1698 Emperor Leopold I persuaded Metropolitan Atanasie to form the Greek Catholic, or Uniate Church. Greek Catholic priests were to receive the same constitutional status as their Catholic and Protestant counterparts, in return for which they had to recognize the Pope as the head of the Church, use unleavened bread for the Eucharist, acknowledge the existence of purgatory and accept the 'Filioque' clause of the Nicean Creed which stated that the Holy Spirit proceeds from both the Father and the Son.³⁷ Not all Orthodox priests agreed with the emperor's proposal, and Transylvania found itself with two very similar churches, only one of which had imperial support. Whereas a clerical elite enjoyed the benefits brought by the Union with Rome, the majority of Romanians clung to Orthodoxy. The Emperor insisted that Transylvanian Romanians now had their own church – a Greek Orthodox one – so he refused to appoint an Orthodox bishop from 1700 until 1761. As Keith Hitchins argues, the discovery that their clergy had changed their religion hit Romanian peasants particularly hard because priests were responsible

---

³⁴ Maner, *Multikonfessionalität*, 61.
³⁵ Ibid., 75.
³⁶ R. J. W. Evans, *The Making of the Habsburg Monarchy, 1550–1700* (Oxford: Clarendon Press, 1979), 235–72.
³⁷ Ibid., 419–24.

for policing the very practices and rituals which bound them together as a community and differentiated them from 'outsiders' such as the Habsburgs. When the 'betrayal' became known, peasants responded with violence. Two of the three peasant rebellions in Transylvania during the eighteenth century were led by monks. The first was triggered by the preaching of a monk from Serbia named Visarion Sarai, whose popularity demonstrated widespread support for Orthodoxy against the Greek Catholic Church. Peasants told imperial officials sent to investigate that they had not known that their priests had converted to Greek Catholicism and they resented it deeply.[38] One old man from Sibiu reportedly said,

> This coat, which I have on, is mine. But if the empress wished to take it from me, I would give it gladly. I have worked day and night with these old arms and legs and with my whole body to pay the tithe. They belong to the empress, and if she wished to take them from me, I could do nothing. But I have only one soul, which I am keeping for God in heaven, and no earthly power may bend it.[39]

The Empress Maria Theresa reorganized Transylvanian Orthodoxy in 1779 through a law known as the *Rescriptu declaratoriu*. She placed the Church firmly under state control, limited the number of priests allowed in each region, demanded higher education for all clergy and introduced lay participation in church governance.[40] These reforms also gave bishops greater independence from their metropolitans, which turned out to be a blessing for Romanian nationalists when Emperor Joseph II subordinated the Orthodox Church in Transylvania to the Metropolitanate of Karlowitz in 1783. The rise of modern nationalism increasingly encouraged the Karlowitz metropolitanate to see itself as a vehicle for Serbian national interests, even if secular Serbian nationalists still believed that the church was too closely allied with the emperor to be an effective advocate for their cause.[41] The first two Orthodox bishops of Transylvania under the new system were Serbian, and the first Romanian to hold the position was Vasile Moga, who was appointed in 1810 after the office had been vacant for fourteen years. Moga worked steadily to represent Romanian interests to the

---

[38] Keith Hitchins, 'Religion and Rumanian National Consciousness in Eighteenth-Century Transylvania', *The Slavonic and East European Review* 57, no. 2 (1979), 234.
[39] Quoted in ibid., 229.
[40] Nicolae Bocşan, 'Nation et confession en Transylvanie au XIXe siècle. Le cas de la Métropolie roumaine', in *Ethnie et confession en Transylvanie (du XIIIe au XIXe siècles)*, ed. Nicolae Bocşan, Ioan Lumperdean and Ioan-Aurel Pop (Cluj-Napoca: Centrul de Studii Transilvane, Fundaţia Culturală Română, 1996), 103–4.
[41] Aleksov, *Religious Dissent*, 37–41.

emperor. He encouraged his priests to preach regular sermons and to build schools and churches. A chronic lack of money hindered his efforts, which were redoubled by his successor, Andrei Şaguna.

Romanians had no constitutional status within the empire and Habsburg law stated that only the Orthodox and Greek-Catholic bishops could represent them before the emperor. As the spokespeople for the Romanian people, Şaguna as the Orthodox bishop, and his Greek Catholic counterpart, Archbishop Alexandru Şterca Şuluţiu, found themselves catapulted to the forefront of the Romanian national movement when revolution broke out in 1848. Şaguna distinguished himself as a talented politician and a tenacious advocate for the Romanian cause despite constant tensions with the lay intellectuals who chafed at having a bishop at the head of what they thought should have been a secular movement. Şaguna consistently argued in favour of a Romanian alliance with the emperor against Hungarian ambitions, a conservative stance that won him few friends inside the national movement and ultimately failed when the court in Vienna abandoned the Romanians in order to compromise with the Hungarians. His efforts to promote Romanian interests nonetheless encouraged many to view the Orthodox Church as a core part of the national movement and of Romanian national identity.[42]

Şaguna also fought to improve the reputation of his Church. He wrote to his superior that 'our Church is completely disorganized and drags everyone down with it because the priests (and even more the protopopes) are completely blinded by personal interests.'[43] As bishop he increased the education levels of his parish priests, reorganized the seminary at Sibiu and established a church newspaper known as *Telegraful român* (*The Romanian Telegraph*). Lay involvement became a central pillar of the Transylvanian church following the *Organic Statute of the Romanian Orthodox Church of Transylvania* of 1868, which built on the *Rescriptu declaratoriu* by enshrining synods as the core feature of church government. Synods were introduced at every level of the church hierarchy, and a third of their members were clergy while two-thirds

---

[42] Keith Hitchins, *Orthodoxy and Nationality: Andreiu Şaguna and the Rumanians of Transylvania, 1846-1873* (Cambridge, MA: Harvard University Press, 1977); Johann Schneider, *Der Hermannstädter Metropolit Andrei von Şaguna: Reform und Erneuerung der orthodoxen Kirche in Siebenbürgen und Ungarn nach 1848* (Köln: Böhlau, 2005), 34–114.

[43] Andreiu Şaguna to Joseph Rajačić, quoted in *Rumänisch-orthodoxe Kirchenordnungen 1786-2008: Siebenbürgen— Bukowina—Rumänien*, ed. Paul Brusanowski, Ulrich A. Wien and Karl W. Schwarz (Köln: Böhlau, 2011), 19.

were laymen.[44] This model continued to evolve over the following decades. It ensured that parish priests had a viable income and placed the administration of local churches under parish committees and synods which were required to keep detailed financial accounts. A strong believer in the importance of lay participation in the church, Șaguna also oversaw the printing of an updated Romanian translation of the Bible and encouraged the British and Foreign Bible Society to distribute literature within Transylvania.[45] The church he left behind upon his death in 1873 was one that placed great importance on the education of priests, which had its own distinctive voice in public affairs, and which was proudly associated with the Romanian national movement.

When Liviu Stan articulated a theology of lay Christianity in 1939 he evoked a tradition of lay leadership in the Transylvanian Orthodox Church dating back to the late 1860s, in which laypeople made up two-thirds of every ecclesiastic administrative body.[46] The Metropolitan Andrei Șaguna had intended lay involvement in the Church as a way of providing political representation to the otherwise disenfranchised Transylvanian Romanians, and Ionuț Biliuță argues that Șaguna's reforms represented the beginning 'of a consciously shaped nationalistic "political Orthodoxy" in order to mobilize the Orthodox intellectuals and clergymen around the same nationalist ideas'.[47] Stan was an active member of the Legion of the Archangel Michael during the 1930s, and he explicitly drew on both Șaguna's heritage and the example of Catholic Action as the inspirations for involving laypeople in a politicized, nationalist approach to Orthodoxy in a way that resonated with Vartolomeu Stănescu's version of Social Christianity.[48]

Șaguna campaigned for several decades to establish Transylvania as a separate metropolitanate independent of Serbian control and finally achieved his goal in 1864, also incorporating two related dioceses – one in Arad and the other in Caransebeș.[49] The bishopric of Bukovina followed suit in 1873, becoming

---

[44] 'Verfassung der Griechisch-Orientalisch-Romanischen Kirche (1868)', in *Rumänisch-orthodoxe Kirchenordnungen*, ed. Brusanowski, Wien, and Schwarz, 40–97.

[45] Schneider, *Der Hermannstädter Metropolit*, 115–41.

[46] Schneider, *Der Hermannstädter Metropolit Andrei von Șaguna*, 200–4; Paul Brusanowski, *Reforma constituțională din Biserica Ortodoxă a Transylvaniei între 1850–1925* (Cluj-Napoca: Presa Universitară Clujeană, 2007), 15–34, 194–207.

[47] Ionuț Biliuță, 'Rejuvenating Orthodox Missionarism among the Laymen: The Romanian Orthodox Fellowship in Transylvania', *Studia Universitatis Babes-Bolyai. Theologia Orthodoxa* 62, no. 2 (2017): 24.

[48] Ibid., 21–38.

[49] Andreea Dăncilă-Ineoan, Marius Eppel and Ovidiu-Emil Iudean, *Voices of the Churches, Voices of the Nationalities: Competing Loyalties in the Upper House of the Hungarian Parliament (1867–1918)* (Berlin: Peter Lang, 2019), 78–9.

its own metropolitanate with its seat in (Austrian) Czernowitz despite Șaguna's insistence that it should have been incorporated into (Hungarian) Transylvania. The Habsburgs had formally annexed Bukovina in 1775 and introduced an Episcopal Council in 1786 to oversee church matters.[50] The Episcopal Council was reorganized in 1869, after Bukovina became part of Cisleithania, the Austrian part of the Austro-Hungarian Empire. Whereas the Transyvlanian church was heavily shaped by lay governance and enjoyed a relative degree of autonomy, the Metropolitanate of Bukovina was under the direct control of the bishop, and above him the emperor, without significant input from protopopes, parish priests, or lay people.[51] A protest meeting of 2,000 leading Romanians in 1870 demanded that the government stop using Romanian taxes to subsidize other churches, stop postponing the Church Congress and allow lay Christians to elect their own bishops. Their requests were opposed by the Bishop of Bukovina, Eugenie Hacman, who disapproved of democratizing the Church, and the emperor used Hacman's opposition as an excuse for even listening to the demands of the Romanian delegation when it tried to present its demands.[52] Hacman was rewarded for his loyalty to the empire by becoming the first metropolitan of Bukovina three years later. Bukovinian Orthodoxy also included large number of ethnic Ruthenians. Moga and Șaguna had seen the Church as a vehicle for Romanian national ambitions because almost all Orthodox Christians in Transylvania were ethnic Romanians, but the multi-ethnic character of Bukovina meant that the national movements there took on a more secular character.[53]

Ethnic Romanians in Bessarabia mostly worshipped within the Russian Orthodox Church after Tsar Alexander I annexed the region in 1812, and its hierarchy was dominated by Russians until the late nineteenth century. It, too, was effectively a branch of the state, with parishes functioning as state administrative units, and lay people being expected to attend church without involving themselves in its business in other ways.[54] The Russians in Bessarabia did allow some Romanian features to continue and provided the Bessarabian church with its own administrative structure. The archbishop's word was law, however, and when he carried out a series of ecclesiastical reforms in 1872,

[50] *Rumänisch-orthodoxe Kirchenordnungen*, ed. Brusanowski, Wien and Scharzet, 208–59.
[51] Ibid., 197, 260–77; Maner, *Multikonfessionalität*, 44.
[52] Paul Brusanowski, *Autonomia și constituționalismul în dezbaterile privind unificarea Bisericii Ortodoxe Române (1919-1925)* (Cluj-Napoca: Presa Universitară Clujeană, 2007), 43.
[53] Maner, *Multikonfessionalität*, 45.
[54] Shevzov, *Russian Orthodoxy on the Eve of Revolution*, 16–27.

Archbishop Pavel Lebedev explained to the congress that it was 'obliged to implment my proposals precisely'.⁵⁵

Romanians increasingly received more freedom to worship in their own language towards the end of the nineteenth century. In 1900 the Orthodox Missionary Brotherhood of the Lord's Birth, established by Bishop Iacob Piatniţki of Chişinău and Hotin, began distributing religious brochures and pamphlets in Romanian, which helped cultivate Romanian national identity as much as it did souls. Piatniţki's successor Vladimir introduced Romanian as the language of instruction at the seminary in Chişinău. Nonetheless, Orthodox priests still complained that limited access to religious services in Romanian was encouraging people to turn to Inochentism and Repenter Christianity.⁵⁶ The Russian revolution of 1905 helped spread democratic and national ideas within the Bessarabian church, which became increasingly decentralized, with parish priests playing a greater role in its governance than they ever had before. Change was slow, however, and when Gurie Grosu began advocating for the Romanian national movement by establishing a printing press and a church newspaper in Romanian he was sent to a monastery in Smolensk – almost 700 miles away.⁵⁷ The legacy of 1905 nonetheless endured and bore fruit in wide-ranging democratic reforms in 1917. The Russian Sobor of 1917 involved large numbers of lay people in church governance for the first time. Led by their ethnically Russian archbishops, most priests in the region did not want their church to join the ROC in March 1918.⁵⁸

In Transylvania Şaguna's immediate successor as metropolitan, Miron Romanul, struggled against a strong opposition in the Synod led by a vicar named Nicolae Popea who played a leading role in the Romanian National Committee. Romanul responded to attempts by the Romanian National Committee to use the Church for its own ends by establishing the more moderate Romanian Constitutional Party and by staunchly defending the Church's autonomy from the national movement. A stalemate developed with Popea's supporters controlling the Synod and the Archdiocesan Council, and the metropolitan dragging his feet to implement their decisions.⁵⁹ Romanul was replaced by Ion Meţianu in 1899, who demanded sweeping reforms of the church administration and used a heavy hand to ensure professionalism among the clergy.

---

⁵⁵ Quoted in Brusanowski, *Autonomia şi constituţionalismul*, 63.
⁵⁶ Vasile Pocitan, *Biserica românească din Basarabia* (Bucharest: Tipografia Albert Baer, 1914).
⁵⁷ Brusanowski, *Autonomia şi constituţionalismul*, 71.
⁵⁸ Veronica Boldişor, *File din viaţa unei biserici şi a unui mitropolit* (Chişinău: Pontos, 2014), 38.
⁵⁹ Hitchins, *Orthodoxy and Nationality*, 232–7.

In addition to the demands of the Romanian national movement, Romanul and Mețianu had to deal with repeated attempts by the Hungarian state to control church affairs. A civil marriage law passed in 1895 moved authority from the Church to the state. While the Catholic Church was able to mount a vehement opposition to the legislation, the Orthodox had to repeatedly back down to avoid accusations of irredentism.[60] Orthodox interpolations in Hungarian political debates were consistently framed in terms of loyalty to the state. In a speech from 1894, for example, Mețianu opposed a law on the free exercise of religion on the grounds that

> Not all the citizens of the homeland live in well regulated conditions, not all of them are blessed, grateful and thankful. There are citizens, maybe even the majority of citizens, who are unhappy with their fate, who are poor, and needful and embittered, people who are heavily tried and who no longer know where to seek help and relief, and thus they seek the empathy of the Church, they appeal with faith to the mercy of God, faith which alone is capable of encouraging people to accept their own mortal fate.[61]

Only the Church, Mețianu suggested, had the moral authority to keep Romanians loyal to the Hungarian state, so the government would do well to agree to its demands. Despite the Transylvanian clergy being better educated and better organized than their counterparts in Romania, low salaries made the priesthood an uninviting career choice and many parishes found themselves without priests.[62] The Hungarian state began paying Orthodox clergy a regular stipend from 1898 onwards, but administered these salaries in ways that many priests considered discriminatory and unfair, including reserving the right to deny salaries to priests suspected of promoting Romanian nationalism.[63] 'While the government offers a small financial allowance with one hand', Mețianu noted, 'with the other hand it claims for itself the right of great interferences into the autonomy of the confessions'.[64]

---

[60] Dăncilă-Ineoan, Eppel, and Iudean, *Voices of the Churches*, 91–106.
[61] Ioan Mețianu at the House of Magnates assembly meeting, 3 October 1894, quoted in ibid., 125.
[62] Brusanowski, *Reforma constituțională*, 15–34, 194–207.
[63] Mircea Păcurariu, *The Policy of the Hungarian State Concerning the Romanian Church in Transylvania Under the Dual Monarchy 1867-1918* (Bucharest: Bible and Mission Institute of the Romanian Orthodox Church, 1986), 82–8; Keith Hitchins, *A Nation Affirmed: The Romanian National Movement in Transylvania 1860/1914* (Bucharest: The Encyclopaedic Publishing House, 1999), 186–9.
[64] Ioan Mețianu at the House of Magnates assembly meeting, 7 June 1898, quoted in Dăncilă-Ineoan et al., *Voices of the Churches*, 135.

Dissatisfaction about the Orthodox Church's treatment by the state also extended to confessional schooling. Whereas most schools in Transylvania had been run by churches in Șaguna's day, three reforms between 1876 and 1907 demanded higher qualifications for teachers and introduced Magyar language and literature as core subjects in all schools. They brought ever-increasing state control over Church schools with them. More than half of the Romanian Orthodox schools closed in the wake of the 1907 reforms because they were unable to sustain themselves without government funding and the Hungarian government would not pay for schools that did not teach Hungarian.[65] Romanian demands for greater autonomy were tightly policed during the late nineteenth century and priests were among those tried and imprisoned for engaging in 'anti-state' propaganda.[66] Their trials and tribulations bolstered popular support for the Church, which thus became strongly associated with the national cause.

Nation-building in Greater Romania

Ion Mețianu died in January 1916, shortly before Romania entered the First World War as an enemy of Austria-Hungary. He was succeeded by Vasile Mangra, who distinguished himself during his two years as metropolitan by collaborating closely with the Hungarian government. Metropolitan Vasile Mangra was on his deathbed when the war ended in November 1918. The National Romanian Central Council, which represented Transylvania's Romanians at this time, included the Bishop of Arad, Ioan I. Pop, the Bishop of Caransebeș, Miron Cristea, and the Greek Catholic Bishop Iuliu Hossu. The Council called for a National Assembly and Cristea was among those who presented the Resolution of the Assembly to King Ferdinand I, incorporating Transylvania into Romania on 1 December 1918.[67] In a prayer during the ceremony at Alba Iulia, he prayed:

> Lord our God. You are our Father. You saw the distress of our parents and you heard their cries, for they had become as flowers covered in frost – their souls bent waiting to be crushed and their bodies pressed against the earth. You have fulfilled among us that which you promised in ages past: I will break your yoke and I will burst your bonds, I will gather you from the peoples, and assemble you

---

[65] Hitchins, *A Nation Affirmed*, 197–220; Paul Brusanowski, *Învățământul confesional ortodox din Transilvania între anii 1848–1918: Între exigențele statului centralizat și principiile autonomieie bisericești* (Cluj-Napoca: Presa Universitară Clujeană, 2005).
[66] Păcurariu, *The Policy of the Hungarian State*, 88–212.
[67] Constantin I. Stan, *Patriarhul Miron Cristea: o viață, un destin* (Bucharest: Editura Paideia, 2009), 145–72; Petcu, *Guvernarea Miron Cristea*, 124–131.

out of the countries where you have been scattered. I will restore your judges as at the first, and your counselors as at the beginning. Yes Lord, you who loose those bound with fetters and raise up those who are cast down, with your help we have won the war with rejoicing and driven out the children of insolence. You have saved us, your people, and the salvation of our God is seen to the ends of the earth.[68]

Cristea saw Romanians as God's chosen people, to whom all of the promises made to the people of Israel now applied.[69] He believed that they were oppressed and that the collapse of the Austro-Hungarian Empire was a divine judgement. As he reminded his listeners, 'the way of sinners is paved with smooth stones, but at its end is the pit of Hades'.[70] He outlined an expansive vision that involved the extension of Romanian territory as far as Romanian speakers could be found: 'Remind us Lord of our brothers [still] in slavery, show them mercy and give them compassion for those who enslaved them.' Romanian control of Transylvania was not internationally recognized at this time, and the country was still waiting anxiously to learn how its claims to the Banat, Crişana, Bukovina and Bessarabia would be received at the peace conferences. The implication that Romanians had now come into possession of their Promised Land caused Cristea to pray that God might 'make straight our paths and our actions that we might live in this land'. We shall never know whether he had in mind the other injunction to given to the people of Israel when they entered Canaan – 'as for the towns of these peoples that the Lord your God is giving you as an inheritance, you must not let anything that breathes remain alive' (Deuteronomy 20:16) – but over the next twenty years Cristea pursued a consistent policy of denying rights to any who were not Romanian Orthodox and at the end of his life he presided over the initial stages of the destruction of Romanian Jewry.[71]

Appointed metropolitan-primate of the Romanian Orthodox Church in February 1920, Cristea threw his support behind the state's nation-building projects. Inflation was a major problem after the war and the government issued bonds in 1920 to help rebuild infrastructure destroyed by the war.[72] Cristea

---

[68] Quoted in Stan, *Patriarhul Miron Cristea*, 155.
[69] In addition to numerous Biblical allusions, Cristea here quoted directly from Isaiah 1:26, Jeremiah 2:20 and Ezekiel 11:17.
[70] Here Cristea was quoting from Sirach 21:10.
[71] Ion Popa, 'Miron Cristea, the Romanian Orthodox Patriarch: His Political and Religious Influence in Deciding the Fate of the Romanian Jews (February 1938–March 1939)', *Yad Vashem Studies* 40, no. 2 (2012): 11–34.
[72] Bogdan Murgescu, *România şi Europa: Acumularea decalajelor economice (1500–2010)* (Iaşi: Polirom, 2010), 223.

ordered that 'it is the duty of all Very Reverend Deans and Priests and all church organs to carry out the most extensive patriotic propaganda in support of this loan'.⁷³ State- and nation-building took pride of place in Cristea's writings during this period. He instructed priests to

> use every opportunity to awaken and develop healthy thinking in the minds of the people about communal obligations and citizenship. [To] make the pastorate into an element of order, submission, love for country and throne, a force for the cultivation of the soil, for the exercising of trades, ready to give to the country all the tributes and sacrifices necessary for ensuring its existence and continual progress.⁷⁴

Worried about the spread of communism, he issued circulars calling on people to support the government and not to listen to those 'false prophets' who had already brought revolution to Russia.⁷⁵ The state took full advantage of the Church's support and asked priests to teach their parishioners to stop stealing telephone wires and vandalizing the electrical boxes 'because it is costing the state a lot of money'.⁷⁶

As Irina Livezeanu has shown, the process of integrating the new provinces involved standardizing and centralizing state administration, imposing the norms and values of the Old Kingdom on to the new provinces, each of which had its own traditions and functionaries.⁷⁷ The government turned to Orthodox priests as potential agents in the state's centralization efforts. The Church responded enthusiastically, offering a 'cultural programme' and promising to collaborate closely with teachers in promoting official policies.⁷⁸ One article from *Biserica și școala* (*Church and School*) argued that 'without its cultural mission, the Romanian Orthodox Church, like many of the Oriental churches, becomes a contemplative, purely dogmatic institution eternally involved in the consecration of its denomination [*cult*] in the most perfect forms, but without any connection with real life. But Christ's church is a living institution, and Christianity is a real part of the culture.'⁷⁹ Involvement in education also

---

73 Miron Cristea, 'Către iubitul cler și popor din Arhiepiscopia Ungro-Vlahiei', in ANIC, Fond Miron Cristea, Dosar 3/1920, f. 11.
74 Miron Cristea, Circular 642/7 February 1922, in ANIC, Fond Miron Cristea, Dosar 3/1920, f. 67.
75 Circular 1461/1920, in ANIC, Fond Miron Cristea, Dosar 3/1920, ff. 12–15.
76 ANIC, Fond MCA, Dosar 2/1921, f. 52.
77 Irina Livezeanu, *Cultural Politics in Greater Romania: Regionalism, Nation Building, and Ethnic Struggle, 1918–1930* (Ithaca: Cornell University Press, 1995).
78 Letter, Consistorul Eparhial Ortodox, Cluj, to the Minister of Education, 22 August 1922, ANIC, Fond Ministerul Instrucțiunii, Dosar 29/1922, f. 60.
79 'Școala confesională', *Biserica și școala*, 1919, 1.

allowed the ROC to influence what was being taught in schools. In an address to the Romanian Orthodox Society in 1911, the renowned geographer Simion Mehedinți had argued that the Church must be given control of public education lest young people believe that science and religion were incompatible.[80] In 1922 the archdiocese of Alba-Iulia and Sibiu published a circular instructing 'all teachers of every specialty to work harmoniously and consistently to develop theist ideas – Christian and Orthodox – in students'. 'Religion', they explained, 'should be the primary focus of all education'.[81]

Standardizing education was particularly difficult in the new territories, and state-building was simultaneously a nationalizing process aimed at imposing the culture of the Old Kingdom on ethnic minority populations.[82] Teachers from minority groups in Bukovina who had taught under the Austro-Hungarian system, for example, found it hard to adapt to Romanian requirements, sometimes refusing to celebrate Romanian commemorations for war heroes or Orthodox religious holidays when both they and their students were Roman Catholics who had fought against Romania during the war.[83] Ethnicity was not always clear-cut. Slovak students attended Polish schools and German students attended Hungarian schools depending on which had been more easily available under the Austro-Hungarians. The state was quick to reduce teaching staff as soon as the number of students at any given minority school dropped.[84] School inspectors from the Old Kingdom found much to criticize in schools from the provinces. A school inspector in Târnava Mare county reported in 1922 that 'Romanian education is as bad as possible. The old oppressive spirit dominates the atmosphere.' He recommended that 'to bring the new current of spiritual regeneration into these schools, to bring new ideas of education and teaching we will need new people, young and well-qualified teachers'.[85] The Ministry of Education agreed, sending both books and personnel to the provinces to replace existing staff.[86]

---

[80] Simion Mehedinți, *Pentru biserica noastră* (Bucharest: Tipografia Gutenberg, 1911).
[81] ANIC, Fond Ministerul Instrucțiunii, Dosar 310/1923, ff. 207–9.
[82] Mariana Hausleitner, *Die Rumänisierung der Bukowina: Die Durchsetzung des nationalstaatlichen Anspruchs Grossrumäniens 1918–1944* (Munich: R. Oldenbourg Verlag, 2001), 12, 344.
[83] Report, Directoratul General pentru Bucovina to the Minister of Education, Cernăuți, 26 December 1922, ANIC, Fond Ministerul Instrucțiunii, Dosar 310/1923, ff. 4–6.
[84] ANIC, Fond Ministerul Instrucțiunii, Dosar 310/1923, ff. 4–6, 33–7.
[85] Report, Revizor Școlar to the Minister of Education, August 1922, ANIC, Fond Ministerul Instrucțiunii, Dosar 29/1922, ff. 61–2.
[86] Livezeanu, *Cultural Politics*, 35–48; Alberto Basciani, *La Difficile Unione: La Bessarabia e La Grande Romania, 1918–1940* (Rome: Aracne, 2007), 166–7.

Seminaries were just as susceptible to regional chauvinism as primary schools. When the University Senate in Iași approved the application for a new theological faculty in Chișinău, for example, it noted that 'Bessarabia needs a superior cultural institute which is not to be only a centre for theoretical learning but also a place which radiates Romanian culture to the great masses of Moldavian people beyond the Prut River'.[87] The hiring committee argued that no one currently teaching in Bessarabia was sufficiently qualified and insisted that the new professors be 'elements of national propaganda'.[88] At the same time, however, the ROC was willing to bend the rules about qualifications when it came to other provinces. When it was discovered that most priests in Dobruja were ethnic Bulgarians they passed a special law dropping the qualification requirements for any Romanian priests willing to move there.[89]

Part of the ROC's willingness to concede the closure of confessional schools despite strong opposition from Nicolae Bălan can be attributed to Cristea's close relationship with the National Liberal Party. Most of the prominent Romanian politicians from the former Austro-Hungarian Empire organized themselves into the Romanian National Party after the war, establishing themselves as the representatives of Transylvania in Greater Romania. In 1919 they entered into an alliance with Ion Mihalache's Peasant Party to form a government, thus breaking the National Liberals' long-standing monopoly on power. The shaky alliance held sporadically until 1926 when the two parties officially merged.[90] Transylvanian politicians thus placed themselves in clear opposition to the established political elite from the Old Kingdom, represented by the National Liberal Party. Confident that Cristea would support their cause, they requested his presence in the Senate whenever an important vote was about to take place.[91] The relationship did not last long. Cristea attracted the ire of his old supporters when he formed a close working relationship with the Liberal Prime Minister Ionel Brătianu in 1921 with the intention, he said, of helping the Liberals gain support in Transylvania.[92]

Over the next few years the government consistently appointed hierarchs with Liberal sympathies and who were embedded in Liberal patronage networks.[93]

---

[87] Meeting of the University Senate of Iași, 10 October 1926, ANIC – Iași, Fond Universitatea A. I. Cuza, Rectoratul, Dosar 1122/1926, f. 37.
[88] Ibid., f. 27.
[89] ANIC, Fond MCA, Dosar 9/1924, f. 13, and Dosar 109/1925, ff. 115–16.
[90] Keith Hitchins, *Rumania, 1866–1947* (Oxford: Oxford University Press, 2007), 386–95.
[91] ANIC, Fond MCA, Dosar 2/1921, f. 63v.
[92] Miron Cristea, *Note ascunse: Însemnări personale (1895–1937)* (Cluj-Napoca: Editura Dacia, 1999), 55.
[93] Ibid., 147.

The National Peasantists, in turn, came to be seen as a party affiliated with the Greek Catholic Church.⁹⁴ Angry at what he saw as Cristea's betrayal, his former patron Octavian Goga turned against him, writing that Cristea

> lacked first and foremost a clear religious belief. In every one of his roles his life betrayed not only a complete absence of any thirst for God, but also an incontestable frivolity that is profoundly disagreeable. He lacks any serious cultural orientation which might have allowed him to cover up his moral failings through intellectual aptitude. His only saving graces were a good-looking appearance and an undeniable aptitude as a provincial orator.⁹⁵

Brătianu's patronage nonetheless paid dividends. When Cristea moved into the metropolitan's residence he found it dirty and dilapidated, so he donated the building to the Society for the Graves of War Heroes and convinced the government to build him a new official residence.⁹⁶

Regional tensions and a new patriarchate

The ROC now had to incorporate the other Orthodox churches from the new provinces, each with its own customs, traditions and laws, into a central administration.⁹⁷ The challenge, as Valer Moldovan pointed out in 1921, was that

> the Metropolitanate of Ardeal as it is organized today under Șaguna's *Organic Statutes*, is an example of the more advanced autonomous and constitutional organizations, while the Church of the Old Kingdom is a model of a state church [*o biserica etatizată*], of a church subjugated to the state, completely lacking any sort of constitutional organization in a democratic and representative sense.

The Church in Bukovina was 'a state church ... subordinated to a foreign state power', and in Bessarabia the Church was 'under foreign control as a nation and country but of the same Orthodox laws'.⁹⁸ As a Transylvanian, Moldovan's

---

⁹⁴ Maner, *Multikonfessionalität*, 106, 121.
⁹⁵ Octavian Goga, 'Însemnări zilnice. Jurnal politic, 31 March 1931', quoted in Gheorghe I. Bodea, 'Cuvânt înainte', in Elie Miron Cristea, *Note ascunse: Însemnări personale (1895–1937)* (Cluj-Napoca: Editura Dacia, 1999), 23.
⁹⁶ Cristea, *Note ascunse*, 84–5.
⁹⁷ *Proiect de Statut Organic pentru organizarea Bisericii Autocefale Ortodoxe Române* (Bucharest: Tipografia Cărților Bisericești, 1921) in ANIC, Fond MCA, Dosar 2/1921, ff. 81–106.
⁹⁸ Valer Moldovan, *Biserica Ortodoxă Română și problema unificări: Studiu de drept bisericesc* (Cluj: Ardealul Institut de Arte Grafice, 1921), 6, 130, 146.

solution was that the ROC as a whole adopt the organizational model of the Transylvanian church.⁹⁹ Florian Kührer-Wielach has noted that the idea that the Old Kingdom should follow Transylvanian leadership was widespread among Transylvanian elites. They believed, he writes, that although 'national freedom gave the Old Kingdom the potential for a higher level of *cultural* development, this was compensated for by the *civilizational* head start of the former Habsburg regions'.¹⁰⁰

The government attempted to unilaterally write the unification of the Church into law in February 1920 but was forced to withdraw the proposal a few days later in the face of spirited protests from representatives of the new provinces.¹⁰¹ Led by Nicolae Bălan, the Transylvanians had advocated for importing their ecclesiastical model into the ROC since 1919, and they now elected Bălan as Metropolitan of Ardeal on a platform of resisting any centralization of the Church that did not preserve the Transylvanian model.¹⁰² In early 1921 the Transylvanian legal expert Lucian Borcia declared that the autonomy the Church had enjoyed in Austria-Hungary was still legally binding and that therefore the Romanian state had no legal right to impose a new structure on the Church. With the support of the Bessarabians, the Transylvanians insisted that they should maintain their own governmental structures unchanged, effectively declaring their autonomy to govern themselves within the ROC.¹⁰³ In Bessarabia the Church elected its own archbishop in an extraordinary congress that included both clerical and lay representatives but which did not have the legal backing of the ROC. The new archbishop, Gurie Grosu, declared that this level of democracy should characterize the Bessarabian church from this point on. 'We want to keep these institutions and practices and to introduce them into Greater Romania as well', he promised.¹⁰⁴ Few politicians or church leaders from the Old Kingdom agreed. They insisted on shaping the entire ROC in their own image, just as they had the schools, the military and other state institutions. Miron Cristea explained that the ROC needed a 'tempered autonomy' unlike the more democratic Transylvanian and Bessarabian systems.¹⁰⁵ For their part, the

---

⁹⁹ Ibid., 155–6.
¹⁰⁰ Kührer-Wielach, *Siebenbürgen ohne Siebenbürger?*, 353.
¹⁰¹ Brusanowski, *Autonomia și constituționalismul*, 113–16; Nicolae Bălan, *Chestiunea bisericească din România și autonomia bisericii noastre* (Sibiu: Tiparul Tipografiei Arhidiecezane, 1910); Nicolae Bălan, *Cuvântări rostite cu ocazia alegerii, sfințirii și investiturii* (Sibiu: Tiparul Tipografiei Arhidiecezane, 1921).
¹⁰² Brusanowski, *Autonomia și constituționalismul*, 73–92, 117–43.
¹⁰³ Ibid., 217–55.
¹⁰⁴ Ibid., 16–19.
¹⁰⁵ Brunsanowski, *Reforma constituțională*, 287.

Bukovinians advocated a slow process of integration that preserved both local autonomy from the Holy Synod and kept the state from interfering in church business, but were quite willing for the metropolitan-primate in Bucharest to dominate church governance.[106]

After months of tense negotiations, church-state relations were ultimately defined by the 1923 constitution. Ionel Brătianu appointed Cristea to the committee that drafted the constitution, along with Vartolomeu Stănescu, the Bishop of Râmnicului Noului Severin, who was there at Cristea's request. Stănescu had been Cristea's rival for the position of metropolitan-primate in 1919 and the two men did not always get along, but he was the only Church leader who openly argued for 'removing the church from under the administration of the state'.[107] Whereas Church leaders such as Cristea preferred to speak of Tradition when negotiating Church-state relations, Stănescu was a sociologist by training, having studied under Émile Durkheim in Paris. Stănescu characterized the state as an arena for political squabbles, but believed that the Church's mission was 'to lay the foundations of the Kingdom of God in this part of the visible world'. That involves, he said, 'refashioning each and every Christian through the power of faith and the moral purification of his life, building the true faith and the most sublime virtues in the spiritual man, which involves ... self-control and denying oneself for one's neighbour'.[108] He argued that the Church needed to be free 'from the tutelage of a state which, through its natural incompetence in holy things takes the clergy away from the service of Christ and places them entirely in the service of moral opportunism and of deviant modern materialism such as party politics'.[109] At the same time, Stănescu thought that an English-style separation of Church and state was impossible in Romania, where 'the two are united as in one being', such that 'the state represents the body for the nation, with its organic needs and strengths, and the Orthodox Church the soul'.[110] Although he claimed to dislike the idea that one church might be 'privileged' over others by having its leaders sit in parliament and being represented at official occasions, he argued

---

[106] Ibid., 145–58.
[107] Vartolomeu Stănescu, 'Principiile pe cari va avea să se întemeieze autonomia Bisericii Ortodoxe de Răsărit în Regatul Român', *Arhiva pentru drept și politica* (1919), reproduced in Stănescu, *Puterile sociale*, 220.
[108] Vartolomeu Stănescu, 'Rostul în lume al Bisericii lui Hristos: Cuvântare rostită cu prilejul Congresului Preoțesc Oltean al Societății "Renașterea" ținut la Turnu Severin în ziua de 7 Octobrie 1930', in Vartolomeu Stănescu, *În lumina cuvântului* (Râmnicu Vâlcea: Editura Sfântul Antim Ivireanul, 2013), 14.
[109] C. 'În jurul alegerii mitropolitului primat. Convorbire cu P. S. Arhiereul Vartolomeiu Băcăoanul', *Dacia* 2, no. 27 (1920): 1, quoted in Raiu, *Democrație și statolatrie*, 98.
[110] Stănescu, 'Principiile pe cari va avea', in Stănescu, *Puterile sociale*, 199.

that Orthodoxy was so deeply embedded in the Romanian nation-state that the dominant status of the ROC was there to stay.[111]

Miron Cristea, on the other hand, was comfortable with state oversight of the Church. In a seminal pamphlet from 1920, he argued that 'the Romanian Orthodox Church has the duty not only to recognize, but to allow and even require that the state and the crown have the right to control and oversee all church administrative affairs in all contexts regardless of their nature and importance'.[112] According to Cristea, his main disagreement with Brătianu over the constitution was that, whereas the prime minister wanted to say that 'the Orthodox Church is the religion of the majority of Romanians', Cristea insisted on the phrase 'the dominant church'. Brătianu then suggested describing both the Romanian Orthodox and the Greek Catholic Churches as 'dominant', but Cristea replied that to call the Greek Catholic Church a national church was impossible so long as they acknowledged a foreigner, the Pope, as their head. The ROC also asked to be allowed to regulate its own activities and administer its own businesses, cultural activities and foundations just as the other major churches in the country did. Brătianu objected that this would mean 'autonomy', and pointed out that Archbishop Gurie Grosu had been allowing his priests to speak Russian and had been using Church funds inappropriately.[113] Cristea promised that he would discipline his subordinates properly, and with these promises the ROC was given more autonomy in its own administration.[114]

Article 22 of the Constitution read:

> Freedom of conscience is absolute. The state guarantees this freedom and protection to all denominations so long as its exercise does not affect public order, good behaviour, and the laws of the state. The Christian Orthodox and Greek Catholic Churches are Romanian churches. The Romanian Orthodox Church, being the religion of the great majority of Romanians, is the dominant church in the Romanian state; and the Greek Catholic Church has primacy over other denominations. The Orthodox Church is and remains autonomous of any

---

[111] Raiu, *Democrație și statolatrie*, 300–24.
[112] Miron Cristea, *Principii fundamentale pentru organizarea unitară a BOR din regatul român* (1920), quoted in Brusanowski, *Autonomia și constituționalismul*, 102.
[113] Grosu was actually an ardent Romanian nationalist and 97 per cent of priests in the episcopate were Romanian speakers, but Bessarabian churches had maintained elements of the Russian liturgy because of their musical appeal to the population. *Anuarul Episcopiei Chișinăului și Hotinului (Basarabia)* (n.p.: n.p., 1922), iv; Simion Moraru, 'Organizarea slujbelor și a cîntării bisericești în timpul Mitropolitului Gurie al Basarabiei', in *Mitropolitul Gurie: Misiunea de credință și cultură*, ed. Silvia Grossu (Chișinău: Epigraf, 2007), 96.
[114] Cristea, *Note ascunse*, 67–78.

foreign hierarchy, while retaining unity with the Eastern Ecumenical Church in matters of dogma. The Christian Orthodox Church will have a unitary organization in the entire Kingdom of Romania, with the participation of all its constitutive elements, lay and clerical. A special law will establish the fundamental principles of this organizational unity, including how the church will regulate, run, and administer its religious, cultural, foundational, and episcopal activities through its own departments and under the control of the state. The spiritual and canonical matters of the Romanian Orthodox Church will be regulated by a single central synodal authority. Metropolitans and bishops of the Romanian Orthodox Church will be chosen according to special laws. The relationships between different denominations and the state will be established by law.[115]

A law organizing the ROC was eventually passed on 5 May 1925, recognizing Cristea as the new patriarch.[116] According to Cristea, the idea of a patriarchate originally came from the historian Nicolae Iorga and was supported by 'the Bessarabians', but he was hesitant to promote it himself until he received the instruction from the prime minister, Ionel Brătianu.[117] A congress of the Bessarabian Church had actually voted for establishing a patriarchate in March 1921, but it is symptomatic of Cristea's centralizing outlook that he saw this move as an indication of support rather than as a policy the ROC needed to implement.[118] A new cathedral, the Church of the Salvation of the Nation, was proposed as the seat of the new patriarchate, but it was not built until 2018.[119]

The process of creating an autocephalous Romanian patriarchate thus embedded a number of festering sores within the Church. Miron Cristea's refusal to incorporate elements of lay church governance from Transylvania and Bessarabia alienated clergy from those regions who were already upset at being treated like second-class citizens by state officials from the Old Kingdom sent to 'Romanianize' them. The Church in Transyvlania and the Banat had championed the national cause for decades, only to find itself pushed aside in Greater Romania. Cristea's alliance with the National Liberal Party further put him at odds with the Transylvanian wing of the Church, which maintained close ties first with the Romanian National Party and then with its successor, the

---

[115] 'Constituția României din 28 martie 1923', *Monitorul oficial*, 29 March 1923.
[116] 'Lege pentru organizarea Bisericii Ortodoxe Române', *Monitorul oficial*, 4 May 1925.
[117] Cristea, *Note ascunse*, 94–5.
[118] Boris Buzilă, 'Patriarhie pentru țara întregită, Mitropolie pentru provincia revenită la sînul Țării', in *Mitropolitul Gurie: Misiunea de credință și cultură*, ed. Silvia Grossu (Chișinău: Epigraf, 2007), 19.
[119] Ibid., 101.

National Peasantist Party. Church support for the state's nation-building project undermined the potential for the ROC to bring Ruthenian and Russian believers in Bukovina and Bessarabia into its fold as they became targets of concerted Romanianization campaigns. Orthodox Christians in both Bukovina and Bessarabia had long watched their churches submit to any and every demand of the state, and discovering that the ROC planned to continue that tradition in order to maintain its position as the 'dominant church' must have been a bitter disappointment.

Part Two

Orthodoxy's Others

4

Reaction

The process of unifying four different churches into a single patriarchate understandably caused some people to worry that something was being lost in the process. Tensions between metropolitans and bishops reflected dissatisfaction among parish clergy and laypeople as well, which in some cases resulted in the formation of new religious movements. As a society experiencing extraordinary social and political upheavals, including new borders, a nationalizing state, industrialization, new communication and transportation networks and new political ideologies, inter-war Romania was a fecund environment for religious innovation. With monasticism in decline and ever higher expectations being placed on both priests and laypeople, two of the most significant new religious movements of the period emerged in regions where monasticism and the monastic approach to spirituality had been strongest. The first, Inochentism, began in Bessarabia just before the First World War. Its apocalyptic belief that the end times were near included a strong criticism of the Church and the state, a critique that transferred smoothly onto the Romanian state and Orthodox Church once the region became part of Greater Romania. The second, Old Calendarism (*Stilism*), emerged in many of the same places, but the two movements developed independently. As a rejection of the Romanian Orthodox Church's (ROC's) decision to change the liturgical calendar in 1924, Old Calendarism expressed a deep hostility towards the ROC and the modern nation-state. Both Inochentism and Old Calendarism were grounded in traditional forms of rural Orthodox piety and sought to worship God more seriously than they believed was possible in the official Church. In many ways their critiques reflected the Church's failure to live up to the standards it taught in its sermons, catechisms and devotional literature.

Inochentism

Inochentism emerged out of the life and teachings of Ion Levizor, better known as Inochentie of Balta. Born in the village of Cosouți in Soroca county – then part of the Russian Empire – in 1875, he became a spiritual leader for thousands of people across Bessarabia. According to a hagiography written by Filimon Postolache in 1924, Inochentie had a religious experience at the age of nineteen when a supernatural voice cried out, 'the time is now, hurry yourself!' Postolache says that Inochentie understood this moment as 'a revelation from heaven that the time when all the injustices of man will be overcome is close and it is time for him to call the people to repent'.[1] After a period spent wandering through Russia, he entered a monastery in Dobrușa, near his home town. He then began to travel, staying at various monasteries and holy sites around Russia for between nine months and three years, including apparently meeting Tsar Nicholas II and witnessing the Bloody Sunday massacre of January 1905. The foremost expert on Inochentism, James Kapaló, writes that during his ten years spent in various Russian monasteries 'Ioan Levizor was undoubtedly exposed to the political and religious currents sweeping Russia and he seems to have developed a profound sense of the impending crisis and its implications.'[2]

Inochentie joined the monastery at Balta around 1906 and received a second spiritual calling during a ceremony for the reburial of the remains of the holy man Feodosie Levițchi. Approaching Feodosie's coffin, Inochentie heard a voice saying 'Inochentie! Take my cross and walk ahead, because fire will come from within it and all devils will be deposed. Call the people to repent as they won't repent of their own free will, they have to be compelled to repent. With fire and sword you will cleanse the world'.[3] He began a powerful preaching career from this point onwards, transforming Balta into a pilgrimage site where people experienced supernatural healings and Inochentie exorcised demons. Concern about Inochentie's activities soon spread, and in 1910 Bishop Serafim of Bessarabia warned that

> He practices rituals of exorcism in the presence of crowds of people and the possessed persons glorify him in their screams. Through this, he created amongst the dark masses of people an image of himself as saint, healer and

---

[1] Filimon Postolache, *În scurt viața și faptele Părintelui Inochentie de la Balta* (Bârlad: Tip. Const. D. Lupașcu, 1924), quoted in Kapaló, *Inochentism*, 20. My account of Inochentism is taken entirely from Kapaló.
[2] Kapaló, *Inochentism*, 23.
[3] Postolache, *Viața și faptele*, quoted in ibid., 26.

prophet. By pronouncing incantations, by using various threats, by practicing open public confessions, hieromonk Inochentie leads many people into a state of ecstasy and illness.[4]

His following and reputation continued to grow despite attempts by the Church to limit it, and he was exiled to Siberia in 1913. A number of his followers accompanied him into exile, 'hiding in the forest and going to him at night when no one could see'.[5] Inochentie died on 30 November 1917, but his movement continued. His followers built a new community in the province of Kherson, near Balta, creating an underground monastery known as the Garden of Paradise. The community was destroyed and hundreds of its inhabitants murdered by the Bolsheviks in 1921.[6]

Inochentism continued in Bessarabia even after the destruction of the Garden of Paradise, taking on strong millenarian features. Nae Ionescu's *Cuvântul*, which was markedly hostile to Inochentism, reported in 1932 that 'where the movement had once been restricted to a single point, now it extended and gained followers in every locality where those who were expelled from Balta are now installed'.[7] Inochentists practised celibacy and sold their possessions to wait for the end times. They likened Inochentie to the prophets Elijah, Enoch and John the Baptist, as well as claiming that he was 'the embodiment of the Holy Spirit'.[8] Inochentists dug and sanctified wells believed to contain holy water, had ecstatic seizures similar to those of epileptics and encouraged women to take an important role in the movement by serving as administrators and evangelists.[9] One Inochentist community established by a monk named Ioan Zlotea criticized both the Church and state for their material wealth and abuses of power. They were well known for fasting regularly and for abstaining from pork, all of which enhanced their reputation in the region.[10]

Defining Inochentism as heretical and 'sectarian', the ROC, the state, the press and Romanian society more generally persecuted them throughout the inter-war period. Newspapers accused Inochentists of ritual murder and sexual deviancy and police often took bizarre and unverified allegations about them at face value.[11] A police report from 1923 wrote that 'they are not just simple religious

---

[4] Quoted in ibid., 30.
[5] Postolache, *Viața și faptele*, quoted in ibid., 46.
[6] Ibid., 47–9.
[7] 'Cum se dezvoltă Inochentismul în Basarabia', *Cuvântul* (1932), quoted in ibid., 107.
[8] Ibid., 57–71.
[9] Ibid., 74–106.
[10] Ibid., 178–88.
[11] Ibid., 107–77.

maniacs, but are real gangs of criminals who corrupt girls 11 and 12 years of age so that they can use water to cleanse them of sin and make saints out of them'.[12]

In addition to showing how peasants interpreted the violence of the First World War and the political upheavals of the Russian Revolution, the story of Inochentism illustrates widespread dissatisfaction with the spirituality available through the Orthodox Church. In particular, Kapaló argues that Inochentism represented 'a radical rejection of the idea of the nation as a vehicle for salvation'.[13] Lay Inochentists embraced monastic spiritual practices such as fasting, celibacy and poverty. They engaged in person-to-person evangelism just as Repenters did. An Inochentist oral tradition recorded by Kapaló in 2014 emphasizes that Inochentists saw their ascetic practices as a critique of what was lacking in the established Church.[14] Both Inochentie and his followers were repeatedly victims of violent state oppression and their literature associated the Orthodox Church closely with the Russian and Romanian states as abusive, authoritarian institutions.

Old Calendarism

Old Calendarism (*Stilism*) emerged in reaction to the ROC's decision to change the religious calendar, including moving saint's days and the date of Easter. In 325 the Council of Nicea decided that Easter should be celebrated on 'the first Sunday after the full moon which coincides with the Spring equinox or immediately thereafter'.[15] The date of Easter thus moves from April to May each year, depending on the lunar cycle. There were various explanations for this movement. The fictional Moş Dragne, for example, learned from his priest that the date of Easter moves 'so that we never celebrate it on the same day the Jews celebrate Passover'.[16] The Julian calendar included too many leap days, however, and over time the date of Easter moved away from the March equinox. The slippage was rectified in the West with a new calendar introduced by Pope Gregory XIII in 1582, but Eastern Orthodox countries retained the Julian calendar. The rise of the scientific worldview and its association with Western modernity caused Romanian elites to worry that the Julian calendar

---

[12] ANIC, Fond MCA, Dosar 117/1923, f. 2.
[13] Kapaló, *Inochentism*, 172.
[14] Ibid., 183.
[15] Quoted in N. Coculescu, *Chestiunea calendarului* (Bucharest: Tipografia Corpului Didactic C. Ispăsescu & G. Brătănescu, 1898), 7.
[16] Călinescu, *Dialog între Moş Dragne*, 49.

made their country look 'backward'. 'We are on the verge of the twentieth century', the astronomer Nicolae Coculescu argued in 1898, 'which we will enter thirteen days later than other civilized nations because we refuse to relinquish a secular error, finding ourselves behind Japan, which will be welcomed into the European concert before *the Belgium of the orient!*'[17] An abortive attempt had been made to change the calendar in 1864, and the Gregorian calendar was adopted by the Romanian state in 1919 without being extended to the Church. The ecumenical patriarch called a pan-Orthodox council in 1923 to find a solution to the problem, which was attended by a Romanian delegation that included Iuliu Scriban and the astronomers George Demestrescu and Petru Drăghici. With several important exceptions, most Eastern Orthodox churches adopted the Gregorian calendar within the next ten years.

When the Romanian Synod introduced the new calendar in 1924 it emphasized that the purpose was not to conform the ROC with the West but to bring the church calendar in line with that of the Romanian state.[18] Miron Cristea distributed a pastoral letter that was to be read in every church. Archbishop Gurie Grosu argued that 'some say that we're copying the Germans ... We are not copying anyone, but truthfully we want the signs of our calendar to align with the signs of the heavens. We are sticking with the Orthodox Church calendar, just without those thirteen days which separate us from the signs of the heavens'.[19] Iuliu Scriban published an article in *Glasul monahilor* (*The Monastic Voice*) aimed at convincing a popular audience. Scriban imagined a fictitious peasant who, on being told of the reform by his parish priest, responded, 'well, if it changes, here in the village we'll kill the mayor first ...'. The peasant's wise interlocutor replied that

> The calendar is not a step that you take, but a path that you follow. And it is not you that follows this path, but the earth around the sun. You just calculate how long this path takes ... See why we have to fix it; if your clothes came back from the tailor a size too large, you give them back and make them smaller. It is the same for us at the moment, we are correcting some sewing from the past which was too large and making time fit, just as they did in the days of the Church Fathers.[20]

---

[17] Coculescu, *Chestiunea calendarului*, 10.
[18] Radu Petre Mureșan, *Stilismul în România (1924-2011)* (Sibiu: Agnos, 2012), 22-5.
[19] Gurie Grosu, *Luminătorul* 25 (1924): 1-4, quoted in Andreea Petruescu, 'Mișcarea stilistă în Basarabia, 1935-1936. Cauze și soluții. Perspective locale', *Caietele CNSAS* 9, no. 1-2(17-18) (2016): 62.
[20] Iuliu Scriban 'Se schimbă calendarul', *Glasul monahilor* 1-6 (1923-4), quoted in Radu Petre Mureșan, *Stilismul în România (1924-2011)* (Sibiu: Agnos, 2012), 31.

Not everyone accepted – or even heard – Scriban's arguments, and a movement emerged in Moldavia and Bessarabia known as Old Calendarism. Old Calendarists argued that the new calendar ignored the natural rhythms of life. 'Everything functions in accordance with the old calendar', they said.

> Look, the cuckoo doesn't sing on Annunciation with the new calendar; it sings with the old calendar. When has the cuckoo always sung? He sings until Midsummer. Now Midsummer passes and he is still singing … The soil follows the old calendar too. No-one sows on the new first day of March, but the old first day of March is perfect.[21]

Old Calendarism was simultaneously a protest against the ROC and the increasing attempts of the modern nation-state to interfere in village life. Thinking about the iconoclastic controversy in the Byzantine Empire, Leslie Brubaker and John Haldon write that 'the relationship between individuals and the holy was redefined at the same time as that between individuals and their ruler'.[22] Much the same argument could be made about other religious movements, including the sixteenth-century wars of religion, the rise of Old Belief in eighteenth-century Russia and the spread of Old Calendarism in 1920s Romania. As Andreea Petruescu notes, 'with time the acceptance of the calendar reform in Bessarabia became synonymous with the acceptance of the national church and the Romanian state'.[23] The ROC recognized this problem and in a pastoral letter from 1925 Gurie Grosu wrote that 'some troublemakers are saying that the calendar reforms come from our Romanian brothers, that they are breaking our laws … But this rumour is not true. For the ones who introduced the calendar reform were the Greeks and the Patriarch of Constantinople in 1922.'[24]

Old Calendarism appeared in many of the same areas that Inochentism was strongest and seems to have taken the authorities by surprise. A history of the movement written by local police in 1948 stated that

---

[21] Silvia Grossu, 'Impactul social al problemei modificării calendarului creștin', in *Mitropolitul Gurie: Misiunea de credință și cultură*, ed. Silvia Grossu (Chișinău: Epigraf, 2007), 150.

[22] Leslie Brubaker and John Haldon, *Byzantium in the Iconoclast Era, c. 680–850: A History* (Cambridge: Cambridge University Press, 2011), 10; quoted in Angie Heo, 'Imagining Holy Personhood: Anthropological Thresholds of the Icon', in *Praying with the Senses: Contemporary Orthodox Christian Spirituality in Practice*, ed. Sonja Luehrmann (Bloomington, IN: Indiana University Press, 2018), 88.

[23] Petruescu, 'Mișcarea stilistă în Basarabia', 62.

[24] Quoted in Boldișor, *File din viața unei biserici*, 64.

In the regions with monasteries and especially where religious mysticism was more widespread, this decision of the Synod [to change the calendar] is seen as a blow to the foundations of the Orthodox faith and so many refuse to accept the new calendar in any way, continuing to hold the feast days according to the old (Julian) calendar. They are known as Old Calendarists. Several monks who have been expelled from the monasteries, whether for inappropriate monastic behaviour or for not recognizing the new calendar, associate themselves with others who do not want to accept the new calendar, organizing them and pushing them even further into religious mysticism. These monks, coming in particular from Baia and Neamț counties, succeed in gathering about 60 percent of the population of these counties around them, building churches and houses of prayer in a number of places. To distinguish the new sect from Orthodox Christians who follow the new calendar, Old Calendarists display their sectarianism by growing large beards.[25]

The problem was complicated by a lack of consensus about the changes even among elites. Alexandru Averescu's People's Party made returning to the old calendar one of its election promises in 1926 and the right-wing National Christian Defence League (LANC) did the same during the early 1930s.[26] Moreover, Gurie Grosu and Visarion Puiu allowed Easter to be celebrated according to the old calendar in 1929, thus undermining the very reform they claimed to support.[27] A group of protesters marched down the village streets of Careii Mari that year chanting, 'Down with the priests! Long live Disorder!'.[28] One newspaper article claimed that the Old Calendarists avoided Orthodox priests, 'not even saying hello', and that 'the churches remain empty of believers'.[29] Newspapers such as *Credința ortodoxă* (*The Orthodox Faith*) combated Old Calendarism and Inochentism by giving advice about Orthodox praxis, such as how to properly cross oneself and the proper ways to fast.[30]

An Old Calendarist protest took place in the village of Fântânele during 1933, when Old Calendarism grew rapidly in the wake of claims that the parish priest was charging too much money for services such as baptisms and funerals. Old Calendarists designated a private house as a 'house of prayer', setting up

---

[25] 'Studiu', in the Archives of the National Council for the Study of the Securitate Archives (henceforth ACNSAS), Fond Documentar, Dosar 9486, vol. 1, f. 238.
[26] Mureșan, *Stilismul în România*, 34; Petruescu, 'Mișcarea stilistă în Basarabia', 71.
[27] Mureșan, *Stilismul în România*, 35. Police complained that Bishop Visarion even supported Old Calendarism. ANIC, Fond MCA, Dosar 125/1935, f. 27.
[28] Mureșan, *Stilismul în România*, 36.
[29] 'Activitatea dezastruoasă a stiliștilor în jud. Baia și Neamț', *Calendarul*, 469 (1933): 3.
[30] *Credința ortodoxă* (1932–40).

icons and prayer books in the courtyard and barricading the gate to prevent the police from entering. Led by an itinerant monk, they claimed to be ready to die for their beliefs and threatened to kill anyone who tried to prevent them worshipping.[31] The conflict between Old Calendarists and the state escalated in 1935 due to increased efforts by police to contain the movement and thanks to the new Bishop of Bălți and Hotin, Tit Simedrea, who worked to enforce Orthodoxy in his episcopate.[32] Old Calendarists locked up Orthodox churches and prevented priests from performing the liturgy according to the new calendar. They provided bodyguards for their own priests who barricaded themselves in their churches to avoid being imprisoned by the gendarmerie.[33] Police targeted Russian minority communities in particular, claiming that they were being supported by White Russian émigrés from Belgrade and Vienna.[34] According to complaints received by the government, worshippers were pulled out of their churches and beaten on the streets while gendarmes watched.[35] A young girl from the village of Cuciurul Mic in Cernăuți county reported seeing a vision in September 1935 in which God told her to keep celebrating the feast days according to the old calendar.[36] Despite low literacy levels in the region, Old Calendarists produced pamphlets defending their beliefs and 'exposing the lies' of the ROC.[37] One pamphlet apparently warned that 'he who accepts the Gregorian Easter and the Papist calendar, be he priest or lay person', may he 'not decay after death but labour for all eternity'.[38]

Both Church and state were eager to wipe the movement out, but each blamed the other for failing to do so. The police complained that Church leaders in the area did nothing to combat Old Calendarism or even to alert them to its presence.[39] This was not quite true. Priests in Oltenița tried getting people to go to church by force. When the Old Calendarists refused to stay for the liturgy the priests began refusing to conduct funerals, leading to a stand-off that the gendarmes had to step in to resolve.[40] Lacking the resources to properly control

---

[31] ACNSAS, Fond Documentar, Dosar 13408, vol. 2, f. 9.
[32] Petruescu, 'Mișcarea stilistă în Basarabia', 72–3.
[33] ANIC, Fond MCA, Dosar 125/1935, f. 5, 92.
[34] Ibid., Dosar 125/1935, ff. 10–11, 27.
[35] ANIC, Fond Ministerul Propagandei Naționale, Dosar 5/1930, ff. 12–13.
[36] 'Nota informativă, 4 octombrie 1935', in ANIC, Fond MCA, Dosar 125/1935, f. 1.
[37] Petruescu, 'Mișcarea stilistă în Basarabia', 70, n. 34.
[38] According to a report from the newspaper *Cuvântul*. Quoted in Mureșan, *Stilismul în România*, 37.
[39] ANIC, Fond MCA, Dosar 125/1935, f. 14.
[40] Ibid., Dosar 20/1924, f. 126.

the problem, gendarmes warned that only 'a military occupation of the region' would wipe it out.[41] In response the Synod argued that Old Calendarism was 'a movement aimed at changing the current regime' and that 'the old calendar is only a platform'.[42] 'Encouraged by the fact that no action is taken against them', Miron Cristea wrote to the Ministry of the Interior, 'these agitators become aggressive and dangerous to the safety and lives of missionary priests and other believers'.[43] According to one report, by 1936 Old Calendarism had over a million adherents.[44]

Over time the movement developed its own rituals and practices. A police report from 1948 noted that Old Calendarists disturbed church services by singing songs appropriate to the old calendar, sanctified wells by throwing crosses into them on particular dates and refused to send their children to school on days that had been feast days in the past.[45] A study on an Old Calendarist community in Slătioara commissioned by the ROC in 1968 wrote that the Old Calendarist leadership were substituting themselves for the ROC hierarchy and labelling the official Church as schismatic. They encouraged believers not to have any contact with Orthodox priests and cultivated a sober attitude on festive occasions such as weddings as well as avoiding going to the cinema. The report said that they gave money to the poor, helped the sick and contributed to the digging of wells. Evangelism was a core element of the movement by this time. Believers spread their message from person to person, through religious celebrations and by door-knocking on the New Year. They refused to work on feast days and did not register marriages with the state.[46]

Separating themselves from Romanian society, and in particular from the secular state and the Orthodox Church that supported it, Inochentists and Old Calendarists engaged in a sustained critique of Church-state relations. They identified the ROC as fallen by avoiding Orthodox priests and by developing their own, higher, standards of holiness. Both movements flourished in a region where dissatisfaction with the Greater Romanian state was highest, and their success can be seen as evidence that for many people the state's failings reflected badly on a church that had tied its fate to an earthly government.

---

[41] 'Aviz nr. 188 din 18 Sept 1935', in ibid., Dosar 125/1935, f. 90v.
[42] Letter, Sfântul Sinod to Ministerul Instrucțiunii, 15 July 1935, in ibid., Dosar 125/1935, ff. 100–5.
[43] Quoted in Petruescu, 'Mișcarea stilistă în Basarabia', 75.
[44] Petruescu, 'Mișcarea stilistă în Basarabia', 62.
[45] '1 Februarie 1948', in ACNSAS, Fond Documentar, Dosar 9486, vol. 1, f. 228.
[46] ANIC, Fond MCA, Dosar 153/1968, ff. 12–45.

5

Catholics

Of all the churches, it was the status of Catholicism that was most bitterly contested by Orthodox leaders during the 1920s. In particular, the negotiation of the 1927 concordat with the Vatican prompted accusations from the Romanian Orthodox Church (ROC) that the government was surrendering control to a foreign power. Between them, Roman and Greek Catholics made up 14.7 per cent of the country's population at the time of the 1930 census. Catholicism was strongly identified with ethnic and regional minorities which had been incorporated into Greater Romania after the First World War. Ninety-five per cent of Greek Catholics came from either Transylvania, Crişana or Maramureş, and only 13.5 per cent of Roman Catholics were from regions that had been part of Romania before 1918.[1] The Roman Catholic Church had only created archdioceses in Bucharest and Iaşi in the 1880s, and was commonly associated with Hungarian-ness because many Roman Catholics identified either as Hungarians or Csangos.[2]

Discussions about the status of Catholicism in Greater Romania had begun in 1920 but were not concluded until 1929.[3] The Orthodox position was that any reconciliation with Catholicism was 'too difficult' and any attempts to make peace should be abandoned. The newspaper *Ţara noastră* (*Our Country*) argued in 1926 that 'we want a union of the two churches too, as does any honest Romanian. But if this union cannot take place through a spontaneous manifestation [of brotherhood], but only through fratricidal fighting, then it is preferable to give up on it.'[4] Orthodox newspapers wrote about 'the pope with all his antichrist tyranny, with all his frightening heresies' and claimed that he put

---

[1] Manuilă, *Recensământul general*, xxiv, xxx.
[2] Maner, *Multikonfessionalität*, 49.
[3] Ibid., 225.
[4] 'Treuga Dei', *Ţara noastră* 7, no. 34 (1926): 1000, quoted in Kührer-Wielach, 'Orthodoxer Jesuitismus', 319.

on 'the airs of a god descended among unfortunate mortals'.[5] *Biserica Ortodoxă Română* stated that Catholics 'praise our weaknesses because of delight and not out of sincere feelings. This Jesuit-Catholic system casts the scale of values into darkness, introduces confusion, makes people unable to recognize the real aspects of life and forces them to think only according to their misleading Catholic patterns.'[6]

Catholicism posed a problem for Romanian nationalists because many of them believed that Romanian-ness was synonymous with Orthodoxy. According to the wisdom of the day, the Romanian people had embraced Christianity thanks either to the preaching of the apostle Andrew or Roman legionaries settling in Dacia at the beginning of the second century. 'We have the Christian faith just as it grew from the first seed, sown in these parts by Christian missionaries', wrote Sebastian Pârvulescu, a parish priest from Cernădia-Gorj in 1911, who used the antiquity of Romanian Christianity to argue that the Orthodox Church had preserved the 'original' faith of the apostles.[7] Nicolae Iorga, the pre-eminent historian of the Romanian nation, argued in the 1928 edition of his *History of the Romanian Churches* that large numbers of the Roman settlers in Dacia were Christians fleeing persecution in Asia Minor. Christianity apparently soon spread among the pagan Dacians as well, and a 'Christianity without canonical bishops' took root in the area, where it survived for the next thousand years. Iorga argued that Greek and Slavic influences first entered Romanian Christianity as part of the cultural renaissance brought about by the creation of the first Bulgarian Orthodox patriarchate in the tenth century. Such influences, he wrote, involved naming sections of the liturgy and memorizing the Creed, and in no way imply that Bulgarian rule extended north of the Danube.[8]

With the blessing and possibly at the urging of the emperor, the ecumenical patriarch collaborated with local rulers in establishing a Metropolitanate of Ungro-Wallachia based in either Curtea de Argeș or Câmpulung in 1359, followed by one at Severin in 1370, and another for Moldavia at Suceava in 1394 (ratified in 1401). Establishing Orthodox Church structures provided international recognition for the newly independent principalities of Wallachia

---

[5] *Misionarul* 2, no. 2 (1930): 132 and *Glasul monahilor* 5, no. 114 (1928): 3, both quoted in Ciprian Ghișa, 'The Image of the Roman Catholic Church in the Orthodox Press of Romania, 1918–1940', in *Eastern Orthodox Encounters of Identity and Otherness: Values, Self-Reflection, Dialogue*, ed. Adreeii Krawchuk and Thomas Bremer (New York: Palgrave Macmillan, 2014), 112.
[6] *Biserica Ortodoxă Română* 13 (1923): 1010, quoted in ibid., 113.
[7] Sebastian Pârvulescu, *Biserica noastră națională în raport cu celelalte confesiuni* (Vălenii de Munte: Tipografia Neamul Românesc, 1911), 18.
[8] Iorga, *Istoria bisericii românești*, vol. 1, 28–33.

and Moldavia and helped protect them from the imperialist designs of their Catholic neighbours.[9] Romanian priests, scholars and rulers began to use Middle Bulgarian as their administrative and liturgical language during the fourteenth century, incorporating Slavic elements into what had hitherto been a Byzantine Christianity.[10] In the early twentieth century Romanians looked back to the fourteenth century as the official beginning of their Church. 'The Romanian Orthodox Church established its hierarchy at the same time as the consolidation of the Romanian lands', the Liberal politician Petru Gârboviceanu wrote. 'Both in Muntenia and in Moldavia, and at roughly the same time. We had both metropolitans and bishops right from the beginning.'[11] History mattered because if Romanian Christianity was extremely ancient and ecclesiastically independent, then to be Romanian was to be Orthodox. Vasile Pocitan, a teacher at two of Bucharest's leading schools and the future Archbishop of Huși, claimed that 'Christianity is just as deeply embedded in the soul of our people as the yeast of Romanian nationhood. There was even a time when we were more Christian than we were Romanian.'[12]

Greek Catholicism

Ironically, it was Greek Catholics who made the story of the Roman origins of the Romanian people into the central founding myth of Romanian nationalism. The Greek Catholic Church had been established by the Holy Roman Emperor in 1698 along with promises that its adherents would receive rights and privileges in return for acknowledging the papacy. After struggling for its first few decades, the Greek Catholic Church eventually flourished in Transylvania between 1729 and 1744 under the leadership of Bishop Ion Inochențiu Micu-Klein. A capable organizer, he moved the seat of the bishopric to Blaj, where he built an impressive cathedral and encouraged Greek Catholic higher education. Klein is remembered today as a tireless advocate for Transylvania's Romanian population. Keith Hitchins points out that Klein used the word *natio* interchangeably to mean 'members of the Uniate Church' or 'a community held

---

[9] Mircea Păcurariu, *Istoria Bisericii Ortodoxe Române* (Sibiu: Patriarhul Bisericii Ortodoxe Române, 1991), 253–85; Keith Hitchins, *A Concise History of Romania* (Cambridge: Cambridge University Press, 2014), 23–4.
[10] Hitchins, *A Concise History*, 37.
[11] Petru Gârboviceanu, *Biserica ortodoxa și cultele străine din regatul român* (Bucharest: Institutul de Arte Grafice, 1904), ix.
[12] Vasile Pocitan, *Patriarhatele Bisericii Ortodoxe* (Bucharest: Tipografiile Române Unite, 1926), 88.

together by common origins, customs, and origins', such that when he said 'Uniates' he also meant 'Romanians'.[13] Klein tried to use the slippage between the two meanings of *natio* to extend the privileges promised by the Habsburgs when they created the Greek Catholic Church to all Romanian speakers.[14] He was not always successful, but the educational privileges that Greek Catholics did enjoy helped them connect with strains of Enlightenment thought that introduced them to modern nationalism.

Thanks to their newfound access to higher education, Greek Catholic scholars such as Samuil Micu-Klein, Petru Maior and Gheorghe Șincai established the intellectual and literary foundations of Romanian nationalism through their works on history and linguistics.[15] In 1774 Bishop Klein's nephew, Samuil Micu-Klein, wrote a sweeping history of Christianity in Transylvania in the hope that the Romanians would receive their own metropolitanate if he could prove that their Church preserved the original faith of the early Roman Christians.[16] Subsequent Orthodox elites appreciated the contributions of the Transylvanian School, as it came to be known, but resented the fact that it had come out of Greek Catholic rather than Orthodox circles. Despite having tied their national heritage to Rome, Romanian Greek Catholic leaders repeatedly resisted attempts to Latinize their Church to the point of provoking talk of 'crises' in their relationship with the papacy. A Greek Catholic metropolitanate of Alba Iulia and Făgăraș was established in 1853, which was independent of Hungarian Catholicism and subordinate only to the Pope, giving them broad autonomy in the years leading up to 1867.[17] A committed Catholic, the Emperor Francis Joseph encouraged ostentatious celebrations of religious holidays such as Corpus Christi, often attending the festivities himself. Thanks to state support, by the late nineteenth century Catholic priests were generally well educated, laypeople had a reasonable grasp of theology and the Church played an important role in secular education.[18]

Despite the emperor's support, the dominance of Catholicism in Hungary was contested by the class of liberal elites who controlled Hungarian politics from

---

[13] Hitchins, 'Religion and Rumanian National Consciousness', 221–223.
[14] Keith Hitchins, *A Nation Discovered: Romanian Intellectuals in Transylvania and the Idea of Nation, 1700–1848* (Bucharest: The Encyclopaedic Publishing House, 1999).
[15] Sorin Mitu, *National Identity of Romanians in Transylvania* (Budapest: Central European University Press, 2001).
[16] Keith Hitchins, 'Samuel Clain and the Rumanian Enlightenment in Transylvania', *Slavic Review* 23, no. 4 (1964): 668.
[17] Dăncilă-Ineoan, Eppel and Iudean, *Voices of the Churches*, 86–7.
[18] Maria Bucur, *Heroes and Victims: Remembering War in Twentieth-Century Romania* (Bloomington: Indiana University Press, 2009), 21, 32.

1848 onwards. The liberals hoped to introduce lay governance in church affairs and to establish a secular state independent of any one church. Empowered by the 1867 Compromise which transformed the Habsburg Monarchy into the Austro-Hungarian Empire, they attempted to introduce religious equality, although only succeeded in introducing a 'hierarchy of privileges' that benefited some churches over others while giving Orthodoxy the status of a 'state church'.[19] The clergy responded to what they saw as an attack on their autonomy and privileges with an organized campaign that culminated in the formation of a Catholic political party in 1895 in the wake of new laws regulating civil and inter-religious marriage. In an encyclical from 1893 Pope Leo XIII encouraged Hungarian Catholics in their struggle, writing that 'we hope that all the Catholics in Hungary will realise the dangerous turn of affairs in their country and will find courage and strength in our solicitude and good will. We hope, too, that on their part they will most conscientiously obey our counsel and admonitions.'[20] While neither the state nor the Church wanted a conflict, the result of these laws was the crystallization of a militant Hungarian middle class eager to assert its Catholic identity against any attempt to promote religious pluralism.[21]

Caught up in the midst of Hungarian Church-state politics, the Orthodox Church found itself at the mercy of the Hungarian state, which interfered in the election of bishops and at times postponed meetings of the Ecclesiastical National Congress.[22] The lawyer Valer Moldovan accused the government of gerrymandering episcopal boundaries. He claimed that the administration was incorporating Romanian speakers into majority Hungarian dioceses as part of a deliberate strategy of 'Magyarization'.[23] As Roman Catholics were predominantly Hungarian, Romanian Greek Catholics typically opposed attempts to guarantee Catholic privilege, which was a not-very-subtle way of saying Hungarian privilege. Orthodox writers largely ignored Greek Catholic support for Romanian issues, however. They constantly reminded their readers that the head of the Catholic Church lived in Rome, and accused Greek Catholics of being 'more papist than the Pope'.[24] One pamphlet from 1910 signed by 'a large

---

[19] Paul Hanebrink, *In Defense of Christian Hungary: Religion, Nationalism, and Antisemitism, 1890–1944* (Ithaca: Cornell University Press, 2006), 12–13.
[20] Constanti Hungarorum Encyclical of Pope Leo XIII on the Church in Hungary, quoted in Dăncilă-Ineoan et al., *Voices of the Churches*, 65.
[21] Ibid., 62–8; Hanebrink, *In Defense of Christian Hungary*, 23–8.
[22] Dăncilă-Ineoan, Eppel and Iudean, *Voices of the Churches*, 81–4.
[23] Valer Moldovan, *Biserica în serviciul maghiarizării* (Brașov: Tipografia A. Mureșeanu, 1913), 14–19.
[24] Petru Ionescu, *Observări critice la opul 'Metropolia românilor ortodoxi din Ungaria și Transilvania' etc. și observări la răspunsul prea cuvioșiei sale Dlui Arhimandrit Dr Ilarion Pușcariu* (Caransebeș: Tiparul Tiografiei Diecesane, 1901), 11.

number of Orthodox' wrote that 'Propaganda is an institution created by the Pope in Rome for spreading Catholicism among the pagans and heretics which, like the Israelite alliance, spreads like a cancer across the whole earth with its agents and missions.'[25]

Greek Catholics attacked the Orthodox in return. In his history of Romanian Orthodoxy from 1910, the Greek Catholic publicist Zenovie Pâclișanu wrote that he was 'filled with pain':

> When we see the immense role that the church has had in developing the national life of the peoples of Western Europe and we think of *the tragic destiny* which cast us into the arms of a church of extraordinary sterility, robed in a soul-destroying Byzantinianism which lacked the power of life, and lacks it even today; when we think that it could have been a powerful wellspring of life if the church hierarchy had had other connections. It could have been a pedestal upon which we could have raised up a string of enlightened peoples.[26]

While the Orthodox believed that the Greek Catholics were 'stealing souls' which were rightfully theirs, Greek Catholics pointed to weakness and corruption within the Orthodox Church and celebrated their own cultural and educational achievements.

Having been a dominant church under the Hungarians, the Greek Catholic Church found itself in the position of a minority religion after the war. In 1918 Alexandru Rusu, who later became the Greek Catholic Bishop of Maramureș, wrote that whereas before the war Greek Catholicism had been a major defender of ethnic Romanians – 'a true shield and watch tower for the strength of our ethnical character' – now it could focus purely on the care of souls.[27] Like the Orthodox, the Greek Catholics introduced a number of initiatives aimed at mobilizing the laity and intensifying spiritual life in their churches. This involved establishing new clerical and lay associations as well as distributing more devotional literature aimed at a popular readership.[28] Most Greek Catholic writings during the inter-war period emphasized the Church's victimhood and

---

[25] Mai mulți ortodoxi, *La 'Ierarchia Românilor din Ardeal și Ungaria'* (Sibiu: Tiparul Tipografiei Archidiecesane, 1905), 1.

[26] Zenovie Pâclișanu, *Biserica și românismul* (Târgu-Lăpuș: Galaxia Gutenberg, 2005), 10.

[27] Alexandru Rusu, 'Noua eră și biserica noastră', *Cultura Creștină* 7, no. 17–20 (1918): 336–7, quoted in Ciprian Ghișa, 'The Greek-Catholic Discourse of Identity in the Inter-War Period: The Relation between the Nation and People's Religious Confession', *Studia Universitatis Babeș-Bolyai Historia* 57, no. 2 (2012): 60.

[28] Sergiu Soica, *Biserica greco-catolică din Banat în perioada anilor 1920–1948* (Timișoara: Editura Eurostampa, 2011), 79–119.

their persecution at the hands of the Orthodox. At the same time, they repeatedly stated their loyalty to the Romanian nation and state. Eugen Stroescu wrote in 1922 that

> on top of the commandments regarding our fellows, God put the duty towards the family, which extends with necessity over the large family, over the nation in which He wanted for each of us to be born in ... As Catholics aware of the divine law, for us, nationalism is not a facultative Evangelical advice from which we can restrain, but a command that we cannot deny without committing a sin.[29]

Roman Catholicism

Romania's territorial expansion after 1918 necessitated a massive reorganization of the Roman Catholic Church, just as it had of the ROC, with dioceses that had previously been under Russian and Austro-Hungarian control now being brought under Romanian administration.[30] Both the Archbishop Raymund Netzhammer of Bucharest and the Papal Nuncio Francesco Marmaggi opposed the subordination of the Transylvanian diocese to the Romanian Catholic hierarchy and were hostile to the Vatican's attempts to arrange a concordat with the Romanian state. But heads of churches now had to be Romanian citizens, so Netzhammer was replaced in 1923 and Marmaggi in 1924. The new archbishop was a Romanian by the name of Alexandru Cisar, who then appointed other Romanians to leading positions within the church, radically changing the ethnic composition of the Roman Catholic hierarchy in Romania.[31] Catholic leaders complained bitterly about having lost a great deal of property during the land reform of 1921, about discrimination against Hungarians in Romania and about the frequent attacks on Catholics in the Orthodox press.[32]

Noting the close relationship between religion and ethnicity, Florian Kührer-Wielach has argued that 'Confessionalism – the political and ideology instrumentalization of religious affiliation', is key to understanding

---

[29] Eugen Stroescu, *Unirea* 6 (1922): 2, quoted in ibid., 66–7.
[30] Marius Oanța, 'Arhidieceza romano-catolică de București între România Mare și Republica Populară Română (1918–1948): Date statistice', *Anuarul Institutului de Istorie George Barițiu din Cluj-Napoca* 57 (2018): 335–44.
[31] R. Chris Davis, *Hungarian Religion, Romanian Blood: A Minority's Struggle for National Belonging, 1920–1945* (Madison: University of Wisconsin Press, 2018), 39.
[32] Ibid., 39.

how Orthodoxy functioned to create a more homogeneous population.[33] Confessional schools had been abolished in the Old Kingdom during the 1860s, and now the government decided that the time had come to close them in the new provinces as well, making schools a pivotal issue in the rivalry between the churches. Opponents of confessional schools argued that their primary role had been to fight the 'race war' for Romanian culture in Hungary and that they were now superfluous in an era of the 'uniform nation-state'.[34] This was a spurious argument, the Catholics responded, because

> the church has established, sustained and defended schools according to its historic right that proceeds from the Saviour's command to teach the nations. It has not only cultivated language and love of one's nation, but above all it sought to shape religious beliefs, from which the spiritual and moral strengths of our nation have always flowed: 'The one who is righteous will live by faith'.
>
> (Gal 3:11)[35]

Angelescu abolished confessional schools entirely in 1925, stating that 'our churches have to realize that the Romanian State that is ours, all of ours, must be strengthened and that this State can only be strengthened by … letting the State mold the souls of all its citizens'.[36] Impassioned protests came from the Roman Catholic, Greek Catholic and Reformed churches, whereas the only major Orthodox protest against the project came from Nicolae Bălan, who was also losing his Orthodox schools in Transylvania.[37]

In 1923 the government legislated that 'Catholic priests may no longer teach religious education in schools in the Old Kingdom'. This was no longer just about regionalism, and Roman Catholics from Roman complained that they were now 'being treated worse than the brothers from the new provinces'.[38] Even when an earlier law had stated that Roman Catholic priests were allowed to teach two hours of religious education a week in Catholic villages, local officials had prevented them from doing so, claiming that no such rights existed.[39] A report

---

[33] Florian Kührer-Wielach, 'Orthodoxer Jesuitismus, katholischer Mystizismus: Konfessionalismus in Rumänien nach dem Ersten Weltkrieg', in *Orthodoxa Confessio?: Konfessionsbildung, Konfessionalisierung und ihre Folgen in der östlichen Christenheit*, ed. Mihai-D. Grigore and Florian Kührer-Wielach (Göttingen: Vandenhoeck & Ruprecht, 2018), 307.

[34] 'Stratificarea învăţământului în Ardeal', *Şcoala nouă* (1922), quoted in Kührer-Wielach, *Siebenbürgen ohne Siebenbürger?*, 146.

[35] Senior, 'Agonia şcoalei confesionale', *Cultura creştină* 13, no. 2 (1924): 34.

[36] Quoted in Livezeanu, *Cultural Politics*, 47.

[37] Maner, *Multikonfessionalität*, 317–19.

[38] Petition to the Minister of Education, 28 February 1924, in ANIC, Fond Ministerul Instrucţiunii, Dosar 289/1924, f. 28.

[39] Letter, Episcopia Catolică de Iaşi to Minister of Education, 13 March 1924, in ibid., f. 39.

by British Presbyterians on the state of Reformed churches in Transylvania after a fact-finding mission in October 1920 concluded that

> Gross and grievous mismanagement has characterized the occupation and the administration of the Hungarian territory now ceded, and ... vindictive race-feeling has prompted and condoned a revolting policy of terrorism, and outrage, and dispossessions, and restraint, of which our Churches and ministers have been conspicuous victims, not, we believe, because they are Protestant or Presbyterian, but because they are Magyar by birth and education, and are regarded as foci of disaffection. Scores of the ministers and office-bearers we examined had been beaten or imprisoned or threatened with death or violence. Men are imprisoned for months, untried and even uncharged, by uncontrolled and irresponsible officials and police. Appeals for justice have been habitually ignored, or repelled and avenged by punishment, as insults to the good name of Rumania.[40]

The Presbyterian report confirmed what became increasingly clear over the next few years – that if Catholicism was to survive in Romania it would need a solid legal framework defining its relationship to the state. To this end the Vatican spent much of the 1920s negotiating a concordat with Romania. Without a concordat, other churches struggled throughout the inter-war period. By 1930 the Lutheran Church discovered that the money it received from the Romanian state was far less than it had become used to in Austria-Hungary. Unable to continue to function otherwise, it began selling Church property and solicited money from Hungary to fund its schools.[41] The Reformed Church found itself in a similar situation and had to rely on charity from churches in Switzerland.[42] Neither of these churches faced the same popular hostility as the Catholics, but they nonetheless suffered from being classified as 'minority religions'.

The 1927 concordat

The Vatican had not been represented at the Paris Peace Conferences. Terrified about the threat of communism, they used concordats as a way to establish political relations with European nation-states, signing ten such agreements

---

[40] William A. Curtis, J. R. Fleming and J. MacDonald Webster, *Report of the Commission Appointed to Visit Churches and to Inquire into Conditions Prevailing in Central Europe, August-October 1920*, in Lambeth Palace Archives, R. T. Davidson Papers, Official Letters, 1920, Vol. 198, f. 12.

[41] ANIC, Fond Ministerul Propagandei Naționale, Dosar 5/1930, ff. 4–7.

[42] Ibid., ff. 24–5.

between 1922 and 1939.⁴³ Despite having been forced to make concessions to Romanian nationalism, most Romanian Roman Catholics responded positively to the concordat signed in 1927 and ratified in 1929.⁴⁴ Greek Catholics further defended it against Orthodox attacks in the press.⁴⁵ The concordat recognized the Catholic churches as churches (*biserici*) instead of denominations (*culte*), provided government salaries for Catholic priests, gave the Catholic Church legal status as a corporate entity, required Romanian citizenship from all teachers in Catholic schools and made Romanian the official Church language. Individual bishops could, however, allow schools and churches within their jurisdictions to speak Hungarian.⁴⁶ Its ratification followed an equally divisive debate over the 1928 Law of Denominations. Whereas Orthodox leaders insisted that churches – not parishes – should control ecclesiastical wealth and that the ROC should receive preferential treatment from the state, other religious leaders insisted that the state ensure freedom of conscience for its citizens.⁴⁷

Orthodox leaders were furious with the outcome of both debates. They argued that 'Catholicism is and remains a dangerous offensive force opposed to Orthodoxism and a formidable power capable of successfully penetrating inside and across the borders of *national* states', and that the state had made too many concessions to the Vatican.⁴⁸ In an angry speech in the Romanian Senate, Nicolae Bălan complained that the concordat undermined the constitution and the Law of Denominations, forced the state to support Catholic proselytism, allowed for too many Catholic episcopates relative to the size of their population and promoted the 'Magyarization' of the Church.⁴⁹ The Greek Catholic Bishop Iuliu Hossu of Gherla responded that a treaty of this nature was necessary to bring episcopal boundaries in line with national boundaries and hoped that the new laws would finally bring Orthodox and Catholic conflicts to a close, emphasizing that 'justice has finally been done'.⁵⁰

---

[43] Giuliana Chamedes, *A Twentieth-Century Crusade: The Vatican's Battle to Remake Christian Europe* (Cambridge, MA: Harvard University Press, 2019), 34–68.

[44] Ciprian Ghişa, 'Întărind vechi alterităţi, ridicând noi frontiere: Concordatul dintre România şi Vatican – 1929', *Studia Universitatis Babeş Bolyai – Theologia Catholica* 55, no. 4 (2010): 43–56.

[45] 'In chestia concordatului', *Unirea*, 6 July 1929, 2–3.

[46] Tudor Popescu, *Concordatul cu Papa* (Bucharest: Institutul de Arte Grafice Răsăritul, 1927), 41–84.

[47] Constantin Schifirneţ ed., *Biserica noastră şi cultele minoritare: Marea discuţie parlamentară în jurul legii cultelor* (Bucharest: Editura Albatros, 2000).

[48] I. Mateiu, *Valoarea concordatului încheiat cu Vaticanul* (Sibiu: Tiparul Tipografiei Arhidiecezane, 1929), 12–13.

[49] Nicolae Bălan, *Biserica împotriva concordatului* (Sibiu: Tiparul Tipografiei Arhidiecezane, 1929).

[50] 'Cuvântarea Prea Sfinţitului Iuliu ţinută în Senat la discuţia ratificării Concordatului cu Sfântul Scaun al Romei', *Curierul creştin*, 1 August 1929, 121–37,

The debate over the concordat also had a wide-ranging impact on the Romanian public sphere. According to Ionuț Biliuță it was the 1927 concordat that disillusioned the Romanian Orthodox clergy with democracy and caused them to turn their sympathies increasingly towards right-wing and fascist politics.[51] Indeed, a new group of writers calling themselves 'Orthodoxists' rose to prominence in the midst of the anti-Catholic sentiment of the late 1920s, pushing Orthodox public discourse further towards ultranationalism.[52] The priest Ion Dobre, better known by his pen name of Nichifor Crainic, established his reputation after the First World War by publishing poetry with nationalist overtones and engaging in debates about Romanian culture with other literary critics. In 1926 he began teaching courses on Christian mysticism at the new theological faculty in Chișinău and started editing the literary magazine *Gândirea (Thought)*.[53] In the pages of *Gândirea* he championed a literary and artistic current he called 'Traditionalism'. Rather than 'a longing for the past', Crainic argued that 'traditionalism does not appear as ... a static force, dead with its back to the future, but as a living, dynamic force, with bursts torrentially forward out of the past towards the growth of new and more adequate forms of its existence'.[54] Crainic's Traditionalism fought for 'a culture created with autochthonous values', maintaining that 'our orientation cannot but be towards the Orient, that is, towards ourselves, towards that which we are through the inheritance of which we are worthy'.[55] Alongside – and in competition with – Crainic, the religious philosopher Nae Ionescu promoted his own brand of 'Orthodoxism' through the newspaper *Cuvântul (The Word)*, which he edited from 1926 onwards. Ionescu established his credentials as an expert on Orthodox Christianity through his celebrated lectures on mysticism at the University of Bucharest from 1924 onwards, though the bulk of these lectures were plagiarized from a book by the English Anglo-Catholic writer Evelyn Underhill.[56] Ionescu equated Protestantism with democracy, capitalism and rationalism, all of which

---

[51] Ionuț Biliuță, 'The Ultranationalist Newsroom: Orthodox "Ecumenism" in the Legionary Ecclesiastical Newspapers', *Review of Ecumenical Studies* 10, no. 2 (2018): 192.
[52] George Călinescu, '"Crinul alb" și "Laurul negru"', *Viața literară*, 3 November 1928, 1–2.
[53] Roland Clark, 'Orthodoxy and Nation-Building: Nichifor Crainic and Religious Nationalism in 1920s Romania', *Nationalities Papers* 40, no. 4 (2012): 525–43.
[54] Nichifor Crainic, 'A doua neatârnare', *Gândirea* 1 (1926), reprinted in Nichifor Crainic, *Puncte cardinale în haos* (Iași: Editura Timpul, 1996), 153.
[55] Nichifor Crainic, 'Sensul tradiției', *Gândirea*, 9, no. 1–2 (1929): 2–3.
[56] Marta Petreu, 'Istoria unui Plagiat: Nae Ionescu – Evelyn Underhill', *România literară* 27, no. 49–50 (1994); Evelyn Underhill, *Mysticism: A Study in the Nature and Development of Man's Spiritual Consciousness* (New York: E. P. Dutton & Company, 1911).

he saw as evils threatening to destroy Romanian culture.[57] Both Crainic and Ionescu claimed to speak on behalf of Orthdoxy, although Ionescu in particular frequently distinguished between 'Orthodoxy' and the actions of the ROC.[58] Orthodoxist polemics encouraged hostile reactions from Catholics, and in 1927 the French Catholic writer Henri Massis defended Western philosophy against what he called the 'German-Asian-Russian' irrationalism of Orthodoxists like Ionescu and Crainic.[59]

Ionescu became embroiled in a bitter debate with the Catholic theologian Iosif Frollo over the relationship between Catholicism and Romanian-ness in 1930. In a discussion about the sister of the writer Cezar Petrescu, Ștefania Petrescu, who had recently converted to Catholicism and entered a convent, Iuliu Scriban used the pages of *Cuvântul* to argue that 'whoever turns to Catholicism ceases to be a good Romanian, and if one enters the monastic life then one becomes perverted to the highest degree so as to become the most dangerous enemy of the Romanian nation'.[60] Frollo responded by listing prominent Greek Catholics from the eighteenth century whose work had been foundational for the ideology of Romanian nationalism, asking rhetorically, 'can a Catholic therefore not be a "good Romanian"?'.[61] No, said Ionescu, 'no one can be Romanian ... unless one achieves concretely, individually, the organizing spiritual structure on the basis of which is the essence of the Romanian nation'.[62] As Chris Davis points out, Ionescu's argument was that 'people's attitude toward God, and the ways in which they experience divinity, were interwoven in the nation's fabric'.[63]

With the ROC now confirmed as the 'dominant' Church in the nation-state, Orthodoxists such as Crainic and Ionescu sought to use their particular brand of Orthodoxy to dominate Romanian culture. By defining ethnicity in religious terms, the Orthodoxists placed religion at the heart of Romanian-ness. In privileging religion, they gave themselves a privileged place in the

---

[57] Romina Surugiu, 'Nae Ionescu on Democracy, Individuality, Leadership and Nation: Philosophical (Re)sources for a Right-Wing Ideology', *Journal for the Study of Religions and Ideologies* 8, no. 23 (2009): 68–81.
[58] Nae Ionescu, 'Ortodoxia răsăriteană și pancreștinismul', *Cuvântul*, 2 May 1926, 1; Nae Ionescu, 'Tot despre Facultatea Chișinăului', *Cuvântul*, 24 September 1926, 1; both republished in Nae Ionescu, *Roza vânturilor* (Bucharest: Editura Roza Vînturilor, 1990), 3–5, 29–33.
[59] Vanhaelemeersch, *Generation 'Without Beliefs'*, 120–1.
[60] Iuliu Scriban, 'Călugărițele catolice nu-și lasă năravul', *Cuvântul*, 1930, quoted in Davis, *Hungarian Religion*, 54.
[61] Iosif Frollo, 'Scrisoare deschisă cătră S.S. Arhimandritul Scriban', *Cuvântul*, 1930, quoted in ibid., 55.
[62] Nae Ionescu, 'A fi "bun român"', *Cuvântul*, 1930, quoted in ibid., 55.
[63] Ibid., 56.

creation of Romanian culture: only they, and not eugenicists, social scientists or bureaucrats truly knew how to reinvigorate Romania. Defining the status of Catholicism thus mattered as much to the Orthodox Church as it did to the Catholic churches. Whereas for the Catholics the concordat was a matter of securing their legal rights in a country where they now found themselves in the minority, for the Orthodox it was about determining which discourses and ideologies would shape the church's future. The idea that nationality should be determined in terms of religion resonated perfectly with the state's drive to unite the population around the idea of Romanian ethnic dominance, thus securing state support for the persecution of religious minorities. Whatever regional tensions remained in the wake of unification were largely put aside in the face of the greater dangers apparently posed by Catholics and Repenters. When it came to securing Orthodox dominance over other religious groups, even those bishops who had most passionately argued in favour of autonomy were more than willing to work together with the state to guarantee Orthodox hegemony in Greater Romania.

6

Repenters

Whereas Inochentists and Old Calendarists rejected the official Church by grounding themselves in recognizably Orthodox patterns of piety, Repenters abandoned Orthodoxy altogether for a personal Saviour who promised them eternal life.[1] They called each other 'brother' and 'sister', cherished the Bible above all else and withdrew from 'worldly' things in their pursuit of holiness. Repenter groups appeared in Romania during the second half of the nineteenth century and spread in various parts of the country. Some claimed simply to follow 'the Repenter religion', but most clearly affiliated themselves with one denomination or another.[2] The spectre of Repenters appeared constantly in Orthodox writings from the 1920s, giving the impression that they were to be found knocking on doors in every village and town. In reality, the number of Repenters at this time was remarkably small, and their presence restricted to only some parts of the country. Baptists were strongest in Arad and Bihor counties, according to the 1930 census, with significant communities throughout western Transylvania and Bessarabia. Dorin Dobrincu writes that 'in 1921 the Baptist Union numbered 21,193 members (14,000 Romanians, 6,223 Hungarians, 670 Germans, and 300 Russians), congregated in 645 churches ... There were 77 ordained pastors ... and 668 unordained leaders'.[3] Romania's estimated population in 1920 was 16 million, meaning that Baptists constituted roughly 0.001 per cent of the population.[4] Brethren were concentrated most strongly in Teleorman, Suceava and Iași, although one could also find them in

---

[1] A thorough overview of the literature on Repenters can be found in Michelson, 'The History of Romanian Evangelicals', 191–234.
[2] Fond MCA, Dosar 178/1923, f. 48.
[3] Dobrincu, 'Sub puterea cezarului', 94.
[4] Direcția Generală a Statistice, *Anuarul statistic al României 1922*, 20.

Muntenia and Bukovina. Pentecostals and Nazarenes, on the other hand, were restricted primarily to the Banat and western Transylvania during the inter-war period.[5]

Baptists

The largest and most visible of the Repenter churches were the Baptists. The first Baptist church was established in Amsterdam in 1609 by English separatists angry at the Archbishop of Canterbury's suppression of reformist Puritanism. During the 1640s Baptists embraced the idea of believer's baptism by immersion, meaning that only people who are old enough to understand the significance of their actions should be baptized and that it should be done by immersing the entire person in water to symbolize them dying and rising from the dead.[6] Believer's baptism became one of the trademarks of the Baptist faith alongside beliefs that Christians are saved by faith alone, that the Bible is the only reliable authority in matters of religion and that congregations should be allowed to govern themselves.

A Baptist pamphlet from 1905 Romania explained that 'God makes himself known to men through the books of the Bible, giving them everything they need to organize faith and life'. Although God created men

> in his image and likeness ... through Satan's cunning the first man fell into sin. Turning away from God he lost the image and likeness of his maker and thus became mere flesh, existing in a state of spiritual death. Given that all men come from the seed of Adam we all partake of his nature, which is totally depraved and sinful. As children of hostility, conceived and born in sin, we oppose everything that is good and, despite ourselves, we seek that which is evil.[7]

Although he is fully God, Jesus Christ took on the form of sinful man for us, suffering and dying on the cross. 'He sacrificed himself for us body and soul, becoming a curse for us when he took the anger of God upon himself as punishment for our sins. We believe that this act of redemption, which has

---

[5] Nicolae Geantă, 'Dinamica teritorială a bisericilor evanghelice din România', in *Omul evanghelic: O explorare a comunităților protestante românești*, ed. Dorin Dobrincu and Dănuț Mănăstireanu (Iași: Polirom, 2018), 536–44.

[6] Stephen Wright, *The Early English Baptists, 1603–49* (Woodbridge: Boydell, 2006).

[7] *Fassiunea credinței și (întocmirea iei): Pentru adunările creștine, cari de comun pórtă numirea de adunări baptiste*, trans. Georgiu Slăvŭ, 2nd edn (n.p.: n.p., 1905).

eternal value, is the only reason why ... all of our sins and transgressions are forgiven and atoned for for all eternity.' Of God's absolutely free will he 'chooses those sinners who, as individuals, accept his offer of salvation and make it their own during their lifetimes, thus inscribing their names in heaven and giving themselves into the hands of the Saviour'. God's choice is 'eternal and unchangeable' once he has made it, and 'those who he has chosen will never be taken out of Christ's hands. Rather, through the power of God, through faith in Christ, and through love they will be kept for eternal glory.' 'This is salvation', the pamphlet said,

> that man, through the living and active word of God awakens from the sleep of death, recognizes his sins and transgressions, is sorry for them and contrite at heart. Feeling Christ's sufferings, he hastens to escape by taking hold of Christ, the only way to salvation and redemption, thus receiving through faith the forgiveness of his sins and faith in his heart that he is a child of God and a partaker of eternal life.[8]

Baptists heard this message in weekly or twice-weekly sermons, proclaimed it in song, preached it to each other during Bible studies, reminded themselves of it in their prayers, told it to their neighbours and discovered it in the Scriptures. They believed that individuals had to make a conscious choice to accept Jesus's offer of eternal life, so they rejected the baptism into the Orthodox Church they had received when they were babies. Confident that Jesus's death and resurrection had saved them once and for all, they no longer felt that they needed to confess to a priest. Discovering that they understood the Bible when they read it for themselves and disappointed that they had never heard this message of salvation from their priests, they stopped trusting the Orthodox Church to interpret Scripture for them. Excited that they could pray directly to God as his beloved children, they stopped praying to the saints or venerating icons and relics. They also refused to pray to the Virgin Mary and held up Protestant missionaries as their heroes in place of the saints who populated the Romanian national pantheon. Striving to live the holiest lives possible, they cut themselves off from the rest of society, shunning alcohol, smoking, swearing and sex outside of marriage, and looked with suspicion on things such as cinema and novels that did not have a religious purpose.

---

[8] *Fassiunea credinței și (întocmirea iei).*

Baptist churches were established in North America during the mid-seventeenth century. The Baptist Missionary Society was founded in 1792, which formed the basis for the international expansion of the movement.[9] A preacher by the name of Johann Gerhard Onken founded the first Baptist church in Germany in 1834 and then baptized the first Swiss Baptists in 1847. Baptist churches appeared in Vienna, Denmark and Sweden during the 1840s, in Bohemia and Hungary during the 1870s and in Bulgaria during the 1880s. They faced persecution in almost every country they found themselves, but the Church continued to grow due to the tenacious efforts of dedicated preachers and a growing acceptance of the idea of religious freedom.[10] It was ethnic Germans in Congress Poland who first introduced Baptist teachings into the Russian Empire during the 1850s. Ten years later ethnic Russians from Transcaucasia who were members of a sect known as Molokans or 'Spiritual Christians' began forming Baptist churches. Also in the 1860s, another new religious movement known as Shtundism appeared in previously Orthodox villages in the Ukraine. Shtundism grew organically out of interactions between Orthodox peasants and German Protestant colonists. Shtundists became known for their 'Bible circles' during which they discussed Bible passages and encouraged each other to live holy lives. Another reformist group, the Pashkovites, spread through St Petersburg's upper classes during the 1870s and, after tentative attempts at collaboration during the 1880s, the Baptists, Shtundists and Pashkovites increasingly decided that their movements were so similar that they should make common cause and organize together as Baptists. Tensions between different strands of Baptism continued throughout the movement's early decades but the faith spread quickly and created deep roots in tight local communities.[11]

The Baptist faith came to Romania from a variety of directions. Karl Johann Scharschmidt, who had been baptized by Onken in Hamburg, arrived in Bucharest in 1856 and a small Baptist church developed around him over the following decade. At first it was composed entirely of ethnic Germans, but ethnic Romanian converts joined during the mid-1890s. In Dobruja the Baptist church was established by German migrants who came from southern Russia

---

[9] William H. Brackney, *Baptists in North America: A Historical Perspective* (Malden: Blackwell, 2006), 8–23; Brian Stanley, *The History of the Baptist Missionary Society 1792–1992* (Edinburgh: T. & T. Clark, 1992).

[10] James Henry Rushbrooke, *The Baptist Movement in the Continent of Europe* (London: The Carey Press, 1923).

[11] Coleman, *Russian Baptists*; Zhuk, *Russia's Lost Reformation*; Catherine Wanner, *Communities of the Converted: Ukrainians and Global Evangelism* (Ithaca: Cornell University Press, 2007), 21–35.

during the 1860s. These congregations gradually increased in size, adding Romanian converts who in turn established their own communities. Although their numbers always remained tiny compared to their presence in the Orthodox press, the Baptist faith was well established in Romania by the early twentieth century. The creation of Greater Romania brought even more Baptists into the fold. Strong Baptist communities existed in Bessarabia, where they had been influenced by the Shtundists, and Baptists in Transylvania had enjoyed a limited degree of state recognition prior to war.[12]

Despite the strength of the Baptist Church in the Russian empire, Baptist beliefs emerged out of Christian experiences in Western Europe and the United States and most Romanians saw them as fundamentally foreign. Dănuț Mănăstireanu argues that twentieth-century Romanian Evangelicalism – a movement in which the Baptists held a central place – was influenced by the Reformation teachings of Martin Luther and John Calvin, Anabaptism, seventeenth-century Pietism and the brand of nineteenth-century Christian rationalism combined with Biblical literalism and dispensationalism that eventually gave birth to American Fundamentalism.[13] Baptists did not particularly care whether their message was 'Romanian' or not. They saw these as universal ideas that applied to everyone regardless of their ethnic origins. Nonetheless, as Iemima Ploșcariu has argued, Baptists and other Repenters went out of their way to emphasize their loyalty to the Romanian nation and state. Despite Orthodoxist claims to the contrary, Baptists desperately wanted to be 'good Romanians'.[14]

During the early twentieth century Repenters were characterized more by their enthusiasm than by their theological training. When a Baptist child from Jegălia died in 1909, no one in the community knew how to run a funeral so they had to send for a preacher from Cernavodă. Confronted by the ridicule of Orthodox family members who were horrified that they would bury someone without a priest, the small group carried the child to the cemetery singing hymns and eventually brought the whole village out for the funeral.[15] Early Baptist gatherings sometimes just involved members reading passages of the Bible out loud. Over time one or two began explaining the readings and

---

[12] Popovici, *Istoria baptiștilor*, vol. 1, 17–179; Dobrincu, 'Sub puterea cezarului', 42–64.
[13] Dănuț Mănăstireanu, 'Identitatea evanghelicilor români: rădăcini, actualitate, perspective', in *Omul evanghelic: O explorare a comunităților protestante românești*, ed. Dorin Dobrincu and Dănuț Mănăstireanu (Iași: Polirom, 2018), 256–64.
[14] Ploscariu, 'Pieties of the Nation'.
[15] Popovici, *Istoria baptiștilor*, vol. 1, 118–19.

drawing practical lessons from them, and people became preachers simply through practice.[16] Regular Bible reading was extremely important. To help people discover the whole Bible, Baptist newspapers would publish daily reading guides with specific passages recommended for morning and evening reading.[17] Many communities struggled to be allowed to register their leaders as preachers or to have their children taught religion by Baptists because the state required that people occupying these positions had either graduated from a recognized theological institute or passed their baccalaureate exams.[18] Few Baptists had. Dorin Dobrincu writes that

> the Baptists had 909 preachers at the beginning of 1927 with the following levels of education: one had university studies, four secondary school, three higher agricultural school, one business school, one four classes of middle school and trade school, six four classes of middle school, and three pedagogical school. Similarly, seven had attended seminary and three a school/Bible course/theological course. The vast majority (880) of preachers had only primary school although they had served in the church for many years.[19]

Instead, Baptists trained preachers through 'Bible courses' that might last anything from a couple of days to nine months.[20] Before a seminary was built in Bucharest in 1923, preachers who wanted further training travelled to seminaries in Budapest or Hamburg.[21]

Baptists spread their message through person-to-person evangelism and by inviting people to witness their church services where they would experience singing, prayers and preaching.[22] Weddings, funerals and baptisms were particularly good occasions for evangelism because they attracted extended family members, and Baptist newspapers reported that these events were 'a good witness' or that non-Baptists had been converted.[23] Stories about conversion experiences that testified to radical changes having taken place in believers' lives provided the pivot around which evangelistic messages were structured.[24] In

---

[16] Ibid., 191.
[17] 'Un text din Sft. Scriptură pentru fiecare zi', *Farul mântuirei*, December 1923, 11.
[18] ANIC, Fond Ministerul Instrucțiunii, Dosar 310/1923, f. 305.
[19] Dobrincu, 'Sub puterea cezarului', 97.
[20] Ilie Craiovean, 'Cursul biblic din Revețiș', *Farul mântuirei*, December 1923, 12.
[21] Dobrincu, 'Sub puterea cezarului', 97–9.
[22] ANIC, Fond Direcția Generală a Poliției (henceforth DGP), Dosar 44/1938, f. 18.
[23] 'Botezuri' and 'Căsătorii', *Farul mântuirei*, January 1923, 7–8.
[24] Heather Coleman, 'Becoming a Russian Baptist: Conversion Narratives and Social Experience', *Russian Review* 61, no. 1 (2002): 94–112; Mihai Curelaru, 'Convertirea religioasă în comunitățile evanghelice – o abordare psihologică', in *Omul evanghelic: O explorare a comunităților protestante românești*, ed. Dorin Dobrincu and Dănuț Mănăstireanu (Iași: Polirom, 2018), 602–40.

addition to Bibles and tracts, they printed their own newspapers that contained information about local communities as well as articles of a devotional or theological nature.²⁵ Itinerant preachers worked as colporteurs, or travelling book salesmen, distributing Repenter literature as a way of supporting their preaching journeys.²⁶

The first Baptist hymn book in Romanian was printed in 1897. It contained 200 songs, but the translations focused more on doctrine than on rhyme, so the words were not always easy to sing. Some communities relied entirely on Orthodox or Greek Catholic song books as people were more used to this style of worship.²⁷ Repenters were willing to use song books produced by other denominations, and their music was influenced by a broad range of Protestant currents, including hymns from German Pietism, English Puritanism, Methodism, Gospel music and songs associated with the Salvation Army and the ministries of Dwight L. Moody and Ira D. Sankey.²⁸ Music became one of the most recognizable features of Repenter gatherings. As Marin Marian-Bălașa argues, 'music does not just express identity, it creates it', and foreign musical influences helped define Repenters as distinctively 'non-Romanian' in the popular imagination.²⁹

Romanian Baptist churches in the United States established close contacts with their co-religionists inside the country. They sent literature and missionaries, and local congregations stayed in touch with Romanian students who went to study in America.³⁰ The most important international contact Baptists had was James Henry Rushbrooke, a British pastor who served as the European Commissioner of the Baptist World Alliance (BWA) from 1920 to 1925, as the Secretary for Eastern Europe from 1925 to 1928, as General Secretary from 1928 to 1939 and then as President from 1939 until his death in 1947.³¹ Rushbrooke visited Romania together with Charles Alvin

---

[25] Popovici, *Istoria baptiștilor*, vol. 1, 204–19.
[26] ACNSAS, Fond Documentar, Dosar 12388, vol. 18, f. 1; Dosar 13408, vol. 1, ff. 160–2, 168.
[27] Ibid., 195–6.
[28] Vilmos Kis-Juhász and Iulian Teodorescu, 'Bazele închinării evanghelice – Cazul evanghelicilor din România', in *Omul evanghelic: O explorare a comunităților protestante românești*, ed. Dorin Dobrincu and Dănuț Mănăstireanu (Iași: Polirom, 2018), 726–33.
[29] Marin Marian-Bălașa, 'Muzica în cadrul bisericilor minore: Funcții, identități și roluri socioculturale', in *Omul evanghelic: O explorare a comunităților protestante românești*, ed. Dorin Dobrincu and Dănuț Mănăstireanu (Iași: Polirom, 2018), 714.
[30] 'La Universitatea Denison', *Farul mântuirei*, December 1923, 10.
[31] Marius Silveșan and Vasile Bel, *Rolul lui James Henry Rushbrooke în obținerea libertății religioase pentru credincioșii baptiști din România între anii 1907–1947* (Cluj-Napoca: Editura Risoprint, 2017), 27–9.

Brooks of the American Baptist Home Mission Society in 1920. The two men were on a 'fact-finding mission' to ascertain the state of Baptist churches in Europe in the wake of the First World War. Their report emphasized how badly the war had devastated Europe – and Eastern Europe in particular – calling on Baptists in Britain and the United States to send material aid to Germany as well as to the rest of the Continent. Rushbrooke was particularly upset about the extent to which Baptists were being persecuted in Romania and they dedicated twelve pages of the report to describing beatings at the hands of police, closed churches and confiscation of buildings and literature. A Romanian delegation to the 1920 BWA conference in London attempted to bring detailed evidence of these atrocities but it was confiscated at the border.[32] Rushbrooke made up to seventeen visits to Romania and tirelessly lobbied both the Romanian and British governments and other churches to introduce religious freedom, thus providing Baptists with a voice at the highest levels of government.[33]

Baptists were the only Repenter denomination that enjoyed this sort of international support. They were also the only denomination to organize effectively on a national level. Despite frequent infighting, the establishment of the Baptist Union of Romania in 1920 provided them with a representative body that could intervene with the authorities on behalf of persecuted local congregations.[34] Official representation was important because Repenters enjoyed almost no rights under the law. A State Ordinance from 1921 denied them the right to worship and the 1923 constitution failed to recognize any Repenter denominations as churches. Laws were often inconsistent and confusing, such as the 1927 legislation that defined Baptists in Transylvania as a denomination because they had been recognized as such in Hungary but Baptists elsewhere in the country only as members of religious associations.[35]

---

[32] Bernard Green, *Tomorrow's Man: A Biography of James Henry Rushbrooke* (Didcot: The Baptist Historical Society, 1997), 73–9, 211 n. 14.

[33] Ibid., 88–110, 148–70; Silveşan and Bel, *Rolul lui James Henry Rushbrooke*; Robert S. Wilson, 'Coming of Age: The Post-War Era and the 1920s', in *Baptists Together in Christ, 1905–2005: A Hundred Year History of the Baptist World Alliance*, ed. Richard V. Pierard (Birmingham, AL: Samford University Press, 2005), 47–72.

[34] ANIC, Fond Ministerul Instrucţiunii, Dosar 1922/29, f. 120; Dosar 289/1924, f. 7. On the history of the Baptist Union, see Dobrincu, 'Sub puterea cezarului', 94–7; Popovici, *Istoria Baptiştilor*, vol. 2, 288–94.

[35] Dobrincu, 'Sub puterea cezarului', 91–3; Green, *Tomorrow's Man*, 151–2.

Brethren

The Brethren (*Creștini după Evanghelie*) were the second largest Repenter denomination. The Brethren faith emerged out of meetings of non-conformist Protestants in Ireland during the late 1820s. Over the next decade it established important hubs in Plymouth, England, and Geneva, Switzerland.[36] The movement experienced a number of schisms, but it was a Swiss missionary from the 'Open Brethren', Francis Berney, who brought the faith to Romania in 1899. After planting a church in Bucharest, Berney was joined by an English missionary, Edmund Hamer Broadbent, and together they carried out missions among ethnic Germans in southern Transylvania in 1902–3. The faith then spread organically within Moldova when soldiers and refugees from the Old Kingdom concentrated there during the First World War.[37]

Brethren placed a strong emphasis on personal prayer, regular Bible study and holy living. Their most distinctive feature was that they rejected the idea of pastors or any organizational structures above the level of the local congregation, preferring to be governed by a loose configuration of 'elders' – usually older men who were well regarded within the church community. Congregations were affiliated with one another through fraternal bonds and membership of the Church was defined by whether or not one was allowed to receive the Eucharist, not through any formal Church structures.[38] When the state demanded that the Brethren demonstrate that they had some sort of church hierarchy in order to receive permission to function, the Brethren decided 'after much prayer and deliberation' that they would prefer to remain outside of the law and suffer the consequences rather than appoint official leaders.[39]

Brethren were also known for the doctrine of dispensationalism, which was first developed by the Brethren pioneer John Nelson Darby. Unlike other early Brethren preachers who taught that the Rapture and Christ's Second Coming would take place after a seven-year period of tribulation, Darby

---

[36] Massimo Introvigne, *The Plymouth Brethren* (Oxford: Oxford University Press, 2018), 18–60.
[37] Dobrincu, 'Sub puterea cezarului', 64–70; Ieremia Rusu, *Cine sunt Creștinii după Evanghelie? Curente teologice care au influențat doctrinele specific ale Bisericilor Creștine după Evanghelie din România în perioada interbelică și comunistă* (Bucharest: Editura Didactică și Pedagogică, 2011).
[38] Eugen Matei, 'Teologia evanghelicilor români: Rădăcini și perspective', in *Omul evanghelic: O explorare a comunităților protestante românești*, ed. Dorin Dobrincu and Dănuț Mănăstireanu (Iași: Polirom, 2018), 433–41.
[39] ACNSAS, Fond Documentar, Dosar 13408, vol. 2, f. 34–5.

argued that the rapture could take place at any time.[40] Darby's particular brand of Brethren theology was not the one that first arrived in Romania, but his dispensationalism was strong in Brethren circles between the wars.[41] In practical terms, the knowledge that the Rapture could take place at any time encouraged a 'watchfulness' and served as an impetus for holy living because one did not want to be caught sinning when Christ returned.

Rather than entrusting preaching to one person with theological training, Brethren elders preached according to the inspiration of the Holy Spirit. They never established seminars or Bible schools in Romania during the inter-war period, although several leaders studied at Brethren seminaries in Switzerland and Germany and some Orthodox priests with theology degrees joined the movement during the 1920s. The Brethren also published their own newspapers and magazines, which disseminated Brethren doctrines to scattered communities.[42] A police report from 1930 stated that in Brașov Brethren 'preachers and colporteurs traverse the town and villages selling different religious literature. They use these occasions to make speeches and convert the weakest [members of society]. These sects are sustained by money donated by their followers and from the sale of literature. Every year these sectarians are visited by foreign missionaries who make propaganda speeches for their sects.'[43] Police reports listing the members of Brethren communities suggest that women were in the majority in most churches.[44] As did all Repenter denominations, the Brethren insisted on clear gender roles for men and women. Only men were allowed to preach or exercise leadership and women were to display their subordination by covering their heads and not wearing jewellery or make-up. There was little that was remarkable about these rules for Romanian Christians, however, and none of the anti-sectarian literature ever commented on Repenter gender roles.

---

[40] Timothy C. F. Stunt, 'John Nelson Darby: Contexts and Perceptions', in *Protestant Millennialism, Evangelicalism, and Irish Society, 1790–2005*, ed. Crawford Gribben and Andrew R. Holmes (Basingstoke: Palgrave Macmillan, 2006), 83–98.
[41] Matei, 'Teologia evanghelicilor români', 441.
[42] Dobrincu, 'Sub puterea cezarului', 101–2.
[43] ANIC – Brașov, Fond Chestura de Poliție Brașov, Serv. Siguranței, Dosar 4/1930, f. 691.
[44] ACNSAS, Fond Documentar, Dosar 13408, vol. 1, ff. 293–8; vol. 2, f. 205–6.

Nazarenes

The founding father of the Nazarenes, Samuel Heinrich Fröhlich, writes that in April 1825, during the Easter vacation from his second year of theological studies at the University of Basel, 'a very soft voice, which was neither terrifying nor depressing but nevertheless very convincing and penetrating, spoke in the depth of my soul, "It cannot remain thus with thee. Thou must change!"'.[45] With a new passion for personal holiness and renewal, Fröhlich returned to his studies temporarily but had to leave university in October for financial reasons. He became a minister in the Swiss Reformed Church in 1828 but was expelled in 1830 for refusing to accept new liturgical reforms, which he said were based 'upon the underlying principles of nature and upon the religion of reason rather than upon faith in Christ'.[46] Fröhlich then embraced the doctrine of believer's baptism and worked with the Baptist Continental Society between 1831 and 1836 before establishing the Neutäufer movement, also known as the Communities of Evangelical Baptists (Evanghelisch Taufgesinnter Gemeinden). The new Church emphasized the importance of repentance and holiness to the point of believing that Christians must be entirely perfect. Fröhlich wrote that when they are born again, Christians

> Receive, in addition to our cleansed *human nature*, the *divine* nature of the Son (Romans 8; 2 Peter 1); and as regenerated children of God we must in our following after Christ, *earn* our *share* in the future glory like Jesus, i.e., we must become *worthy* of it by our *obedience* to the will of God in our efforts and sufferings, although it is to Him alone that we owe our *share* in the salvation, because of his obedience to death on the cross. But if we are not faithful and do not suffer with Him and *conquer* the world and the devil, *remaining constant unto the end*, then we cannot be raised to glory with Him, although He died for us (2 Timothy 2:10ff; Romans 8:17ff).[47]

From the late 1830s onward, the Neutäufer movement spread across Switzerland, Alsace and southern Germany as well as through the Hungarian regions of the Habsburg Empire. Increasingly known as Nazarenes, communities of Fröhlich's

---

[45] Quoted in Joseph F. Pfeiffer, 'Between Remnant and Renewal: A Historical and Comparative Study of the "Apostolic Christian Church" among Neo-Anabaptist Renewal Movements in Europe and America' (MA diss., Associated Mennonite Biblical Seminary, Elkhart, Indiana, 2010), 53.
[46] Ibid., 59.
[47] Quoted in ibid., 70.

followers consolidated in Hungary under the leadership of Louis Hencsey in particular, including converts from Roman Catholicism, the Hungarian Reformed Church, Slovak Lutheranism and Serbian Orthodoxy.[48] The denomination spread to the United States in 1847 where it became known as the Apostolic Christian Church of America.[49] A second wave of Nazarene migrants fled to America to escape communist persecution following the Second World War.[50] Non-resistance became a core feature of Nazarene teaching during the second half of the nineteenth century, bringing them closer to traditional Anabaptist teachings while exposing them to increased state persecution because of their refusal to bear arms.[51]

A number of Nazarenes became Romanian citizens following the territorial shifts after the First World War. The Romanian state soon classified them as Repenters and took a decidedly hostile attitude towards them. One police report stated:

> This sect, originally known as 'the New Church' and later as 'the Nazarene community', adopting the name of Nazarenes because they confess that they seek to follow Christ the Nazarene in their life and actions. This sect originates among the Hungarians and entered Romania following the union with the Transylvanian provinces. Large concentrations of the sect are in the Banat, Bukovina, Cluj, and in Dobruja. Their doctrine consists primarily of affirming the interior church, rejecting outward acts of religiosity. They believe in baptizing only adults; they refuse to take oaths or serve in the military. They do not recognize the priesthood, and they call our church 'the old Babylon' in the propaganda. They hide under the name of Baptists. Their propaganda organ is a pamphlet called *The New Harlot of Zion* in which they defame the church.[52]

The most serious quarrel that Romanian officials had with the Nazarenes was that they would not bear arms. They pointed out that many Nazarenes had refused to fight for Austria-Hungary during the First World War and had even been executed for it.[53] Nazarenes responded that their faith actually made them ideal citizens, because 'we submit to all the obligations of citizenship and wish

---

[48] Aleksov, *Religious Dissent*, 87–116.
[49] Aleksandra Djurić-Milovanić, '"Our Father is Good, but Strict": The Transformation of the Apostolic Christian Church-Nazarene in North America', *Journal of Amish and Plain Anabaptist Studies* 6, no. 1 (2018): 61–72.
[50] Perry Klopfenstein, *Marching to Zion: A History of the Apostolic Christian Church of America*, 2nd edn (Eureka, IL: Apostolic Christian Church of America, 2008).
[51] Pfeiffer, 'Between Remnant and Renewal', 91–2.
[52] ACNSAS, Fond Documentar, Dosar 10727, vol. 2, f. 3.
[53] ANIC, Fond MCA, Dosar 136/1922, ff. 1, 5, 21.

to contribute to the consolidation and happiness of the national Romanian state with our modest abilities. Our faith teaches us not to ruffle even a hair on anyone's head. We preach true love for one's neighbour in our Lord Jesus Christ.'[54] Nazarenes operated with a different vision of the state to that of the police. Whereas the Nazarenes believed that the state should leave them alone so long as they obeyed its laws, the modern nation-state expected them to become active supporters of its ideological programme of national chauvinism, which is something they and other Repenters were not always willing to do.[55]

Pentecostals

The Pentecostal movement was characterized by speaking in tongues, a focus on supernatural healing, a literal reading of the Bible and a strong emphasis on holy living. It had its roots in the Holiness movement, Protestant faith healing and the revivalism of the Keswick convention in England, but as a denomination it emerged out of a series of charismatic revivals in North America, Wales, India and Korea at the beginning of the twentieth century. The most famous of these revivals took place at Azusa Street in Los Angeles, California, between 1906 and 1915.[56] Pentecostalism arrived in the western Balkans almost immediately after the Azusa Street revival began.[57]

In Romania there were reports of Pentecostals in Moldavia as early as 1908 and the first Pentecostal church was established in Bukovina in 1918 by individuals who had encountered Pentecostalism while serving on the Eastern Front during the First World War. Other Romanians discovered Pentecostalism in the United States through various preachers, including the founder of the International Church of the Foursquare Gospel, Aimee Semple McPherson, whose healing meetings in Los Angeles made her a household name in America.[58] As a denomination centred around faith healing and speaking in tongues, Pentecostalism was usually spread by people who had experienced

---

[54] Ibid., f. 6. They added that, although they did teach people not to bear arms, the choice to do so was an individual one and so the Nazarene denomination as a whole should not be punished for it. Ibid., f. 21.
[55] See ibid., Dosar 178/1923, f. 114.
[56] Allan Heaton Anderson, *An Introduction to Pentecostalism* (Cambridge: Cambridge University Press, 2014), 19–39.
[57] Driton Krasniqi, 'The Development of Pentecostalism in South-Eastern European Nations: Albania, Bosnia and Herzegovina, Greece, Macedonia, Montenegro, Kosovo, Serbia', in *European Pentecostalism*, ed. William K. Kay and Anne E. Dyer (Leiden: Brill, 2011), 205–24.
[58] Bălăban, *Istoria bisericii pentecostale*, 15–16; Dobrincu, 'Sub puterea cezarului', 70–2.

these phenomena at a Pentecostal meeting. Thus empowered, they would return to their own communities and pray that others might experience these 'gifts' as well. In Romania most early Pentecostals were converts from Baptist churches who broke away from their local congregations to form their own churches once they had gathered a few people who were enthusiastic about this new style of worship.[59]

Two of the earliest Pentecostal leaders in Romania were a husband and wife, Gheorghe and Persiada Bradin, who had left their local Baptist church because of doctrinal differences. In 1923 they heard about 'baptism in the Holy Spirit' and wrote to Romanian Baptists in Cleveland asking for details. Their friends in America sent them a pamphlet and they prayed to be baptized in the Holy Spirit. Persiada Bradin had been suffering from tuberculosis and water retention for three years. She received gifts of prophecy and speaking in tongues as well as being miraculously healed. The couple subsequently established a Pentecostal church in their village of Pauliș, in Arad county. From here Pentecostalism spread throughout the country until by 1931 they could claim 169 churches with a total of 3,560 members. The Bradins preached a particularly strict doctrine of holiness and separation from 'the world', to the extent that early Pentecostals did not wear ties and shaved their heads to avoid becoming proud of their appearance.[60]

Pentecostal congregations were typically smaller than most Baptist or Brethren churches during the inter-war period and police reports suggest that the average member was relatively younger.[61] In addition to preachers, Pentecostals also recognized prophets, presbyters, deacons and deaconesses in their churches, each of which had clearly defined roles to play in making the church function.[62] Although every Christian receives gifts of wisdom, knowledge and faith, Pentecostals argued, not everyone will be able to speak in tongues or heal people. Whether or not an individual received such a gift was at the discretion of the Holy Spirit.[63]

The authorities were initially quite worried about the impact of Pentecostalism on society. A circular from the Ministry of the Interior from 1934 asked local police to report

---

[59] ACNSAS, Fond Documentar, Dosar 12388, vol. 21, f. 43; Dosar 10727, vol. 2, ff. 7–8.
[60] Bălăban, *Istoria bisericii pentecostale*, 18–19; Dobrincu, 'Sub puterea cezarului', 72–9.
[61] ACNSAS, Fond Documentar, Dosar 12388, vol. 21, f. 16.
[62] *Scurta expunere a principiilor de credință a "Bisericii lui Dumnezeu Apostolice" (Penticostale) din România* (Arad: Editura Vestitorul Evangheliei, 1947), 22–3.
[63] Ibid., 19–20.

1) If their belief in an outpouring of the Holy Spirit on certain people has a disastrous impact on these believers; that is to say whether it provokes a religious psychosis which manifests through extremely contagious psycho-mystical ecstasies. In other words, whether there are frequent cases of mental illness among them.
2) If their belief in healing through prayer and anointing with oil causes them to stop going to the doctor and reject normal sanitary measures such as refusing to vaccinate their children, etc.
3) What the attitude of these believers is towards the authorities and the laws of the state in general.[64]

All reports consistently came back saying that Pentecostals were not a threat to law and order in any way but they were nonetheless persecuted by police to the extent that several early Pentecostals were beaten to death.[65] Not allowed to have church buildings, they met in secret in homes with blacked-out windows, in fields or in the mountains and at night.[66]

Pentecostals were aware that they were frequently misunderstood and ridiculed, even by other Repenters.[67] An exposition of their beliefs from 1947 is instructive because it shows the extent to which Pentecostal beliefs about spiritual gifts were related to their understanding of the end times, as well as their desire to demonstrate that this was an international phenomenon, in no way restricted to Romania. They wrote,

> Once again the Gospel is being spread among sinful people with ever greater power. The time when the Lord Jesus will come again is drawing near, though he cannot come until those who live on earth are made aware of what is coming. Precisely for this reason the Lord Jesus has begun to work in miraculous ways, raising up chosen people who are preaching the Gospel with the passion of Christians from ages past. Humanity has begun to awaken after ages of slumber; Christian churches based on repentance are being established everywhere. Great works of the Holy Spirit are appearing in churches once again. Apostolic Christianity has once again begun to move multitudes of faithful souls with enthusiasm. The apostolic faith is beginning to work with

---

[64] ACNSAS, Fond Documentar, Dosar 13408, vol. 2, f. 97.
[65] Bălăban, *Istoria bisericii penticostale*, 42–50.
[66] Dobrincu, 'Sub puterea cezarului', 77.
[67] On the polemics between Pentecostals, Baptists and Brethren, see Bălăban, *Istoria bisericii penticostale*, 27–32.
[68] *Scurta expunere*, 3.

the same power that it had in the time of the apostles, bringing thousands, and hundreds of thousands of souls to the Lord Jesus.⁶⁸

A schism divided Romanian Pentecostalism only a few years after the movement began. Whereas Gheorghe Bradin led the Pentecostals in Arad, the churches in Bukovina were led by a former Baptist pastor named Eugen Bodor. Bodor invited the Russian and Eastern European Mission (REEM) to collaborate in the work in Romania, but Bradin clashed with REEM's representative, Gustav Herbert Schmidt, an Assemblies of God missionary from Poland. Bradin insisted that believers should wash each other's feet before participating in the Eucharist and that they never touch alcohol, and he differed with Schmidt over whether there were two different types of baptism in the Holy Spirit. Bodor and Schmidt found themselves unable to collaborate with Bradin and, despite several attempts at reconciliation, the movement split in 1931, beginning over a decade of infighting and factionalism.⁶⁹

Seventh-Day Adventists

Seventh-Day Adventism began in the United States. In 1833 a Baptist preacher by the name of William Miller predicted that the Second Coming of Christ would take place on 22 October 1844, a day that came to be known as the Great Disappointment. No one saw anything out of the ordinary happen that day, but Ellen Gould Harmon, a Methodist, had a vision in which it was revealed that this was when Christ began judging the dead. When he finishes he will return to earth. James White, an itinerant preacher who later married Harmon, supported her message and she continued having visions throughout her life. Together they founded the Seventh-Day Adventist Church.⁷⁰ The faith was first preached in Romania during 1868 by Mihail Czechowski, a former Roman Catholic priest who had converted to Adventism while visiting the United States. Czechowski made only twelve converts in Pitești, but visits from American Adventist leaders kept the community alive. Ludvig Conradi, another American missionary, converted several people in Cluj during the mid-1890s before helping a group of German Adventist settlers who had moved from the Crimea to establish a church in Constanța county. Adventism came to Bucharest in 1904 through

---

⁶⁹ Bălăban, *Istoria bisericii pentecostale*, 50–69; Dobrincu, 'Sub puterea cezarului', 105–11.
⁷⁰ Laura L. Vance, 'God's Messenger: Ellen G. White', in *Female Leaders in New Religious Movements*, ed. Inga B. Tøllefsen and Christian Giudice (New York: Palgrave Macmillan, 2017), 29–49.

Johann Ginter, an evangelist from Russia who was expelled from the country, but not before establishing a small church and sending two Romanians – Petru Paulini and Ștefan Demetrescu – to study at an Adventist training school in Germany. Paulini and Demetrescu began organizing conferences in 1907 and there were roughly 2,000 Adventists in Romania by the time they founded the Romanian Union Conference in 1919. An Adventist press in Germany printed Romanian-language literature between 1908 and 1920, when Adventists set up the Adventist Publishing House in Bucharest. By 1923 the church had its own training school in Romania.[71] Adventists received state recognition in 1928 and by 1930 they had 7,700 members, 65 ministers and 290 houses of prayer.[72]

A police report on Ion Solea, a preacher from Târgoviște who was arrested in the home of Pantazică Stoica in a village 45 miles away, gives us some idea of what Adventist gatherings looked like. 'In the evening', the report said,

> while he was giving some advice to Mr. and Mrs. Stoica several women and children arrived who listened to the sermon. He read several parables from Holy Scripture, about the beggar and the poisoned bread and the sacrifice of Abraham and Isaac and about how pork is unclean and should not be eaten. After this he sang the usual songs which are part of their prayers.[73]

The fact that Solea was arrested so far from home reminds us that small, rural Adventist communities did not always have their own ministers and underlines the importance of travelling preachers in keeping the movement alive.[74]

Adventists held a number of beliefs that set them apart from Orthodox Christians and from other Repenters. Demetrescu elaborated on these beliefs in a 1915 tract *What We Adventists Believe*, which focused on clarifying the differences between Adventism and Romanian Orthodoxy. Rather than worshipping on Sunday as other Christians did, Seventh-Day Adventists kept 'the seventh day' – Saturday – holy, in accordance with the fourth Commandment. They were happy to acknowledge the possibility that saints really were holy, but pointed out that if this was true only God would know anyway. 'Their holiness only helps them', Demetrescu wrote, 'not helping anyone else except as an example to

---

[71] Gary Land, *Historical Dictionary of Seventh-Day Adventists* (Lanham, MA: Scarecrow Press, 2005), 252.
[72] Earl A. Pope, 'Protestantism in Romania', in *Protestantism and Politics in Eastern Europe and Russia: The Communist and Postcommunist Eras*, ed. Sabrina Petra Ramet (Durham: Duke University Press, 1992), 186.
[73] ACNSAS, Fond Documentar, Dosar 9486, vol. 1, ff. 48–9.
[74] Police reports often noted that Adventist communities were sustained by visiting ministers. ANIC, Fond MCA, Dosar 131/1922, f. 14.

follow because everyone has to answer before God for their actions themselves'. Adventists did not venerate icons, but Demetrescu insisted that they did not ridicule the Orthodox for doing so. Moreover, they believed in a strict separation of Church and state so they paid their ministers and did not expect state salaries, quoting the words of 1 Corinthians 9:14 that 'those who proclaim the gospel should get their living by the gospel'. Demetrescu mentioned that Adventists 'abstain completely from all forms of intoxicating drink, from smoking tobacco, from consuming food that stimulates and weakens the nerves [i.e., meat], and from any sort of bad habits'. 'For us renewing our health goes hand in hand with renewing and strengthening our faith', he said. 'It even constitutes the first step in preparing us for the higher life to which the Lord Jesus has called all men: purifying and keeping the human body healthy – this wonderful temple, the only one in which God dwells through his Spirit – being the first step towards a life worthy of the divine presence living in the heart of man.' A former army officer himself, Demetrescu denied the frequent accusations that Adventists refused to serve in the military, as well as distancing his denomination from both philosemitism and antisemitism. 'Explosions of hate are and remain proof of weakness', he said, 'which makes one think given that they come from [Orthodox] church leaders in the form of pastoral letters that claim that we are Jews who want to dominate the country spiritually. These attacks do the country more harm than people realize.'[75]

Legal recognition did not always stop police and gendarmes from harassing Adventists. As the General Secretary of the Evangelical Union of Seventh Day Adventist Communities, Demetrescu frequently found himself writing to the government requesting that they remind the authorities that Adventists had a legal right to worship.[76] Whenever a conflict developed between Adventists and Orthodox Christians the police consistently sided with the Orthodox. According to an Adventist complaint from 1923 when two drunks disturbed an Adventist worship service in Turtucaia, the local policeman – who was already on the scene – entered the church and began beating the preacher 'to keep the peace'. A few days later secret policemen disrupted another one of their services, hitting people with their own Bibles.[77] Elsewhere Adventists were imprisoned for weeks at a time for actions such as 'insulting the Mother of God during a funerary

---

[75] Ștefan Demetrescu, *Ce credem noi adventiștii: Răspuns calomniilor debitate despre noi de către cei interesați* (Bucharest: Atelierele grafice SOCEC, 1915).
[76] ACNSAS, Fond Documentar, Dosar 9486, vol. 1, f. 3; ANIC, Fond MCA, Dosar 131/1922, ff. 36–7.
[77] ANIC, Fond MCA, Dosar 131/1922, ff. 42–4.

vigil [*priveghere*] in the church'.⁷⁸ Adventist preachers and colporteurs were arrested and their literature confiscated any time they were found not carrying government-issued documents proving they had permission to preach. These authorizations had to be stamped, contain the individual's photograph and be renewed every three years.⁷⁹ Orthodox priests used the widespread distrust of Repenters to make life as difficult as possible for them. The parish priest in Alexandria wrote to the police in 1922 that

> two colporteurs – Adventist propagandists – came into our town a few days ago. They went from house to house on the pretext that they were selling Bibles but in reality they were doing Adventist propaganda; criticizing and insulting our church and clergy, deceiving people that they are not Adventists but 'Orthodox Christians'; threatening women and children that if they did not buy the books all the punishments and plagues of Egypt would come upon them, and more.⁸⁰

Although the Romanian Adventist church might have been small, it was well organized on a regional scale, which made people suspect that Adventists were in the pay of foreign countries.⁸¹ According to one book catalogue confiscated by police, Adventists distributed literature in Romanian, Hungarian, Serbian, Slovak, Russian, Polish, Greek, Hebrew, Armenian, Croatian, Czech, German, French, Bulgarian, Ruthenian, Turkish and Italian.⁸² The police were not particularly discerning when it came to confiscating literature and one Orthodox bookseller wrote to the Ministry of Denominations in 1926 complaining that they were even confiscating Bibles and religious books that had been edited by the Ministry itself.⁸³

Bible Students and Jehovah's Witnesses

The founder of the Bible Students, Charles Taze Russell, was influenced by Adventism and other Christian millenarian teachings. He worked together with Adventist preachers in Pennsylvania before starting out on his own in 1879 with the newspaper *Zion's Watch Tower and Herald of Christ's Presence*. Russell taught that the Christian Church had lost its way since the time of the Apostles and

---

⁷⁸ Ibid., Dosar 131/1922, ff. 52–3.
⁷⁹ Ibid., Dosar 146/1936, ff. 1–32, 186–92.
⁸⁰ Ibid., Dosar 131/1922, f. 32.
⁸¹ Ibid., Dosar 131/1922, f. 73.
⁸² Ibid., Dosar 146/1936, f. 35.
⁸³ Ibid., Dosar 119/1926, f. 193.

only now, through a close study of the Bible, was it returning to its true path. His arguments found a ripe audience in late nineteenth-century America, which soon blossomed into a robust Church.[84] Russell believed that he was living in the last days and warned that the world was entering a time of tribulation and persecution for Christians. There is, he wrote,

> a great and severe trial of faith coming with increasing force upon the church – 'the fire of that day' which 'shall try every man's work of what sort it is'. We saw that this fiery trial then coming, aimed to destroy the very foundation of Christian faith and hope, the first principles of the doctrine of Christ – 'How that Christ died for our sins according to the Scriptures' (1 Corinthians 15:3) and that he thus redeemed, ransomed, bought us with his own precious blood.[85]

Political and social upheavals were all evidence of the birth pains of a new age, Russell said, as were changes to the climate and the environment as the earth was being 'prepared' like 'the garden of Eden to be a fit home for perfect man'.[86] Russell rejected the concept of the Trinity, 'an idea so absurd that its very absurdity is taken as proof of its divine authority, though not a text of scripture can be quoted in its support'.[87] He also explained that hell would not involve eternal torment, but 'the tomb is spoken of as a great "prison house", in which the captives of death (the Adamic, or first death) await deliverance. Though dissolved in death, the identity of each being is preserved in the mind and power of God, and will be reproduced in due time by resurrection power'.[88] Not quite understanding this doctrine and consistently thinking in nationalist terms, Romanian police wrote that Bible Student pamphlets taught that the souls of those who died in the war would not go to heaven but were now disembodied spirits because they had perished in bloodshed.[89]

Russell toured Europe during the 1890s. Bible Students began outreach in Berlin in 1897, establishing an office there in 1903 and one in Warsaw in 1910. Adolf Erwin Weber began outreach in Switzerland in 1895, in Belgium in 1901 and in France in 1906.[90] Several Hungarian Bible Students returned

---

[84] M. James Prenton, *Apocalypse Delayed: The Story of Jehovah's Witnesses*, 3rd edn (Toronto: University of Toronto Press, 2015), 13–68.
[85] 'An Inconsistent Contemporary', *Zion's Watch Tower*, January 1886, 2.
[86] 'View from the Tower', *Zion's Watch Tower*, September 1886, 1.
[87] 'The Lord Your God Proveth You', *Zion's Watch Tower*, June 1885, 7.
[88] 'The Lake of Fire and Brimstone which is the Second Death', *Zion's Watch Tower*, October 1886, 5.
[89] ANIC, Fond MCA, Dosar 137/1922, f. 10.
[90] Gerhard Besier and Katarzyna Stoklosa eds, *Jehovas Zeugen in Europa – Geschichte und Gegenwart: Band 1. Belgien, Frankreich, Griechenland, Italien, Luxemburg, Niederlande, Portugal und Spanien* (Münster: Lit Verlag, 2013).

to Austria-Hungary from the United States in the early years of the twentieth century. One of these was Károly Szabó, who carried out mission work in Mureş county from 1911 onwards.[91] The movement soon established an office in Cluj, which moved to Bucharest in 1925.[92] Ilie Groza converted in 1919 and began holding Bible studies in Bessarabia with his family, which soon expanded into a regional movement. By 1921 they could claim 200 members in Bessarabia and 2,000 in Romania as a whole.[93] Romanian Bible Students had five conditions for membership:

1) Belief in God as the supreme, intelligent Creator and Maker of the Universe;
2) Belief in the Son of God, our Lord Jesus Christ, as the Saviour of mankind and thus the personal Saviour of each individual;
3) Belief in the inspiration of the Bible as the Word of God and an unreserved acceptance of it as the sole belief of the Christian;
4) A complete consecration to doing God's holy will;
5) A holy, noble, and irreproachable life.[94]

Each congregation was led by a group of elders who were appointed after a test on Bible knowledge. Individuals had to answer 19 out of 22 questions correctly before being eligible to become elders.[95]

Romanian-language literature was published in New York and distributed throughout the country via the office in Cluj.[96] Iacob Sima, who had returned to Cluj from America after the war, did the Romanian translations, although they had to pay someone to translate their literature into Hungarian.[97] Police claimed that Bible Students exploited 'any difficult economic situation or national or international political conflict, claiming that these problems were predicted as the beginning of a cataclysm, following which the "Kingdom of God" will appear, which will last one thousand years'.[98] Most early missionaries had to work full time to support their evangelism. In 1920 the American leadership

---

[91] Tudor Petcu and Andy Besuden, 'The History of Jehovah's Witnesses in Hungary', *Studia humana* 7, no. 2 (2018): 45–6.
[92] ACNSAS, Fond Documentar, Dosar 10727, vol. 1, f. 7.
[93] ANIC, Fond MCA, Dosar 137/1922, f. 64; Emily B. Baran, *Dissent on the Margins: How Soviet Jehovah's Witnesses Defied Communism and Lived to Preach about It* (Oxford: Oxford University Press, 2014), 23–4.
[94] ANIC, Fond MCA, Dosar 137/1922, f. 65.
[95] Ibid., Dosar 137/1922, f. 65.
[96] ANIC, Fond MCA, Dosar 137/1922, ff. 9–12; ACNSAS, Fond Documentar, Dosar 10727, vol. 1, f. 7.
[97] ANIC, Fond MCA, Dosar 137/1922, f. 13; ACNSAS, Fond Documentar, Dosar 10727, vol. 1, f. 13.
[98] ACNSAS, Fond Documentar, Dosar 10727, vol. 1, f. 7.

gave the Romanian branch a gift of $25, which was used to buy a suit for an evangelist to wear while preaching.[99]

Leadership struggles wracked the movement in the United States during the First World War. Russell's death brought James Franklin Rutherford to power as the uncontested leader of the movement, but not before large numbers of people left to form their own groups in protest at Rutherford's autocratic style.[100] Romanians were largely cut off from the tensions between Russell, Rutherford and other leaders. They remained loyal to Rutherford throughout the inter-war period.[101] In 1931 he changed the name of the Watch Tower and Tract Society to the Jehovah's Witnesses, which is how they are most recognizable today.[102]

Bible Students were harshly persecuted by police and by 1927 some groups were meeting in the woods to avoid repression.[103] Persecution was compounded by the fact that the authorities frequently misunderstood or distorted Bible Student teachings. In 1921 police reported that they were 'socialist because they are against militarism and monarchies. Their primary tendency is Judaism [*jidovismul*], which is to say that everyone should celebrate Saturday because then a great and unique people will form. Only then will the Messiah come who has been awaited by the Jews for 6,000 years.'[104] Romanian police focused in particular on the potential political implications of their teachings, reporting that

> They teach that after Adam fell into sin, Jehovah sent angels to turn the human nations from the rule of Lucifer; that angels have the power to take on human bodies on earth, that they took human women as wives and gave birth to the giants that were destroyed by God and their parents thrown into Tartar. They also say in their propaganda that Judgement Day began in the middle of the nineteenth century, when demons were again given the ability to take on human bodies and gave birth to giants, who in their minds are the great kings, statesmen, generals, scientists, and capitalists who demoralize the world. They believe that God in his anger punishes these people with revolutions and wars. Their doctrine is based on communism.[105]

---

[99] Baran, *Dissent on the Margins*, 22.
[100] Prenton, *Apocalypse Delayed*, 69–80.
[101] ANIC, Fond MCA, Dosar 137/1922, f. 13.
[102] Prenton, *Apocalypse Delayed*, 86–7.
[103] Baran, *Dissent on the Margins*, 24.
[104] ANIC, Fond MCA, Dosar 137/1922, f. 10.
[105] ACNSAS, Fond Documentar, Dosar 10727, vol. 2, f. 3.

Another police summary of Witness teachings from the 1930s stated that their key doctrines were:

1) Belief in the millennium (they say that Jesus Christ will come to earth where he will reign for a thousand years);
2) All human organization is of the devil and the rulers of countries serve the devil;
3) Refusal to submit to the laws, which come from the devil;
4) The end of the world will come at the end of the millennium, when everything will be destroyed and only those who believe in Jehovah will live forever.[106]

Most policemen were Orthodox Christians, and they looked on Repenters with deep mistrust. Largely convinced by arguments that to be Romanian was to be Orthodox, they saw Repenters as traitors to the nation who were spreading foreign propaganda. The foreign origins of these movements did little to allay such fears. Despite the fact that most Repenters did their utmost to obey any and every law that did not explicitly contradict their beliefs, they were consistently persecuted by both the Church and the state throughout the inter-war period.

---

[106] Ibid., vol. 1, f. 13.

7

Missionaries

Evangelical groups such as Baptists, Brethren, Pentecostals and Nazarenes saw an enormous difference between themselves and other Repenters such as Seventh-Day Adventists and Bible Students. The Romanian police did not. They categorized all Repenters as criminals, together with a number of other illegal religious movements including Inochentists and Old Calendarists. Officials often confused the Bible Students with Nazarenes in particular, although both movements took pains to distance themselves from each other.[1] One report from 1923 claimed that Inochentists and Adventists from Piatra village in Orhei county became over-excited when they saw two rockets in the sky that had been launched by a military unit nearby as part of a celebration. Believing that the Holy Spirit had come to earth, they attacked the gendarme station, the post office, the priest and a Jew.[2] As Kapaló has shown, such reports had little basis in reality. This one was copied almost verbatim from a sensationalist newspaper article in *Universul* and the facts were not verified until five years later, when another report confirmed that nothing of the sort had happened.[3]

Many of the groups that police equated with Repenters were Russian movements such as Shtundists, Dukhobors, Molokans and Old Believers (Lipoveni). According to the police, Reapers (Secerătorii) believed that they were living in the last days and that Jesus would soon return to gather them to heaven. They refused to take oaths or to serve in the military. Karaimites were Jewish Christians who practised circumcision, Skoptsy castrated themselves entirely and Khlysts (also known as Milenarişti) were apparently pantheists who believed that God communicates directly with all of creation. If one believes the police reports, they engaged in ecstatic dances to gain supernatural visions and indulged in night-time orgies. The Swedenborgians followed the teachings of the

---

[1] ANIC, Fond MCA, Dosar 137/1922, ff. 13, 18.
[2] Ibid., Dosar 177/1923, f. 9.
[3] Kapaló, *Inochentism*, 156–9.

eighteenth-century mystic Emanuel Swedenborg; the Quakers (Tremurătorii) worshipped by dancing, jumping and weeping in order to gain illumination; and the New Israelites tried to convert Christians to Judaism. Finally, Salvationism – or the Salvation Army – 'is a military organization with ranks, decorations, marches, parades, etc., including uniforms for both men and women. They conduct propaganda through singing and fanfare'.[4] One heresy gave birth to another, Vartolomeu Stănescu said, and heretics made sins into virtues, such that Inochentists supposedly treated sexual immorality as a means of salvation.[5] Convinced that Repenters were a threat to society, individual gendarmes abused their power to prevent them receiving permission to open churches, to stop children attending school, or arresting and beating men, women and children attending prayer meetings.[6] Particularly zealous gendarmes occasionally closed Reformed or Lutheran churches as well, and these churches had to write to the ministry reminding them that they were legally recognized denominations.[7]

The international connections Repenters enjoyed made them particularly susceptible to accusations that they were 'not Romanian'. Occasionally, priests wrote entire pamphlets about the dangers of Khlysts and Mormons even though there were very few Khlysts and no Mormons in the country.[8] These pamphlets used fear campaigns about Mormons spreading polygamy to tar all 'sectarians' with the same brush. Repenters in Broscăuți, in Dorohoi county, reported that the priest and teacher were planning to murder them and throw their bodies into the river. Other priests encouraged their parishioners to attack Repenters, disrupting weddings, vandalizing prayer houses and beating preachers.[9]

The earliest coordinated Orthodox attempt to combat Repenter Christianity in Romania was the Romanian Orthodox Association, founded in 1885 to fight 'foreign propaganda', which it said was being distributed freely by Repenter evangelists.[10] During the inter-war period the Romanian Orthodox Church (ROC) appointed anti-sectarian missionaries whose role was to work in rural communities combating the influence of Repenters and trying to convert them back to Orthodoxy. They produced a vast quantity of anti-sectarian writings

---

[4] ACNSAS, Fond Documentar, Dosar 10727, vol. 2, ff. 3–6.
[5] Vartolomeu Stănescu, 'Ce sunt ereziile creștine și din ce cauza se nasc ele?' *Misionarul* 2, no. 6 (1930): 499.
[6] Dobrincu, 'Sub puterea cezarului', 116–19.
[7] ACNSAS, Fond Documentar, Dosar 13408, vol. 1, f. 250.
[8] Vasile Loichița, *Chiliasmul (Milenarismul): Expunere și critică dogmatică* (Cernăuți: Editura Autorului, 1926); Marin Iliescu, *Poligamiea în America: Secta mormonilor: Doctrina, obieceiurile și istoria lor* (Alexandria: Tipografia Alecsandri, 1932).
[9] Dobrincu, 'Sub puterea cezarului', 121.
[10] Ursul, 'From Political Freedom', 233.

attacking and defaming Repenters.[11] Vasile G. Ispir was appointed Professor of Sectology at the University of Bucharest in 1922, publishing sermons, pamphlets and textbooks attacking Repenters and describing missionary strategies.[12] In addition to his active role as a preacher and teacher, on Sunday mornings Ispir organized teams of students to run 'Sunday Schools' in primary schools on the outskirts of Bucharest. Their goal was 'to touch those chords of the soul which develop in children with appropriate dispositions [simțăminte alese] and to cultivate a noble character and a respect towards holy things'.[13]

Other Orthodox churches had tried similar missionary initiatives during the nineteenth century. From 1885 onwards Serbian priests in Austria-Hungary began holding congresses to discuss how to combat the popularity of the Nazarenes. These were grassroots initiatives by parish priests. They began by calling for harsher state repression, but by the mid-1890s these assemblies began looking inward and argued that people were becoming Repenters because Orthodox priests were not doing enough to combat the threats of Western liberalism, the secular intelligentsia, civil servants and the press.[14] Their arguments focused on Orthodox failures, national identity and foreign threats, and the solutions they proposed consistently involved changing Orthodoxy itself. This was as much a debate about the relationship between Orthodoxy and modernity as it was about actual conversions. The Russian Orthodox Church organized 'internal missions' between 1886 and 1917, which were specifically focused on preventing the spread of Repenters and other non-Orthodox religions.[15] Metropolitan Evlogii

---

[11] Representative titles of this literature include Const. Nazarie, *Duminica, botezul și ierarhia bisericească după adventiști* (Bucharest: Tipografia 'Cărților Bisericești', 1910); Const. Gr. Chirică, *Lupi rapitori în piei de oi* (Galați: Institutul de Arte Grafice 'Energia', n.d.); Ioan Cotârlă, *Sf. Cruce, Sf. Icoane, luminările și tămâia* (Arad: Tiparul Tigpografie Diecezane, 1929); Mina Gașpar, *Legea lui Moise, sâmbăta evreilor și duminica creștinilor* (Arad: Tiparul Tigpografie Diecezane, 1929); Vasile Gheorghiu, *Despre botezul 'cu Spirit Sfânt și cu foc' și darurile harismatice* (Arad: Tiparul Tipografiei Diecezane, 1929); I. N. Dăvărescu, *Feriți-vă de adventiști și de toți rătăciții vremurilor noastre!* (Arad: Tiparul Tipografiei Diecezane, 1930); Ilarion V. Felea, *Critica ereziei baptiste* (Sibiu, 1937); V. Dolinescu, *Lupta contra sectelor religioase* (Bârlad: Atelierele Grafice N. Peiu, 1939).

[12] Vasile Gh. Ispir, *Bibliografia subiectelor tratate în Seminarul de Sectologie de sub direcțiunea d-lui Profesor Dr. V. Gh. Ispir, în anii 1932/33, 1933/34 și 1934/35* (Bucharest: Tipografia Ziarului, 1936); Vasile Gh. Ispir, *Curs de sectologie* (Bucharest: Facultatea de Teologie din București, 1938); Vasile Gh. Ispir, *Sectele religioase. Un pericol național și social* (Bucharest: Tipografia 'Cărților Bisericești', 1942).

[13] *Asociația Misionară a Studenților Creștini Ortodocși. Zece ani de activitate (1926-1936)* (Bucharest, 1936).

[14] Aleksov, *Religious Dissent*, 135–41.

[15] J. Eugene Clay, 'Orthodox Missionaries', 38–69; Heather J. Coleman, 'Defining Heresy: The Fourth Missionary Congress and the Problem of Cultural Power after 1905 in Russia,' *Jahrbücher für Geschichte Osteuropas* 52, no. 1 (2004): 70–91; Heather J. Coleman, 'Theology on the Ground: Dmitrii Bogoliubov, the Orthodox Anti-Sectarian Mission, and the Russian Soul', in *Thinking Orthodox in Modern Russia: Culture, History, Context*, ed. Patrick Lally Michelson and Judith Deutsch Kornblatt (Madison, WI: University of Wisconsin Press, 2014), 64–84.

wrote that 'in the dioceses, in Church circles, [the missionaries] were feared, but they were not loved nor were they trusted'.¹⁶ Associated with Konstantin Pobedonostsev, the Ober-Procurator of the Holy Synod, the missionary endeavour in Russia was about reinforcing a close relationship between Church and state to prevent the spread of political dissent in any form.

Bishop Gurie Grosu established a Romanian missionary society in Bessarabia in 1899 under the auspices of Russian anti-sectarian missions. This was equally an attempt to distribute religious literature in the Romanian language in a region that sorely lacked it. He reported on his efforts in 1922 that

> A popular library has been established in the parish of Văncicăuți, Hotin county. Over twenty issues of a missionary newspaper have been edited in Romanian and Russian, each in at least 5,000 copies. Twenty lectures have been held and over 100 discussions and debates with sectarians in front of the people. Choirs of priests and children from church schools were organized for these occasions. Last autumn courses for missionary priests taught by missionary bishops were held for over a month. A choir was formed of priests and cantors from Chișinău, which gave several public concerts to raise money for the poor.¹⁷

Inochentism was particularly strong in Bessarabia at this time and Orthodox missionaries focused on combating Inochentism as much as they did on Repenters.¹⁸ There were clear continuities between the pre-war Russian missionary movement and Romanian efforts of the 1920s. James Kapaló even notes that 'some of the missionary priests who had been active in the same role in the Russian Orthodox Church continued to work for the Romanian Church'.¹⁹ Missionary priests in inter-war Romania were attached to individual bishoprics and had no central authority directing their ministry.²⁰ They held regular congresses from 1928 onwards where they encouraged missionary priests and discussed new strategies for combating Repenters.²¹ Grosu suggested publishing a newspaper for the movement at the 1928 congress and began printing *Missionarul (The Missionary)* on the press at Chișinău the following year.²²

---

[16] Quoted in Coleman, 'Theology on the Ground', 65.
[17] *Anuarul Episcopiei Chișinăulu*.
[18] Kapaló, *Inochentism*, 56–68.
[19] Ibid., 117.
[20] Ic. St I. Andronic, 'Ne trebuie un organ central de conducerea operei misionare,' *Misionarul*, 6 October 1929, 39–40.
[21] 'Într'un ceas bun', *Misionarul*, 6 October 1929, 1.
[22] Boldișor, *File din viața unei biserici*, 51–2.

Grigorie Comșa, who served as Bishop of Arad between 1925 and 1935, was the most prolific and active of Romanian missionary priests. Most anti-sectarian literature was published either in Arad as part of Comșa's 'Christian Orthodox Library' series (Biblioteca Creștinului Ortodox) or under the supervision of Gurie Grosu in Chișinău, who had his own series entitled 'The Library of the Right-Believing Christian' (Biblioteca Creștinului Drept-Credincios). Attacks on Repenters could be found in almost every issue of every Orthodox Church newspaper during the inter-war period, but Comșa almost single-handedly shaped the Orthodox discourse on Repenters through his vitriol, his prestige and the sheer number of his publications. In addition to providing arguments for missionaries Comșa hoped that Repenters themselves would read his tracts and be converted by the power of his arguments.[23] According to Comșa, 'mission includes all those things that missionaries do to proclaim the word, to fortify believers, those wavering or indifferent to religion and morals, but mission is also about preventing heretical diseases and forming a force of aware and devoted believers in the Church'.[24] He distinguished missionary endeavours from the pastoral work of priests. 'Carrying out the Holy liturgy, a baptism, anointing the sick, a wedding or a funeral', he said, 'is not enough'.[25] In addition, the Church had to preach the word of God. Comșa strongly encouraged preaching, which for him lay at the heart of the missionary endeavour.[26] What he said in his sermons depended on his audience. 'Evangelistic letters' that he wrote to prominent public figures in 1934 emphasized that Christianity was the key to a vibrant and healthy society and encouraged his correspondents to integrate the Church ever more deeply into their professional lives.[27] His message to Orthodox believers can be summed up by his imperatives 'to show that Christ is the Lord of our lives, and not human foibles' and 'to extend the Kingdom of God on earth without anything standing in its way'.[28] His anti-sectarian sermons, on the other hand, identified Repenters as 'false prophets' and 'lying heretics' who must be eradicated for the safety of the Church. His

---

[23] Grigorie Comșa, *Combaterea catehismului baptiștilor* (Arad: Tiparul Tipografiei Diecezane, 1926), 4.
[24] Comșa, *Ființa și necesitatea misionarismului*, 11.
[25] Gheorghe Comșa, *Istoria predicei la români* (Bucharest: Tipografia Cărților Bisericești, 1921), 4.
[26] Collection of Comșa's own sermons include Grigorie Comșa, *Predici pentru toate duminicile de peste an și alte ocaziuni* (Arad: Tiparul Tipografiei Diecezane, 1918); Grigorie Comșa, *Pentru neam și lege: Patruzeci cuvântări de învățătură împotriva adventiștilor și baptiștilor* (Caransebeș: Editura 'Librăriei Decezane', 1923).
[27] Grigorie Comșa, *Scrisori creștinești* (Arad: Tiparul Tipografiei Diecezane, 1934).
[28] Grigorie Comșa, *Glasul pietrelor: Principii călăuzitoare pentru ortodoxia activa* (Chișinău: Tipografia Eparhială 'Cartea Românească', 1931), 7, 31.

goal was 'to tear the mask off the faces of the Adventists', accusing Repenters of a wide variety of dishonourable practices.[29]

According to Comșa, priests differed from missionaries in that they ministered only to believers who already recognized their authority, whereas missionaries were there to spread the Gospel. Only ordained priests were able to do pastoral work, but laypeople could become missionaries. In 1930 students at the University of Bucharest formed a Student Missionary Society and dedicated their summer holidays to carrying out missionary work in rural communities.[30] The goal of the missionary, Comșa said, was 'Christianization in general, in particular the interiorization of religious life, the deepening of Christian thought and feeling, increasing Christian activities, [and] the discipleship of deeds'.[31] Missionaries in Arad would hold three-day festivals in which they would set up a large number of icons outside a monastery, then preach sermons, hear confessions and administer the Eucharist.[32]

What missionary priests did from day to day varied considerably. Gala Galaction fulfilled his duties as a missionary priest in Bucharest by having Teodor Popescu defrocked as a heretic (see chapter 9).[33] In a report from 1935, Ilie Imbrescu described his first year of missionary activity in Dobruja as having involved petitioning the patriarch for the establishment of a new monastery in his region, holding a religious service on the location of the proposed monastery, spending three days travelling around Repenter communities and resolving to establish 'centres' where he would systematically refute Repenters in the future.[34] In Chișinău missionary priests were supposed to be active preachers, lead collective singing in churches, give public lectures and establish missionary circles in communities with a strong Repenter presence. They were to cooperate with the local authorities, mobilize monasteries and religious youth groups and distribute anti-sectarian literature.[35]

Missionaries in Hotin showed a film, *The Life and Passions of the Saviour*, accompanied by choirs, prayers, the lighting of candles and sermons against

---

[29] Comșa, *Pentru neam și lege*, 8, 17 and passim.
[30] ACNSAS, Fond Documentar, Dosar 12694, vol. 3, ff. 1–4.
[31] Comșa, *Ființa și necesitatea*, 13.
[32] Toma Gherasimescu, *Propaganda religioasă prin cinematograf: Cum se poate face ea cu o cheltuială foarte mică* (Roman: Editura Autorului, 1930), 1.
[33] Galaction, *Jurnal*, vol. 3, 158–65; Gala Galaction, *Piatra din capul unghiului: Scrisori teologice* (Bucharest: Tipografiile Române Unite, 1926).
[34] Ilie I. Imbrescu, *Misionarul eparhial al Tomisului: Gânduri după un an de încercări* (Bazargic: Tip. 'Gutenberg' Hristo Radilof, 1935), 14–16.
[35] 'Planul activității misionare stabilit în eparhia Chișinăului de Secția Culturală,' *Misionarul*, 6 October 1929, 109–12.

Seventh-Day Adventism.³⁶ Clerical reactions to new technology were mixed. Irineu Mihălcescu, for example, welcomed the introduction of cinema into Romania, seeing it as a possible vehicle for public education and moral teaching, provided that it was used properly. When asked whether the liturgy should be broadcast on the radio, however, he replied that

> it is the greatest impiety, the most profound sacrilege, a true profanation ... Wouldn't it be ridiculous to have a baptism, an unction, a wedding or an ordination on the radio? What sort of mystery would it be if the recipient was not there to participate in it, to see it, to receive the laying on of hands, the blessing and other rites through which the grace of the Holy Spirit is shared?³⁷

Most missionaries liked the idea of using films, but these were expensive to buy and hard to transport. Suitable religious films were rare and few villages had appropriate buildings in which to project them. It was only once Pathé-Baby projectors were imported at the end of the 1920s that this became a realistic option.³⁸

Comșa wrote that when he became an assistant director at the Ministry of Denominations in 1920 he 'was amazed at the high number of Repenter preachers who were requesting authorization to preach'.³⁹ Unlike Orthodox, Greek Catholic, Roman Catholic, Lutheran priests or Jewish rabbis, every Repenter had to receive permission as an individual if he or she wished to preach.⁴⁰ From the perspective of a clerk this law meant that large numbers of requests from Repenter preachers would have come across Comșa's desk. Moreover, Comșa said, there were many more Repenters than first met the eye because they were often difficult to identify.⁴¹ When Imbrescu tried collecting statistics on Repenters in Dobruja he discovered that the protopresbyters had no real idea how many were living in their parishes.⁴² Comșa saw sectarianism as being a result of 'excessive liberty', a natural desire to rebel against authority and the fact that people saw the Church as representative of an oppressive socio-economic

---

³⁶ 'Conferințe misionare cu cinematograf în județul Hotin,' *Misionarul*, 6 October 1929, 116–18.
³⁷ Quoted in Vicovan, *Ioan Irineu Mihălcescu*, 492.
³⁸ Gherasimescu, *Propaganda religioasă*, 2–3.
³⁹ Grigorie Comșa, *Zece ani de luptă împotriva baptiștilor* (Arad: Tiparul Tipografiei Diecezane, 1930), 5.
⁴⁰ Marius Silveșan, *Bisericile creștine baptiste din România între persecuție, acomodare și rezistența (1948–1965)* (Târgoviște: Editura Cetatea de Scaun, 2012), 96–7.
⁴¹ Grigorie Comșa, *Cheia sectelor religioase din România* (Arad: Tiparul Tipografiei Diecezane, 1930), 1.
⁴² Imbrescu, *Misionarul eparhial*, 7. The police also kept statistics of Repenter communities which were much more detailed than those Imbrescu managed to obtain from his protopresbyters.

order they wanted to escape. He argued that the Orthodox Church was in a particularly difficult position because, despite its support for the state, nineteenth-century reforms had successively stripped it of its wealth and now parish priests had too many souls in their care, which is why people turned to Repenter churches, which promised more personal pastoral care.[43] Not content to take souls away from the Orthodox Church, the Repenter emphasis on the priesthood of all believers apparently masked their intention to do away with the clerical class entirely even though they too had priests, known as 'ministers'.[44]

Comșa repeatedly used military symbolism and references to spiritual warfare in his writings, comparing Baptists to 'the Yids who murdered the Author of life' and calling missionaries 'to arm ourselves and to join the holy war for the defence of the faith and the Nation'.[45] He claimed that 'we never attacked, but we did defend ourselves'.[46] This is not quite true. Comșa was quite comfortable appealing to the authorities to shut down Repenter groups and the first Pentecostal tortured to death by police was arrested at Comșa's instigation in 1927.[47] Other Orthodox writers admitted quite openly that missionaries frequently requested gendarmes to repress Repenters by force.[48] Missionaries targeted Greek Catholics as well as Repenters, and in a harsh critique of Orthodox missionary methods, Greek Catholic writers argued that

> If it really believes in the true teaching 'Go and make disciples …' [Matthew 28:19-20], every Church is and should be like that of Rome: to seek to win souls. 'Only those who do not believe can turn their backs on mission', as the Most Reverend Bălan proclaimed at the FOR [Romanian Orthodox Brotherhood] congress. There is nonetheless an enormous difference between peaceful 'mission' based on conviction, enlightenment, winning people over through persuasion, the power of the truth and good works … and demagogic proselytism, which disturbs public order and is practiced with money and axes, with envy and deceit, with the illegal intervention of the authorities.[49]

Comșa described the growth of Repenter communities in the early 1920s as a diabolical continuation of the First World War using 'the flaming arrows of the evil one' (Ephesians 6:16). Repenters, he wrote, were disgusted by the pleasure-driven

---

[43] Comșa, *Cheia sectelor religioase*, 11-17; Comșa, *Ființa și necesitatea*, 6-9.
[44] Comșa, *Combaterea catehismului*, 25, 43-50.
[45] Ibid., 18; Comșa, *Glasul pietrelor*, 39.
[46] Comșa, *Zece ani de luptă*, 15. Note that by the following year he was demanding that 'we need to attack. Defence is not enough'. Comșa, *Glasul pietrelor*, 36.
[47] Bălăban, *Istoria bisericii penticostale*, 41.
[48] Ioan G. Savin, *Iconoclaști și apostați contemporani* (Bucharest: Editura Anastasia, 1995), 47.
[49] 'Cartea frăției', *Unirea* (1934), quoted in Kührer-Wielach, 'Orthodoxer Jesuitismus', 314.

society around them and wanted to create a new society, separate from the old.⁵⁰ The implication here was that they also sought to separate themselves from the nation-state. Comșa spoke about the 'sins' that Baptist leaders had 'towards the Romanian people' (*patimile ce le au față de neamul românesc*).⁵¹ By this he meant that converts publicly claimed their parents were irreligious, that Baptists did not acknowledge the important contributions Orthodox Church leaders had made to Romanian nation-building in centuries past and that they did not participate in national celebrations. He argued consistently that Repenters 'were a danger to the state and to the spiritual union of Romanians'.⁵² Other Orthodox voices agreed. The theologian Ioan Savin wrote in 1932 that 'not only Orthodoxy but nationality is targeted and under threat by sectarian propaganda'.⁵³

Repenters were dangerous because they encouraged Romanians to mix with Hungarians and were allowed to teach religious studies in schools when they themselves had not graduated primary school. They also refused 'to swear military oaths and to bear arms even in the barracks, let alone in times of war'.⁵⁴ Moreover, Repenter preaching caused Orthodox believers to doubt their faith and turn to atheism.⁵⁵ Repenters, he said, claimed that primitive Christianity had been corrupted by Judaism and Paganism, meaning that Baptists who went back to Scripture had more in common with the early Church than did the Orthodox, who claimed apostolic continuity.⁵⁶ In some places Baptists apparently taught communism to children while at the same time refusing to baptize them regardless of the implications their unbaptized state had on their eternal destinies.⁵⁷

Comșa and his colleagues argued that the ROC was under attack from foreigners just as the Russian Church was suffering under 'Judeo-Bolshevik' anti-clericalism. Social democracy, according to Comșa, was 'the greatest enemy of the Church', and it was no accident that Repenter communities were essentially democratic.⁵⁸ Emphasizing the Jewish and Hungarian origins of some Baptist preachers, he claimed that Repenters represented a foreign attempt to undermine the creation of Greater Romania.⁵⁹ Comșa said that individuals who became

---

⁵⁰ Comșa, *Cheia sectelor religioase*, 13.
⁵¹ Comșa, *Zece ani de luptă*, 10.
⁵² Comșa, *Zece ani de luptă*, 16.
⁵³ Savin, *Iconoclaști și apostăți*, 51.
⁵⁴ Comșa, *Cheia sectelor religioase*, 5–7.
⁵⁵ Comșa, *Ființa și necesitatea*, 18.
⁵⁶ Comșa, *Combaterea catehismului*, 38.
⁵⁷ Comșa, *Ființa și necesitatea*, 18–20; Comșa, *Combaterea catehismului*, 23.
⁵⁸ Comșa, *Istoria predicei*, 3.
⁵⁹ Comșa, *Zece ani de luptă*, 6–8, 20–22.

Baptists even stopped wearing Romanian peasant garb and began dressing like Germans.[60] As one missionary wrote to his colleagues in 1929, 'the whole world knows that Baptist proselytism happens with foreign money'.[61] Comșa agreed, pointing out that Romanian-language publications were often financed by American donors.[62] In 1930 he told a remarkable story about a meeting he had apparently had on a train heading towards Oradea nineteen years earlier:

> Sitting in my compartment, I heard songs that I had never heard before. In the next carriage there were scores of women and men singing Baptist hymns. Curiosity drove me to them and suddenly a baptised Yid, their preacher Mayer Carol, comes up to me and asks me who I am. Learning that I was a graduate of the Theological Institute in Sibiu, he took me into the corridor and said: 'You could make a lot of money if you become a Baptist. Look, I left my parents to sell needles and buttons and shoelaces in Budapest, I became a Baptist and even at my baptism I immediately received 2,000 crowns.'[63]

In case the reader had failed to notice that these were 'women and men', not 'men and women', that the train was heading to an area with a strong Hungarian presence and that the preacher was a 'baptised Yid' who came from Budapest, Comșa then pointed out on the next page that the Baptists were on their way to a baptism that was to take place 'in a Hungarian Baptist meeting hall in Oradea-Mare'.

Not all Repenter money came from abroad. As Gheorghe Livovschi pointed out, the Jews who were apparently behind Seventh-Day Adventism did not like spending their own money to achieve their goals so they collected money from Adventist converts to spread the religion.[64] Money was a frequent problem raised in these polemics. Comșa complained that Repenters accused Orthodox bishops of receiving money for sanctifying churches. This was untrue, Comșa insisted. In reality, he said, bishops gave money away to the poor. Repenters apparently lied about themselves, too. They claimed that they did not drink alcohol, but Comșa insisted that they would have if they could afford it.[65]

Comșa saw the fact that many early Pentecostals originally came from Baptist churches as evidence that Repenters were not deeply committed to their

---

[60] Comșa, *Combaterea catehismului*, 5.
[61] Nicolae A. Murea, 'Pentru congresul general al misionarilor ortodocși români din țară', *Misionarul*, 6 October 1929, 64.
[62] Comșa, *Combaterea catehismului*, 7; Comșa, *Pentru neam și lege*, 14.
[63] Comșa, *Zece ani de luptă*, 1.
[64] Gh. Livovschi, 'Iudaism și adventism. Rolul iudaismului în mișcarea sectei cunoscute sub numele de Adventism", *Misionarul*, 6 October 1929, 81.
[65] Comșa, *Zece ani de luptă*, 18–19.

denominations, repeatedly telling stories about preachers who moved from one denomination to another.[66] Their schismatic tendencies as well as their ecclesiology convinced Comșa that Repenters did not believe that the Church was one body and that Repenter congregations were not actually part of the Church.[67] Comșa also quarrelled directly with Repenter beliefs. His polemical tone consistently patronized Repenters, who he considered simple and uneducated, in need of his extensive education. He accused them of playing God by expelling sinners from their churches when only God has the right to separate the wheat from the weeds (see Matthew 13:30). But ultimately for Comșa this doctrine was just another example of Repenter hypocrisy because, he wrote, 'they proclaim loudly: there are only pure members in our assemblies because we have shown sinners the door', but in fact he knew of one sinner who Repenters claimed they had expelled when in reality 'not even a hair on his head moved'.[68]

Adventists apparently cared so little for the Bible that they changed the text to suit their own doctrines and Comșa showed that Baptists did not really believe in *sola scriptura* (the authority of Scripture alone) because their own catechism admitted that the Gospel was passed down through word of mouth as well as in written form and they taught the 'entirely unscriptural' doctrine that only 'ordained pastors' could baptize people.[69] Similarly, Baptists taught that baptism takes place *after* one believes, whereas St Paul said that 'you were washed, you were sanctified, you were justified' (1 Cor. 6:11), putting baptism *before* sanctification and justification.[70] Moreover, said Comșa, if salvation is a miracle, why does God have to wait until one turns fifteen, which was when Baptists baptized young people?[71]

Baptists refused to recognize Orthodox sacraments such as the Eucharist. Not realizing that God forgives sin here and now, they claimed that He forgave sins at the time of the resurrection and just 'remembered' their salvation when taking the Lord's Supper.[72] Comșa condemned Baptists both for their divergences with Romanian Orthodoxy and for their similarities. He complained that Baptists had 'stolen' their beliefs from the Orthodox Church because they, too,

---

[66] Ibid., 12.
[67] Comșa, *Combaterea catehismului*, 19–22.
[68] Grigorie Comșa, *Pedepsirea păcătoșilor și scoaterea din adunările Baptiste* (Arad: Tiparul Tipografiei Diecezane, 1929), 4.
[69] Comșa, *Pentru neam și lege*, 13; Comșa, *Combaterea catehismului*, 8–10, 27.
[70] Comșa, *Combaterea catehismului*, 33.
[71] Ibid., 41.
[72] Ibid., 51–8.

used the Apostles' Creed.⁷³ At the same time, Baptists believed that they could understand God's word by themselves, without help from nineteen centuries of wise Christian teachers – a claim that Comșa thought ludicrous because Baptists themselves admitted that the human mind is incapable of understanding all of God's mysteries.⁷⁴

Comșa was concerned with what he perceived as widespread irreligion in the villages, which produced ignorance about Orthodoxy and subsequently made people vulnerable to Repenter proselytism. 'In church life', he wrote in 1920, 'we see indifference about indifference. We are painfully aware that there are even priests who have taken up commerce. People don't really go to church any more; the laws and commandments of the church are ignored. Adultery is spreading, the name of God is mocked, the holy mysteries are trodden underfoot and sectarianism runs rampant'.⁷⁵ In the cities, Comșa said, 'we have printed pornography, frivolous literature; in schools there are people teaching evolution and Darwinism, monism continues, free thinking exists, [and] Masonic humanitarianism and atheism are winning all the prizes'.⁷⁶ He argued that 'we are called to show that our people is not only religious in terms of patriarchal village traditions, but also through education and religious instruction'.⁷⁷ Others were not so pessimistic and saw in sectarianism evidence that people really did long for greater religious involvement. The missionary priest Mihail Madan wrote in 1929 that

> Even while atheist and non-Christian propaganda spreads we find that many people long for religious truth. The very spread of the sects is evidence of a religious movement among the people. We should not see the sick growth of the sects as a sign of spiritual death. If the social organism was dead then diseases would not show up on the body. The fact that there are diseases shows that the organism is alive.⁷⁸

Greek Catholic writers echoed the same ideas that could be found in Comșa's works. Nicolae Brânzeu described the spread of Adventism as 'one of the sad results of the war'.⁷⁹ He equated Adventists with Bible Students and warned that 'in five to ten years villages and entire regions will end up with empty churches,

---

⁷³ Ibid., 11–13.
⁷⁴ Ibid., 14–17.
⁷⁵ Comșa, *Istoria predicei*, 3.
⁷⁶ Comșa, *Glasul pietrelor*, 15.
⁷⁷ Comșa, *Ființa și necesitatea*, 1.
⁷⁸ Mihail Madan, 'O nouă eră pentru activitatea misionară', *Misionarul*, 6 October 1929, 60.
⁷⁹ Nicolae Brânzeu, 'Adventismul și combaterea aceluia', *Cultura creștină* 11, no. 7–8 (1922): 223.

and even worse, this religious revolution implies a complete social revolution!'⁸⁰ Like the Orthodox, Greek Catholics argued that evangelism was the only solution to the spread of Repenter Christianity. 'Catechize, brothers!' wrote Iuliu of Gherla in 1927. 'Preach every Sunday and holiday. Catechize the adults in church, catechize children in school. Proclaim the Gospel in all its power. Establish the Kingdom of God in people's souls ... *There is no other way for the people to be reborn*'.⁸¹

Despite the best efforts of missionaries, the number of Repenter groups continued to grow. Their apparent failure led to constant debates about the best ways to combat the threat. Iosif Trifa argued in 1926 that 'there is no other way to combat sectarianism than a great movement of evangelism'.⁸² Comșa taught that successful missionaries needed to be well organized, popular with the local priests, persistent in prayer and mindful of the needs of parishioners.⁸³ With the aim of creating what he called 'a militant church', he suggested modelling Orthodox missions on the youth wing of Catholic Action that developed in Mussolini's Italy in the late 1920s as a way of strengthening lay activism.⁸⁴ Others insisted that philanthropy was the key to winning hearts and souls and encouraged their colleagues to make this a core part of their ministries.⁸⁵ Still others worried that 'not every representative of the clergy is prepared [to combat sectarianism] and furthermore, we lack the material needed to carry on the fight'.⁸⁶ By this the author meant that Romanians still lacked a reliable translation of the Bible, commentaries, theological works and published antisectarian polemics.

Not all Orthodox leaders agreed with using force against Repenters. Vartolomeu Stănescu in particular was outspoken against the use of violence to persecute religious minorities.

> Our Romanian state, so new and with such a young social life, so buffeted inside and out by disturbances for such as time, *is obligated* more than any other state, *to prepare a peaceful future for itself in religious matters, now and in the most urgent manner*. Its first duty is to stand by its church, which has been privileged

---

[80] Nicolae Brânzeu, 'Adventismul și combaterea lui', *Cultura creștină* 11, no. 11–12 (1922): 308.
[81] 'Calea renașterii', *Unirea* 37, no. 4 (1927): 1.
[82] Ioan Trifa, 'Viața Bisericească: Probleme actuale', *Revistă teologică* 16, no. 1 (1926): 24.
[83] Grigorie Comșa, 'Secretul misionarismului', *Misionarul*, 6 October 1929, 7–10.
[84] Comșa, *Glasul pietrelor*, 18–22, 31ff.
[85] I. Puiul, 'Activitatea filantropică', *Misionarul*, 6 October 1929, 29–31.
[86] Al. Bogdaneț, 'Un început bun', *Misionarul*, 6 October 1929, 90.

up until now in both *confessional* and *constitutional* terms, but to renounce oppression *decidedly* and *in its entirety*.[87]

The problem, Stănescu believed, was that Orthodox Church services did not engage laypeople enough. 'In our churches', he wrote, 'Orthodox Christians are just an audience, stuck on their feet for hours on end during a service which they often don't even understand the words of'.[88] His solution to the problem of Repenters was to encourage both priests and laypeople to read and discuss the Bible, to establish Orthodox choirs and cultural associations and for the Church to increase its charity work to the poor.[89]

After an unsuccessful year of missionary work Ilie Imbrescu concluded that arguing with Repenters was futile and that the Orthodox Church would combat sectarianism much more effectively by having wise and sensitive priests, church printing presses, bookstores, candle factories and by giving to the poor.[90] Representatives at the 1928 Congress agreed with him, suggesting innovations such as establishing Sunday schools, choirs and cultural committees in every parish, making monasteries into religious tourist attractions for young people, distributing popular Bibles and icons, selling religious tracts, founding 'moral committees' in parishes to combat sin and setting up cinemas.[91] In many ways these strategies were a deepening and continuation of ordinary, everyday Orthodox ministry. The state eventually withdrew funding from the missionary programme in 1931, but the strategies and hatreds promoted by Comșa lived on in organizations such as the Lord's Army and in the missionary committees, youth groups, catechism courses and university courses missionaries had established over the last decade.[92]

What missionary writings rarely mentioned was the role of the police and gendarmerie in preventing the spread of Repenters. Repenters were frequently beaten, arrested, tortured and even killed by the authorities, often at the instigation of missionaries or parish priests. Anti-Repenter activities involved close cooperation between the Church and the state, which saw Repenters as a common threat. Both Church and state embraced the Orthodoxist doctrine that to be Romanian was to be Orthodox, and persecuted Repenters accordingly.

---

[87] Quoted in Raiu, *Democrație și statolatrie*, 303–4.
[88] Vartolomeu Stănescu, 'Mijloacele pentru preîntâmpinarea ereziilor', *Biserica Ortodoxă Română* 40, no. 2 (1921): 129–32, reprinted in Stănescu, *Puterile sociale*, 332.
[89] Ibid., 336–7.
[90] Imbrescu, *Misionarul eparhial*, 17–20.
[91] 'Dezideratele Congresului general misionar din Arad, sesiunea 1928', *Misionarul*, 6 October 1929, 104–5.
[92] Comșa, *Glasul pietrelor*, 9–11.

The changing and uncertain legal status of Repenter denominations further exacerbated the situation, giving local gendarmes the perfect excuse to persecute Repenter communities even when they were legally allowed to operate.

A common anti-Repenter rhetoric also helped overcome regional tensions within the Church to a certain extent, bringing Orthodox leaders in Arad, Oltenia and Bessarabia into close cooperation and creating a platform that no Orthodox leader could challenge. Visarion Puiu tried to expand on this success by writing to Orthodox leaders across the region and suggesting that the difficult situation the Church now found itself in meant that it was time for all of the Orthodox churches to unite across national borders. His initiative was welcomed but had no lasting impact.[93] Although evangelism, lay involvement and holiness movements lay at the heart of the anti-Repenter agenda, fears about Repenters simultaneously cast doubts over the orthodoxy of such practices. Part Three is concerned precisely with that tension between promoting individual piety as a solution to the scourge of Repenters and the concern that all such practices were quintessentially Protestant.

---

[93] Const N. Tomescu, 'Spre unire in Domnul', *Misionarul* 2, no. 19 (1930): 887–909.

Part Three

Renewal Movements

8

The Lord's Army

The most successful attempt to revive rural spirituality was known as the Lord's Army (Oastea Domnului). It was led by Iosif Trifa from the Transylvanian city of Sibiu and based around the newspaper *Lumina satelor* (*The Light of the Villages*). Nicolae Bălan edited a newspaper called *Gazeta poporului* (*The People's Gazette*) between 1918 and 1920, and in 1922 he invited Trifa to establish a new Church newspaper aimed at a peasant audience. Trifa considered his new newspaper to be a direct successor of *Gazeta poporului* and sent sample copies of *Lumina satelor* to everyone who had subscribed to Bălan's newspaper.[1] Trifa had studied under Bălan as a student, standing out because of his newspaper articles on the difficulties faced by Romanian peasants in Transylvania.[2] Trifa later claimed that Bălan had taught him the necessity of 'sharing with the people the supreme reality of the spiritual life; of bringing it into contact with Christ, with life in Christ', which is indeed something that Bălan had been teaching based on his published sermons.[3]

Trifa served as a village priest in Vidra de Sus in Alba county from 1911 until 1921, where he established a village cooperative, founded a cultural centre and wrote regular articles in the local newspaper defending the rights of the local peasants.[4] He published a successful collection of sermons in 1919, and one of his former teachers, Ion Lupaș, invited him to move to Cluj to pursue an academic career. Trifa rejected the offer because 'to me the word "priest" is a grace, a gift, and a great responsibility, not a burden that can easily be set aside'.[5] That same year Bălan offered him an administrative post in Sibiu where he

---

[1] Iosif Trifa, '1000', *Lumina satelor*, 19 February 1922, 1.
[2] Gheorghe Gogan, 'Viața și activitatea predicatorială a preotului Iosif Trifa' (MA diss., Universitatea 'Aurel Vlaicu', Arad, 2003), 11–12.
[3] *Oastea Domnului* 10, no. 24 (1931): 1; cf. Nicolae Bălan, *Problema religiósă în timpul de azi* (Sibiu: Tiparul Tipografiei Arhidiecezane, 1906), 52.
[4] Gogan, 'Viața și activitatea', 13.
[5] *Biserica și școala*, 26 September 1920.

served as a chaplain at the theological academy, director of a church orphanage and published *Lumina satelor*.[66] Transylvania already had a successful rural newspaper known as *Libertatea* (*Liberty*), but *Lumina satelor* was to have a more explicitly religious focus and was under Bălan's direct authority.[7] In an enthusiastic article praising the new newspaper, the priest Ioan Crăciun noted that what set *Lumina satelor* apart from its competitors was that it was written specifically with 'the enlightenment of the people' in mind and did not serve the interests of particular individuals or political parties.[8]

Sibiu was the seat of the metropolitan of Ardeal and boasted one of the country's best seminaries. Fifty-two per cent of the 194,600 people who lived in Sibiu county at the time of the 1930 census were Orthodox, 28 per cent were Lutherans and 13 per cent Greek Catholics. There were only 47 Seventh-Day Adventists and 408 Baptists.[9] Only 48,000 people lived in Sibiu itself, the rest being scattered throughout the county's 89 villages, but there was no marked migration from the countryside to the city.[10] The city boasted good road and rail connections, good hospitals, a central library with over 66,400 books, 19 primary schools and 22 secondary schools; the only post-secondary institution being the Andreiană Theological Academy for training Orthodox priests. Someone looking for a religious service could find an Orthodox cathedral, three Orthodox churches, one Greek Catholic church, two Lutheran churches, two Roman Catholic churches, one Reformed church and two synagogues. All three of Sibiu's monasteries were Roman Catholic. A city with a strong civil society, it had 37 newspapers and magazines, of which seven were religious publications and 21 were printed in Romanian. The county had a relatively high literacy rate in 1930, with 87.9 per cent of men and 82.6 per cent of women over the age of seven able to read.[11]

Nicolae Bălan had completed his doctoral studies in theology at the University of Czernowitz and studied Protestant and Catholic theology in Breslău. He established *Revista teologică* (*The Theological Magazine*) soon after returning to Romania in an effort to deepen and professionalize Romanian

---

[6] Gogan, 'Viața și activitatea', 15.
[7] Ioan Moța, *42 de ani de gazetărie* (Orăștie: Tipografia Astra, 1935); Nicolae Bălan, 'Binecuvântare arhierească', *Lumina satelor*, 2 January 1922, 1.
[8] Ioan Crăciun, 'Lumina satelor', *Telegraful român*, 26 April 1922, 3.
[9] Manuila, *Recensământul din 1930*, vol. 2, lxxxiv–lxxxv.
[10] Ministerul Industriei și Comerțului, *Anuarul statistic al României: 1922* (Bucharest: Tipografia Curții Regale, 1923), 23.
[11] Dimitrie Gusti ed., *Enciclopedia României*, vol. 2 (Bucharest: Imprimeria Națională, 1938). Available online: http://romaniainterbelica.memoria.ro/judete/sibiu/ (accessed 9 October 2019).

theological research. Believing that the early twentieth century was witnessing a widespread turn towards religion and a fresh engagement with Christianity, Bălan strove to increase theological literacy among Romanians by promoting Bible study and supporting the distribution of popularized Bibles designed for newly literate peasants.[12] Bălan worked to establish his metropolitanate as one of the most important in the country and called a 'Bible Congress' to discuss new possibilities for evangelism in the region.[13] The impetus for establishing *Lumina satelor* came from Bălan, who initially supported Trifa's efforts to establish the Lord's Army, only to attempt to co-opt it for his own purposes at the end of the decade.

Trifa's early articles in *Lumina satelor* were concerned with building the Romanian Orthodox Church (ROC) in Transylvania into a strong and viable Church. He celebrated the fact that Ardeal now had its own metropolitanate and complained bitterly that the state was taking control of church schools.[14] Like Bălan, Trifa considered Greek Catholics to be a threat and had no patience when they complained about being unjustly treated by the state.[15] Bălan took part in ecumenical talks with the Anglican Church in 1923. Trifa praised this initiative, writing that 'if this relationship is made, our Orthodox Church will gain a great deal because the Anglican Church is ahead of everyone else, with its church schools and its methods of spreading the gospel of Christ. Everyone would rejoice at it; only the Pope in Rome would mourn'.[16] Trifa also agreed with Bălan that the 1927 concordat with the Vatican was the gift of a 'Catholic' government to Rome.[17] Trifa maintained a consistently anti-Catholic attitude throughout his career, provoking bitter responses from the Greek Catholic press.[18]

Excited about the country's expansion after the First World War, Trifa worried that if Greater Romania was to last it needed a moral as well as a political transformation. In a collection of sermons he published in 1919 he argued that 'the people which wins the war will be the one which, aided by more faith and

---

[12] Bălan, *Problema religióså*, 4–5; Nicolae Bălan, *Un congres românesc biblic* (Sibiu: Tiparul Tipografiei Arhidiecezane, 1912); Nicolae Bălan, *În chestia 'micii Biblii'* (Sibiu: Tiparul Tipografiei Arhidiecezane, 1914).
[13] Gogan, *Viața și activitatea*, 15.
[14] Iosif Trifa, 'Moștenirea anului 1921', *Lumina satelor*, 9 January 1922, 2; Iosif Trifa, 'Și cu cei fărădelege împreună s'au socotit', *Lumina satelor*, 29 January 1922, 1–2.
[15] Iosif Trifa, 'Cum merge împărțirea pământului', *Lumina satelor*, 28 May 1922, 3.
[16] Iosif Trifa, 'Englezii vreau să-și împreune biserica cu a noastră', *Lumina satelor*, 18 February 1923, 4.
[17] 'Un dar de 6 luni de guvernare: Concordatul', *Lumina satelor*, 26 May 1929, 5.
[18] 'Papa dela Roma s'a întovărășit cu bolșevicii', *Lumina satelor*, 21 December 1924, 8; 'Un praznic al trufei face Papa dela Roma', *Lumina satelor*, 11 January 1925, 2. For the Greek Catholic response, see 'Știrile săptămânii', *Unirea poporului*, 5 July 1925, 4; 'Poșta gazetei', *Unirea poporului*, 12 May 1929, 7.

purer habits, will be able to halt the decay of morals and traditions that has dangerously begun'.[19] During a brief war scare in January 1923 Trifa complained that, instead of uniting Romanians behind 'spiritual borders', his government was squabbling amongst itself about which 'political borders' would most effectively prevent a Hungarian invasion.[20] He worried that the League of Nations would be ineffective at preventing war because it invited bankers and industrialists to its meetings but not Church leaders, 'the spiritual leaders of the peoples'.[21]

Comparing Romanians to the ancient Israelites, who were delivered from Egypt only to spend forty years in the wilderness, Trifa wrote,

> We have escaped from slavery, but behold we have not reached Canaan, the land of milk and honey ... We too have arrived in the wilderness of misfortune and lack. God wants it to be like this, because after we escaped from foreign slavery we too destroyed our habits and behaviour ... We even have a golden calf. An insane greed has seized many people, who only think about making money, often through the subjection, tears and privation of the poor. What else can this be but an idol that many bow down to, even those whose duty and calling it is to smash it? Then we have gambling and merrymaking surrounding the calf: everywhere you hear waves of parties, pleasures and sins that are spreading further and further out, poisoning the clean living of our villages of yesteryear.[22]

He identified the moral decadence of the inter-war years particularly with the urban centres of the Old Kingdom. Gheorghe Greavu, a cantor from a village in north-western Transylvania, wrote to Trifa in 1925 that, during a recent visit to Bucharest, 'I saw that he who has money spends it on balls, coffee shops, and many other useless things. Then the poor suffer from lack of bread and clothing, in cold and nakedness, and from many other problems'.[23] Trifa witnessed similar behaviour in Sibiu and wondered who was sicker – the poor who suffered in the hospitals he visited or the rich who debauched themselves at parties every night.[24] Trifa warned that, just as in the fable of Master Manole, a stonemason who cemented his wife into the walls of a church he was building, modern Romanians were building their state by burying war widows and orphans in

---

[19] Iosif Trifa, *Spre Canaan ... 15 predici în legatură cu răsboiul și vremile noastre* (Arad: Tipografia Diecezană, 1919), 12.
[20] Iosif Trifa, 'Ne trebuie și fronturi sufletești', *Lumina satelor*, 28 January 1923, 1.
[21] 'După sfătul dela Genova', *Lumina satelor*, 28 May 1922, 1.
[22] Trifa, *Spre Canaan*, 26. Trifa developed this metaphor at length in Iosif Trifa, 'România Mare – unele pricini de ce nu este așa cum o credeam și așteptam', *Lumina satelor*, 1 January 1922, 1–2.
[23] 'Încă unul a intrat în oastea noastră', *Lumina satelor*, 25 February 1925, 3.
[24] 'La spital și la bal', *Lumina satelor*, 11 February 1923, 2.

its foundations.²⁵ Those who were corrupting the state were blaspheming the sacrifices of those who had died during the war.²⁶

Trifa's concern with establishing a viable Romanian nation-state focused first and foremost on how it would impact peasants. He deplored politicians who were only concerned with enriching themselves and condemned political infighting as a spiritual illness.²⁷ Trifa kept a close eye on legislation concerning land redistribution after the war and promised to fight for the rights of any villages that felt they had been defrauded.²⁸ He also campaigned for halting imports and for eliminating export taxes so that Romanian farmers could find markets for their produce.²⁹

Both Trifa and Bălan attacked Repenters and Inochentists, although *Lumina satelor* included fewer anti-sectarian articles than most Orthodox publications. The newspaper argued that many Adventist and Baptist preachers were actually 'Yids' (*jidani*) and accused them of selling secrets to the Bolsheviks.³⁰ Despite his hostility towards Repenters, Trifa was reading Protestant writings himself and many of his sermon illustrations and devotional stories were based in England or America.³¹ His concern with preaching was a direct result of his anti-sectarianism. Trifa argued that 'without a doubt the most powerful and effective weapon against the sectarians is the preaching, proclamation, and exposition of the Word … The majority of our children who go astray and cross over to the sectarians do so because there they read and explain the Scriptures, even if they do it badly'.³² Trifa worked with Grigore Cristescu to translate excerpts from the sermons of the Indian preacher Sadhu Sundar Singh into a language that Romanian peasants could understand.³³ Singh was an Anglican

---

[25] Iosif Trifa, 'Văduvele şi orfanii de răsboiu', *Lumina satelor*, 5 February 1922, 1. On the story of Manole, see Mircea Eliade, *Zalmoxis, The Vanishing God: Comparative Studies in the Religions and Folklore of Dacia and Eastern Europe* (Chicago: University of Chicago Press, 1972), 164–9; and Paul G. Brewster, 'The Foundation Sacrifice Motif in Legend, Folksong, Game, and Dance', in *The Walled-Up Wife: A Casebook*, ed. Alan Dundes (University of Wisconsin Press, Madison, 1996), 42–6.
[26] Iosif Trifa, 'Un păcat neiertat', *Lumina satelor*, 9 February 1922, 1.
[27] 'Politica de partid este opera lui Satan', *Lumina satelor*, 26 June 1927, 1; Iosif Trifa, *25 povestiri şi istorioare morale* (Sibiu: Dacia Traiana, 1927), 15.
[28] 'Reforma agrară', *Lumina satelor*, 1 January 1922, 5.
[29] 'De ce nu-s destui bani', *Lumina satelor*, 29 January 1922, 4; 'Se aproprie noua recoltă', *Lumina satelor*, 26 June 1927, 1.
[30] T. Povaţa, 'Despre pocăiţii aşa numiţi adventişti', *Lumina satelor*, 23 April 1922, 1–2; Şerban Brâncoveanu, 'Sectarismul, sionismul şi bolsevismul', *Lumina satelor*, 5 June 1927, 2.
[31] 'Este tata la cârmă?' *Lumina satelor*, 23 July 1922, 1; Iosif Trifa, 'Stai în loc şi-ţi fă socoată!' *Lumina satelor*, 14 January 1923, 1; Iosif Trifa, 'Un dar sufletesc', *Lumina satelor*, 4 March 1923, 1.
[32] Iosif Trifa, 'Sectarismul religios', *Revista teologică* 11, no. 6–7 (1921): 192.
[33] Sadhu Sundar Singh, *La picioarele stăpânului meu* (Sibiu: Tiparul Tipografiei Arhidiecezane, 1928).

but he presented Christianity in terms of Indian culture, making him exotic enough not to threaten Orthodox sensibilities. Pamphlets such as Singh's were particularly successful in inter-war Romania because of the growing literacy rates in rural areas. Trifa took advantage of the fact that more and more people could read by distributing Bibles and writing short sermons and exegeses aimed at peasant audiences.[34] Bălan considered the newspaper's first year to have been a great success and at the end of 1922 he awarded Trifa with an honorary red silk belt.[35]

Trifa published attacks on drunkenness from the beginning and the Lord's Army became a temperance movement in 1923.[36] Trifa writes that, while he was thinking about his past year's work late one night at the end of 1922, 'a crowd of drunks passed by my window shouting loudly. This increased my pain. I fell to my knees in tears and wept, begging God to give me success in my labours'.[37] God inspired him to ask his readers to take an oath, Trifa said, abstaining from alcohol and from swearing. New Year celebrations in Romania were not very Christian, Trifa wrote in the first issue of 1923. 'At any price, whatever the cost, we hold on to our ignorant, pagan tradition: for the new year to find us drunk and to get drunk again in the new year'. He wrote that Satan wants us 'to enter the new year with the same sins that we left the last one with, so that we might enter the next year, and eventually the grave, with these same sins'.[38] In the next few issues Trifa began to refer to those who took the oath to give up drinking as 'soldiers' (*ostași*) and the idea soon developed that they constituted 'the Lord's Army'.

Temperance was not a new idea in Romania. In Transylvania, where Trifa worked, temperance movements had emerged in the second half of the nineteenth century. In 1912 Vasile Oana encouraged his readers to admit that

> Our people are alcoholic, and that alcohol addiction, with all its sad outcomes, has developed strong and deep roots. And from sin, sin is born; while the fair and certain price is moral death ... In our case, as well as in the case of

---

[34] Iosif Trifa, *Ce este Oastea Domnului?* 5th edn (Sibiu: Editura Oastea Domnului, 1934), 92ff; Iosif Trifa, *Cetiri și tâlcuiri din Biblie* (Sibiu: Editura Archdiecezană, 1924).
[35] 'Informațiuni', *Biserica și școala*, 15/28 January 1923, 7.
[36] 'Știrile săptămânii', *Lumina satelor*, 9 January 1922, 4; Leo Tolstoi, 'Cine a iscodit rachiul?' *Lumina satelor*, 5 February 1922, 2–3; Neculce, 'O ciudată pedeapsă americană', *Lumina satelor*, 25 June 1922, 3.
[37] Trifa, *Ce este Oastea Domnului?*, 231.
[38] Iosif Trifa, 'Să facem o intrare creștinească în anul cel nou cu hotărâre și întovărășire de luptă împotriva sudalmelor și bețiilor', *Lumina satelor*, 14 January 1923, 1.

other nations, alcohol addiction has surpassed all the differences in social position, age, or gender; as our intellectual class and the common people, the elder and the young, men and women, all together drink alcohol in an abusive manner.[39]

A doctor from Brașov had established a Society for the Enemies of Alcohol and Nicotine only a month before Trifa launched the Lord's Army.[40] Temperance was so popular, in fact, that Miron Cristea introduced a 'Temperance Day' in 1930, involving a festival in the middle of Bucharest with 'educational and anti-alcoholic' activities.[41] Orthodox preachers quite often attacked drunkenness and swearing along with smoking and disrespecting Sundays. Gurie Grosu, for example, echoed Trifa's comments about how Romanians celebrated Sundays and holidays:

> Instead of staying home with their families and going to the church service in the village, they leave for the market with rent, produce, vegetables, fruits and cereals. And here, as the pubs are open, they turn to drunkenness. Returning home late at night they look for reasons to argue with those who stayed home, starting quarrels and vomiting filthy words out of hearts full of drink.[42]

Another priest, Gheorghe Chirițescu, blamed the fact that evening dances took place next to taverns and said that young people started drinking once the dancing was over, led astray by their drunken elders. He complained that alcoholics spread stories that drink was actually healthy and wrote, 'I have seen women, young and old, carrying eggs – food for their little children – in their aprons and receiving brandy in return. They hide it at home somewhere, in a barrel of beans or bran and drink it when things get too bad. Even sadder, I have even seen mothers give this poison to babies who are still breastfeeding!' Chirițescu warned that 'the spirit of brandy destroys the fragile connection between the brain and the spinal cord, which is why almost all drunks are broken

---

[39] Vasile Oana, 'Prefață', in Augustin Egger, *Clerul și chestiunea alcoolismului* (1912), quoted in Marius Rotar, 'Alcoholism in Transylvania in the Second Half of the Nineteenth Century and Early Twentieth Century', *The International Journal of Regional and Local Studies* 3, no. 2 (2007): 44.

[40] 'Societatea dușmanii alcoolului și nicotinei', *Gazeta Transilvaniei*, 1 December 1922, in ANIC – Brașov, Fond Personal Gyurgyevich, Dosar 3, f. 5.

[41] ANIC – Craiova, Fond Parohia Bisericii Obedeanu Craiova, Dosar 57/1930, f. 26.

[42] Grosu Gurie, *I - Cinstirea Duminicei și a serbatorilor, II – Păcatul sudalmilor și vorbilor urâte* (Chișinău: Tipografia Eparhială, 1923), 3. See also Grosu Gurie, *I. Păcatul dela umblarea la iarmaroace în zilele de Duminecă. II. Păcatul fumatului de tutun* (Chișinău: Tipografia Eparhială, 1924).

of mind and body'.[43] Alcohol was, the teacher Iuliu Grofşorean argued, one of the devil's greatest weapons, taking both people's health and their money.[44]

The tavern was frequently placed in competition with the church and preachers assumed that alcohol was the main reason for a lack of religiosity. In one sermon a priest told of a legend:

> The devil saw that people had begun to build houses of prayer, with high towers pointing to the heavens and that they called them churches, which means the house of God because in church everyone comes together to offer up prayers of thanksgiving to God and to bring sacrifices for all the good things that he gives to us. The devil wracked his brains to find a way to have a church for himself and to get slaves and faithful servants on earth.
>
> With this in mind he asked God to let him build himself a house of prayer to meet his needs. It would not be called a church, but a tavern. God knew that he had given holy and godly commandments to men so that they knew what to embrace and what to avoid. 'You have before you fire and water, good and evil', says Holy Scripture, 'choose'.[45] Neither drinkers nor drunks will inherit the Kingdom of God, as if one were to say 'don't go to the tavern for danger lurks there'.
>
> Knowing that men had enough commandments that would stop them going to the church of the devil, or the tavern, God allowed the devil to build a tavern. For men also have enough brains, unlike the dumb animals, to know to avoid the tavern like a 'murderous cross' ...
>
> The devil put a Jew [in the tavern] in place of a priest, brought from Galicia for this purpose, or from somewhere else but never from the village, knowing that people love foreign publicans more than their own people. They called their first priest 'Master' (*jupâne*) just as one would call a priest 'Father', and he was from Galicia, with sidelocks (*payot*) and a big beard and a kippa on his head. They called him 'Master Frankenstein'. Sharp as pepper and crafty as a fox.[46]

As did other Orthodox preachers, Trifa frequently associated Jews with taverns to show that alcoholism was a foreign evil and was in no way connected to Christianity. Jews ran the taverns in all of Trifa's stories and he insisted that most Repenter preachers were actually 'Yids' in disguise.[47] 'Most publicans are Yids',

---

[43] Gheorghe Chirițescu, *Otrava vieții* (Târgu Neamț: Tipgrafiei Monastirii Neamțu, 1924), 11, 16.
[44] Iuliu Grofşorean, *Scrieri pentru popor* (Arad: Tiparul Diecezane Gr-Or. Rom., 1906), 3–6.
[45] The allusion is to Deuteronomy 30:19, but this is actually a quote from Caesarius of Arles, *The Fathers of the Church: St. Caesarius of Arles, Sermons*, vol. 2. (Washington, DC: The Catholic University of America Press, 1963), 329.
[46] B. Podoabă, 'Povestea cârciumei: Conferință ținută la adunarea despărțământul Astrei la Dezmir, de B. Podoabă', in ANIC, Fond Miron Cristea, Dosar 1902/1, f. 63.
[47] Ibid., Povața, 'Despre pocăiții așa numiți adventiști'; 'Visul bețivului', *Lumina satelor*, 28 January 1923, 5.

he wrote, 'and the taverns are full of fake drinks which make people very ill. They have caught Yids in Maramureș, in Brașov [and] Orade[a] who make up the brandy with lime, sulfuric acid and ash'.[48] The heroes of many of the short stories Trifa printed in *Lumina satelor* were poor but righteous peasants who, when confronted with learned or wealthy atheists from the towns, rejected their disbelief and challenged them to change their ways – usually with amazing success.[49] The villains were often Jews. Thinking back to when Transylvania was part of Hungary, Trifa wrote that '[Buda]Pest was a real Babylon, destroyed thanks to the Judaism that ruled in those days that we despised', and complained that now Jews had corrupted Bucharest as well.[50] Although the newspaper was otherwise apolitical, during the 1920s Trifa praised the antisemitic student movement and A. C. Cuza's National Christian Defense League.[51]

Despite the number of Orthodox sermons condemning drinking and smoking, Repenters were the only religious group to consistently practice temperance. Confronted by Repenters who considered Orthodox believers to be 'a herd of drunkards and debauchers', Trifa offered temperance as a first step in morally reforming the Church.[52] A farm worker (*plugar*) identified as N. T. wrote to Trifa:

> I wanted to repent because I have long liked the good habits of the Repenters who don't swear and don't drink and I worried about what I should do. Often I would wake up in the night and think about repenting but when I went to sleep again all sorts of visions and nightmares appeared. I woke up terrified and it seemed like I had woken my ancestors from the grave, who shook my house in anger that I would want to abandon their ways. But now I thank God that *Lumina satelor* has freed me from my evil thoughts and has brought home to me a decision to renounce swearing and drunkenness with hate and disgust.[53]

As the name suggests, Trifa saw the Lord's Army as 'a declaration of spiritual warfare against the tricks of the devil, against darkness and evil'.[54] He explicitly

---

[48] Trifa, *Ce este Oastea Domnului?*, 106. In fact, only 2.1 per cent of publicans were Jewish. Andrei Oișteanu, *Inventing the Jew: Antisemitic Stereotypes in Romanian and Other Central-East European Cultures*, trans. Mirela Adăscăliței (Lincoln: University of Nebaska Press, 2009), 176.

[49] Iosif Trifa, 'Să începem dela început', *Lumina satelor*, 1 January 1922, 3; Traian Scorobeț, 'Țara fericită', *Lumina satelor*, 1 January 1922, 2–5; 'Țăranul și necredinciosul', *Lumina satelor*, 9 July 1922, 3; 'Cum a păcălit un om pe dracul', *Lumina satelor*, 17 May 1925, 5; Trifa, *25 povestiri*.

[50] 'Jos Sodoma și Gomora', *Lumina satelor*, 25 June 1922, 2.

[51] 'Mișcarea împotriva jidanilor', *Lumina satelor*, 11 February 1923, 2; 'Ce mai e nou în viața politică?' *Lumina satelor*, 8 May 1927, 2. On the newspaper's official political position, see 'Credința noastră politică', *Lumina satelor*, 1 January 1922, 2.

[52] T. Povața, 'Despre pocăiți', *Lumina satelor*, 18 June 1922, 1.

[53] N. T., 'Și eu am vrut să mă pocăesc', *Lumina satelor*, 28 January 1923, 5.

[54] Trifa, *Ce este Oastea Domnului?*, 6.

drew the comparison with the heroism of wartime, saying that 'faith weakened after the Great War, Christian love went cold and evil-doing increased terribly'.[55] The Lord's Army grew rapidly. It claimed 10,000 members by April 1927 and 20,000 by 1928.[56] *Lumina satelor* reported that the movement had 60,000 members in 1932, and in 1934 Trifa said that 'over 100,000 soldiers are now gathered beneath the flag of the Saviour'.[57] Villages sometimes had substantial communities of over fifty members. Supporters donated their money and time to distribute pamphlets and Bibles to communities where the movement had not yet penetrated.[58] Trifa never asked for membership fees or compulsory contributions – members used their money to buy pamphlets that they distributed for free.[59] Others gave large, unsolicited donations which Trifa then publicized on the front page of the newspaper.[60] Accusations that he was extorting money from people nonetheless dogged the movement from its beginnings.[61]

Lumina satelor created what Candy Gunther Brown calls a 'textual community'. Brown writes that Evangelical Christians in nineteenth-century America used newspapers and books to form a national – even international – community based on shared values, common relationships and collective goals rather than focused on local congregations. Letters to the editor, book reviews and news about large events reminded Evangelicals that there were people in other parts of the country who were just like them and allowed them to participate in a community of people they would never meet face to face.[62] D. Voniga, a priest who had also worked in the temperance movement, wrote in 1925 that 'today the press, as a medium for spiritual mediation and cultural propaganda, as a defensive weapon in the battle for the national interests, as creator of spiritual unity, of an intellectual community and public opinion, is considered the most powerful factor of all for battle and for public activity, for all sorts of initiatives,

---

[55] Ibid., 5.
[56] '"Lumina Satelor" a strâns 10 mii de abonați', *Lumina satelor*, 24 April 1927, 1; Gogan, 'Viața și activitatea', 19.
[57] Gh. Șoima, 'Cele două feluri de adunări', *Lumina satelor*, 26 June 1932, 1; Trifa, *Ce este Oastea Domnului?*, 224.
[58] '"Lumina satelor" în ajutorul Asociațiunii', *Lumina satelor*, 4 February 1923, 2; Iosif Trifa, 'Un dar sufletesc', *Lumina satelor*, 4 March 1923, 1; 'Gazeta "Beiușul" din Beiuș', *Lumina satelor*, 25 March 1925, 2; 'Din fronturile Oastea Domnului', *Lumina satelor*, 7 June 1929, 2.
[59] Iosif Trifa, *Munca și lenea văzute în lumina evangheliei* (n.p.: n.p., n.d.), 42.
[60] 'Un dar de 1000 lei pentru societatea ostașilor lui Isus Hristos', *Lumina satelor*, 8 February 1925, 1; 'O altă înștiințare cu 1000 lei pentru societatea celor din Oastea Domnului', *Lumina satelor*, 1 March 1925, 1.
[61] Trifa, *Ce este Oastea Domnului?*, 154.
[62] Candy Gunther Brown, *The Word in the World: Evangelical Writing, Publishing, and Reading in America, 1789–1880* (Chapel Hill: University of North Carolina Press, 2004), 9–15.

progress and victories'.[63] As Voniga was aware, Christians were not the only people using the press to win Romanian souls, and newspapers were also a key vehicle for creating grassroots political movements, especially on the far right.[64] The model worked particularly well for Trifa. Peasants signed an oath and posted it to the newspaper when they joined the Lord's Army and *Lumina satelor* published a regular rubric welcoming new members by name, publishing their letters and giving news about Lord's Army gatherings across the country.[65] Sometimes entire villages joined the movement at once and in one village so many people boycotted the tavern that it went bankrupt.[66]

Thanks to a generous donor from America the newspaper was also able to offer prizes of money and books to subscribers, drawn once a month, as well as other prizes for answering questions about the Bible.[67] Most of the letters Trifa published were apparently from people who worked with their hands, but the list of winners from the first prize draw from 1925 perhaps gives us a more accurate picture of who his subscribers were. Among the seventy names drawn were eight priests, three cantors, a parish officer, an administrator, a teacher, a notary, a shopkeeper, a forester and a farmer.[68] Individuals associated with the church and village intellectuals were thus closely associated with the movement during its early years, though they were far from being in the majority.

Books and pamphlets were the glue that held the Lord's Army together. Trifa loved recounting stories of people being converted through his writings. He told of one person who joined the movement after finding a copy of *Lumina satelor* that someone had left on a train. 'He took it', Trifa wrote, 'read it, liked it, subscribed to it, and today is full of passion for the Lord and for his soul'. 'A sweet story, a Bible, a religious newspaper, a good book, etc., are all gentle calls through which the Spirit of the Lord seeks to awaken sinners to new life'.[69] The ROC agreed. The official newspaper of the episcopate of Caransebeș, *Foaia diecezană*

---

[63] D. Voniga, *Presa bisericească: Importanța ei și mijloace de întreținere* (Timișoara: Tipografia Huniadi, 1925), 5–6.
[64] Roland Clark, *Holy Legionary Youth: Fascist Activism in Interwar Romania* (Ithaca: Cornell University Press, 2015), 122–50; Biliuță, 'The Ultranationalist Newsroom', 186–211.
[65] 'Oastea noastra crește', *Lumina satelor*, 29 December 1924, 3.
[66] 'Hotărârea poporului din satul Botean', *Lumina satelor*, 12 April 1925, 1; 'Ascultați ce lucru cuminte a făcut un sat', *Lumina satelor*, 10 May 1925, 1.
[67] 'Pe anul viitor "Lumina satelor" pune premii de mii de lei', *Lumina satelor*, 21 December 1924, 8; 'Prietenul nostru, Ilie Laza, din America', *Lumina satelor*, 11 January 1925, 1.
[68] 'Tragerea premiilor gazetei "Lumina satelor"', *Lumina satelor*, 8 February 1925, 1; 'Tragerea premiilor gazetei "Lumina satelor"', *Lumina satelor*, 15 February 1925, 2.
[69] Iosif Trifa, *Oglinda inimii omului* (Sibiu: Tiparul Tipografiei Arhidiecezane, 1927), 14.

(*The Diocesian Paper*), celebrated the publication of two of Trifa's collections of sermons in 1925, telling its readers that

> Father I. Trifa pours so much Christian feeling into the hearts of believers wanting to know and hear the word of God. His holiness has the gift and the skill of explaining the most profound teachings of Holy Scripture beautifully and in a way that is easy to understand. In today's critical times, when the faithful flock is tossed back and forth by the temptations of life, these two pamphlets are true spiritual food not only for ordinary people but for all who need spiritual nourishment and comfort.[70]

Trifa's writings were heartily endorsed by a large number of church newspapers during the 1920s, including by the Greek Catholic press.[71]

Although they were primarily connected through printed words, members of the Lord's Army did meet each other. Nicolae Bălan organized a pilgrimage to Jerusalem in 1925 and Trifa joined the 160 pilgrims (mostly priests) who accompanied him, publishing a book-length account of the journey. Trifa wrote of how the journey brought the pilgrims together as 'brothers on the road, brothers in suffering and in the joys that awaited us'. He described reading prayer books and the writings of the Church Fathers on the train and groups of people gathered together praying by candlelight.[72] More than just a travel account, this book provided a template for how his soldiers were to behave when they met. *Lumina satelor* also published details about propaganda meetings held by the Lord's Army. In 1925 a priest named Cornel Magler led thirteen 'soldiers' from his village in a propaganda march to a village in a neighbouring county. The visit had been arranged with the other priest and 'the whole village' turned out to greet them. A number of people preached about topics such as the second coming of Christ, the problem of sectarianism and what was expected of people who joined the Lord's Army. They led prayers and recited poetry from *Lumina satelor*. Forty people joined the movement following this particular excursion.[73] A couple of years later Magler became a missionary priest, combining his work for the Lord's Army with his official anti-sectarian duties.[74] In 1929 members began organizing regional gatherings at which a hundred or so people would

---

[70] 'Două cărți bune', *Foaia diecezană*, 15 February 1925, 4.
[71] 'Cărți și reviste', *Unirea*, 23 April 1927, 9–10.
[72] Iosif Trifa, *Pe urmele Mântuitorului: Însemnări din călătoria la Ierusalim* (Sibiu: Tiparul Institutului de Arte Grafice, 1928), 4–5.
[73] 'Oastea Domnului din Cermeiu în o nouă ofensivă', *Lumina satelor*, 25 October 1925, 4.
[74] 'Ofensiva Oastei în Bihor', *Lumina satelor*, 26 June 1927, 4.

meet to hear sermons and sing songs. The preachers at these occasions were invariably priests and songs were performed by organized choirs.[75]

The Lord's Army established itself in different ways in each place. A police report from 1949 on the city of Călărași wrote that the Lord's Army was started here in 1927 by Ana Ion Scutaru, who received and distributed literature from Trifa. Trifa himself visited in 1930 in order to bless the movement's flag. This was a significant occasion and he was met by members from six different villages. The report stated that the movement took on a life of its own after Trifa's visit, becoming increasingly independent of the ROC.[76] In a confession from 1954 the preacher Vasile Axinuța said that he entered the Lord's Army in 1935 because his parish priest had been distributing Trifa's books and pamphlets. As well as going to church more regularly, he started attending meetings 'where they sang religious poems, prayed and read various lovely teachings from the Bible'.[77]

Members of the Lord's Army were easily identifiable by their behaviour. As well as giving up drinking, swearing and smoking, they sought to live holy lives in their everyday communities. 'The Lord's Army is a movement of cleansing and renewal, completely changing the lives of those who join it. In the Lord's Army we preach a spiritual rebirth; we preach a change in life's foundations; we preach a new life'.[78] Every soldier was expected to own a Bible and to read it regularly.[79] Following the example of the Apostle Paul – and imitating Repenter practices – Trifa's followers called each other 'brother' and 'sister' in their gatherings and their writings. They greeted each other with the words 'Peace be with you!' (*Pacea Domnului!*) and responded, 'And also with you!' (*Să fie cu noi cu toți!*).[80] Encouraging what Max Weber called a Protestant work ethic, Trifa preached that 'work is good for the body and the soul. Laziness is a spiritual and a physical disease'.[81] Soldiers could buy a 'medal' in the form of a cross engraved with 'In the Lord's Army' and the words of 2 Timothy 2:3: 'Share in suffering like a good soldier of Christ Jesus'.[82] As Trifa explained, 'the symbol of the medallion is very useful for travelling as well. On trains, at markets, etc., brothers who wear the same symbol will know each other immediately and will rejoice in the Lord'.[83]

---

[75] 'Serbarea Oastei Domnului din Câmpuri-Surduc', *Lumina satelor*, 7 July 1929, 6.
[76] ACNSAS, Fond Documentar, Dosar 9486, vol. 1, f. 317.
[77] ACNSAS, Fond Penal, Dosar 1882, ff. 8–9.
[78] Trifa, *Ce este Oastea Domnului?*, 122.
[79] Ibid., 163.
[80] Ibid., 218, 226–7.
[81] Trifa, *Munca și lenea*, 46.
[82] 'Semnul celor intrați în Oastea Domnului', *Lumina satelor*, 19 April 1925, 7.
[83] Trifa, *Ce este Oastea Domnului?*, 174.

They also celebrated differently. Trifa wrote that

> A soldier of the Lord does not go to parties, dances, or balls because the way that people party these days (with drunkenness and crazy games) is almost completely in the service of the devil ... A soldier of the Lord will only go to the sorts of parties that do not have alcohol and dancing (concerts, theatre) ... A soldier of the Lord will not attend the evenings, discussions, and gatherings that take place especially during winter in the taverns or at people's houses. They will not go because these too have come into the devil's service. Today's gatherings are full of alcohol, filthy talk and dancing from which Satan reaps a rich harvest.[84]

These were not just empty words. A priest from the village of Hălchiu in Brașov county wrote in 1928 that 'all members of the society, led by the priest and his wife, ended the year singing religious and national songs, reading from Father Trifa's books, and with a great deal of laughter and good cheer. At 11:45pm all of the young people went to the church, where they rang the bells for a quarter of an hour'.[85] *Lumina satelor* reported that peasants sometimes resisted the Lord's Army, assuming that it was a Repenter sect.[86] Trifa assured his readers that far from being 'a new sect', 'we, soldiers of the Lord, *want to live out the Gospel ... just as the first Christians did. That is the whole "novelty" of the Lord's Army*'.[87] Moreover, he published letters from former Adventists who had converted to Orthodoxy because of the Lord's Army and told stories of entire villages of Nazarenes who had been brought back to Orthodoxy by his books.[88]

Trifa wrote that a person's conversion should be visible to everyone around them.

> Look at this man from the village. His life has changed completely. Everyone is amazed at difference. Arrogant and conceited before, now see him full of humility, like a different man. From a lover of alcohol and worldly pleasures, see him suddenly withdraw from taverns, parties, gatherings and from everything that reflects the spirit of this world. Now he doesn't like anything unless it is connected to the Gospel and his soul. The tavern used to be his 'church'; now he loves the church, the school and anything that can provide food for his soul and mind.[89]

---

[84] Ibid., 168.
[85] Gh. Constantin, 'Cercul tinerimii adulte Sf-tul Gheorghe din comuna Hălchiu', *Gazeta Transilvaniei*, 11 January 1928, 2.
[86] 'Din fronturile Oastei Domnului', *Lumina satelor*, 7 July 1929, 2.
[87] Trifa, *Ce este Oastea Domnului?*, 217.
[88] 'S'au întors la biserica străbună', *Lumina satelor*, 15 March 1925, 2; 'Pentru "Renașterea" din Cluj și alți criticanți', *Lumina satelor*, 7 July 1929, 6.
[89] Iosif Trifa, *Oglinda inimii omului* (Sibiu: Tiparul Tipografiei Arhidiecezane, 1927), 28.

Trifa insisted on lay leadership of the Lord's Army. There was to be no hierarchy for this was a lay movement whose goal was to 'help' priests rather than to replace them. 'Every soul who has truly found the Lord becomes a preacher of the Lord', Trifa argued. 'If lay people are not allowed to preach during services', he pointed out, 'they still have the right to preach in church when there are not services being held and even more to preach outside the church'.⁹⁰ The idea of lay ministry was not new, he insisted, quoting the Apostle James, the fourth century preacher John Chrysostom, and the Russian émigré theologian Sergei Bulgakov in his support.⁹¹ Preachers were usually laypeople. Trifa wrote that the two most successful preachers in Sibiu were a bricklayer and a carpenter. He commented that when he was a village priest peasants came preaching Repenter Christianity 'with their Bibles in their hands and the people loved listening to them. A peasant preacher is attractive and praiseworthy. But when these peasants came back again, this time dressed in gentlemen's clothes and calling themselves "preachers", no one listened to them. Everyone said that they were preaching for money. Dollars from America destroyed everything'.⁹²

By the mid-1920s Trifa's preaching had moved from the usual Orthodox interest in attending church and abstaining from particular sins to one focused on personal conversion that was only possible because of Jesus's death on the cross. He expected his soldiers to have individual conversion experiences that they could tell others about. 'Everyone who turns to God has his own story about how he woke from the sleep of sinners and rose again to a new life', he wrote.⁹³ Whereas the church as the Body of Christ lay at the heart of Orthodox teachings about salvation, Trifa said that 'it is not enough for someone to know the church. They must also be built up by the gifts which it administers. It is not enough for a church to sit in the middle of every village when people go to the tavern every Sunday.'⁹⁴ He saw his task as a preacher as being about making people aware of their sins and offering them new life in Christ. 'People do not lose their souls and eternal life because of sins', he argued, 'but because they are not aware of sin, they are not horrified by their sinfulness, they do not let the Spirit of the Lord work in them to awaken them to a new life'.⁹⁵

---

⁹⁰ Trifa, *Ce este Oastea Domnului?*, 138.
⁹¹ Ibid., 129–38.
⁹² Trifa, *Munca și lenea*, 44.
⁹³ Trifa, *Oglinda inimii omului*, 17.
⁹⁴ Trifa, *Ce este Oastea Domnului?*, 84.
⁹⁵ Trifa, *Oglinda inimii omului*, 20.

Genuine repentance was the first step to embracing new life. 'To enter the Lord's Army does not mean to resolve to give up evil', Trifa preached.

> It means being struck down by sin and evil at the feet of the cross … To fall weeping at the feet of the cross just as you are, full of evil … At the feet of the cross you don't just open the eyes of your mind, you receive a gift, a power and help from above which changes your life. Standing at the feet of the cross, a power from above changes your life. It changes your speech, your thoughts, your paths and all your actions. The sacrifice changes you from an 'old man' into a 'new man', from a 'worldly man' into a 'spiritual man'.[96]

Trifa repeated the same ideas again and again in his writing, often reformulating the same phrase through various permutations for half a page or more. When his articles are read out loud his style is that of a preacher giving his audience time to reflect on an important point from different angles before moving on.

Salvation was an existential question for Trifa, resolved by a decision to become a follower of Jesus. In language remarkably similar to that being used by Repenter preachers, he wrote that 'our victory rests on accepting the Lord. It hangs on the question: Have you truly accepted the Lord and his gifts, or not?'[97] In a book comparing the spiritual journey to the Israelites' exodus from Egypt, Trifa noted that after Christians break with the world and escape from slavery they face 'the great school of the wilderness' where they must learn to live as Christians before entering the promised land.[98] Trifa warned that temptations would continue to worry his soldiers after they had been saved but he reminded them that Christ was mightier than the devil. Trifa envisaged the spiritual life as one long battle with evil and explained that 'every sin is a new channel for Satan; it is lost territory in the war for our souls; it is a banner of the devil planted on our battleground'.[99] Not everyone who joined the Lord's Army was ready for the battle, Trifa said, and some would fall along the wayside. Constant vigilance was therefore needed to help the whole army reach the heavenly kingdom.[100]

Members of the Lord's Army did not only use prayer books to pray, because 'praying with your own words is a sign of the work of the Holy Spirit'.[101] They sang together and the movement had its own song book. Trifa wrote, 'as well as

---

[96] Trifa, *Ce este Oastea Domnului?*, 74, 76.
[97] Ibid., 61.
[98] Iosif Trifa, *Spre Canaan* (Sibiu: n.p., 1936), 60.
[99] Trifa, *Ce este Oastea Domnului?*, 57.
[100] Iosif Trifa, *Spre Canaan* (1936), 42.
[101] Trifa, *Ce este Oastea Domnului?*, 179.

[singing] you can read from religious books, recite religious poetry, give speeches, advice and other useful things. Come together in the name of the Lord and the Holy Spirit will show you what to do, what to say, how to sing and how to "build up each other" (1 Thessalonians 5:11)'.[102] *Lumina satelor* frequently published poetry written by members of the movement. These poems were usually upbeat with simple rhyming schemes, encouraging others to continue 'fighting the good fight'.[103] Others wrote poetry instead of letters when they joined the movement. Iuon Doreanu, a bricklayer from Câmpulung Moldovenesc wrote:

> As a master bricklayer
> One never builds for no reason.
> But I build myself
> Into the army of God.
> Help me Lord, Iuon
> Awaken me from slumber
> And make me useful
> Under the flag of Christ the Lord.[104]

By the late 1930s most of the songs used in their gatherings were written by three of Trifa's followers – Ioan Marini, Traian Dorz and Simion Paraschiv. The movement does not seem to have used existing Orthodox songbooks.[105] After the Second World War the music of another Lord's Army songwriter, Nicolae Moldoveanu, would become popular in Repenter circles throughout the country.[106] Songs sung by the Lord's Army reflected an intimate, friendly relationship with a loving God on whom they depended to meet their every need. As statements of belief that were repeated again and again, out loud and in public, Lord's Army songs defined the movement's theology almost as strongly as Trifa's writings did. The words to their songs reflected Trifa's message succinctly and powerfully. In one song, Marini wrote

> O Jesus, my beloved – my beloved
> In this world I have erred – I have erred.
> Till I met you – met you

---

[102] Ibid., 179.
[103] 'Alte poezii pentru cei din Oastea Domnului', *Lumina satelor*, 4 January 1925, 3.
[104] 'De vorba cu cei ce s'au hotărât la o viață nouă', *Lumina satelor*, 11 January 1925, 3.
[105] Traian Dorz, *Din lupta Domnului. Popasuri în 'istoria unei jertfe'. Poezii religioase. Cartea III* (Oradea: Grafica, 1939); Ioan Marini and Traian Dorz, *Să cântăm Domnului: Carte de cântări religioase* (Oradea: Grafica, 1940).
[106] Kis-Juhász and Teodorescu, 'Bazele închinării evanghelice', 733.

> Only evil did I do – did I do.
> But now my only wish – my only wish
> Is to be as God wants me – as God wants me.[107]

Music-making was a collective endeavour, such as the following song which was written by 'the sisters from Potlogi-Dâmbovița' and put to music by Paraschiv.

> I want to sing, to sing with joy,
> From now until the end,
> For I know that I belong to Christ
> And that I'm saved by him.
> *I will sing for all eternity,*
> *Of Jesus my Beloved Saviour.*
>
> For he was put upon a cross,
> And torture he endured,
> The sin that oppressed my life
> Was washed clean by his blood.
> *I will sing ...*[108]

The melodies were simple, without harmonies and within a vocal range that could comfortably be sung by most altos or sopranos. Communal singing thus did not need any musical accompaniment and could be done anywhere at any time.

Although the Lord's Army developed its own devotional literature and made use of readings that Trifa thought would be widely accepted by an Orthodox audience, it was not always clear where his ideas originated. Trifa was not the only preacher who encountered this problem. Few of the stories and arguments found in Romanian sermons during the 1920s originated in Orthodox circles. In one of his writings Trifa described a book called *The Mirror of the Soul* (*Oglinda inimii omului celui din lăuntru*) that had been popular in Orthodox circles at one time. He said,

> It was a translation from Slavic done by a monk named Macarie. The monk Macarie said that this *Reflection* was written by a Russian monk. The truth is that this book was written in France before 1820 by a certain I. Gossner in the spirit of Roman Catholicism. The author was probably a Roman Catholic priest or

---

[107] Ioan Marini and Simion Paraschiv, 'O Isuse', in Marini and Dorz, *Să cântăm Domnului*, 11.
[108] Simion Paraschiv, 'Eu vreau să cânt', in ibid., 12.

monk. The Slavic translation made only minor changes. This book has appeared again in a Romanian translation in Bucharest in recent years. The new edition is being distributed by sectarians in particular, giving people the (incorrect) impression that it is a 'Repenter book' (the devil is a great charlatan: he keeps people away from the Bible and other spiritual books by spreading the word that they are 'Repenter books').[109]

The original author was actually Johannes Gossner, a Roman Catholic priest from Germany who wrote it in 1812 before being defrocked fourteen years later for converting to Protestantism. Gossner later became an important influence on Evangelical Protestant missions. The book's illustrations drew on a Flemish iconographic tradition and reflected a pessimistic turning away from a corrupt society towards internal piety.[110] Trifa rewrote the book in his own distinctive style, reusing many of its illustrations not only here but in a number of his other books as well. Assuming that Trifa's account of how Romanian audiences responded to Gossner's book is accurate, the story shows that it was not so much the ideas in a book that mattered but the author's reputation. Most Orthodox readers would accept a book they believed had been written by a Russian monk but rejected the same book if it was distributed by Repenters. Trifa, on the other hand, appears to have been willing to turn a blind eye to where his ideas came from so long as they resonated with his message.

So many of Trifa's ideas looked and sounded like Evangelical Protestantism, but his Orthodoxy was not questioned within Transylvania so long as he enjoyed the patronage of Nicolae Bălan and the support of the Church press. But when allegations appeared that Trifa had become a 'sectarian' they spread quickly. *Libertatea* reported that the secret police began surveillance of Trifa in April 1929 on the grounds that he was the leader of a new sect. A newspaper known for its antisemitism, *Libertatea* mockingly assumed that the secret police were working on behalf of Jewish publicans whose business had been threatened by Trifa's temperance movement.[111] His enemies agreed that there was something wrong with his theology, however, and on 26 May the Bessarabian newspaper *Glasul monahilor* wrote that

> We often hear people talking – and some people even ask us – if what is written in [*Lumina satelor*] flows out of a true Christian Orthodox spirit or whether it

---

[109] Trifa, *Oglinda inimii omului*, 1.
[110] Helmut Renders, 'As origens do livro emblemático *O coração do ser humano* (1812) de Johannes Evangelista Gossner: continuidade e releituras da religio cordis nos séculos 16 a 19', *Protestantismo em Revista* 29 (2012): 65–78.
[111] 'Săraci cu duhul', *Libertatea*, 30 May 1929, 3.

is Protestant. We admit that the question surprised us, but a lot of people are saying: 'Why don't we see anything written about the Holy Virgin Mary, the Mother of our God and Saviour, our about the saints, whom we know fought vigorously for the light and truth of the Holy Gospels to come to us?'[112]

Iuliu Scriban later wrote that the accusations against Trifa originated with Hieromonk Dionisie Lungu, the editor of *Glasul monahilor*, 'whose insolence propels him to involve himself in things he doesn't understand' (*care-i dă obrăznic cu gura înainte în treburile despre cari nu se pricepe două boabe*).[113] *Renașterea* (*Rebirth*) from Cluj picked up the question and in May 1930 a general episcopal assembly at Cluj requested that the Holy Synod examine Trifa's orthodoxy.[114] Trifa retained the public support of Bălan and Scriban, however, and nothing came of these accusations.

Trifa eventually broke with the ROC over money, not theology. According to Trifa, his troubles began when he bought a new printing press from Germany in November 1929. The press was for a new magazine, *Oastea Domnului* (*The Lord's Army*). Funded by donations and out of Trifa's own pocket it sent him into debt just when his health began to fail. Trifa writes that he was physically drained from having spent several years writing almost night and day to publish *Lumina satelor* and all of his books and pamphlets. He collapsed while visiting a school, coughing up blood. Ironically, it was while he was in hospital that he met a young teacher named Ioan Marini, who was in the same hospital also with lung problems. Marini left his job soon after being discharged from hospital and began working at *Lumina satelor*. He remained a loyal follower of Trifa and became one of the movement's key leaders after his death.[115] As soon as Trifa bought the new printing press, the archdiocese of Sibiu demanded that he pay his debts to their press immediately. No longer able to pay the rent for the bookstore to the archdiocese, he had to close it temporarily. Trifa then asked Bălan if he could print *Lumina satelor* on his own press instead of that of the archdiocese for two or three months to save money. Bălan refused, apparently asking him with a smile, 'You're sorry that you bought the press now, aren't you?' According to Trifa, Bălan 'hated the press from the beginning. The proof is that

---

[112] *Glasul monahilor*, 26 May 1929, quoted in 'Cronica', *Renașterea* (Cluj), 30 June 1929, 6.
[113] Iuliu Scriban, 'Așa zisul Protestantism al "Oștii Domnului"', *Revista teologică* 21, no. 8–9 (1931): 297.
[114] *Actele Adunării Eparhiale Ordinare a Eparhiei Vadului, Feleacului, și Clujului ținută la Cluj în anul 1930* (Cluj: Tiparul Tipografiei Eparh. Ort. Rom., 1930), 21–2.
[115] Nicolae Marini, *Învățătorul Ioan Marini: O viață de apostol* (Sibiu: Editura Oastea Domnului, 2002), 15.

in five years His Holiness did not come down to see where the press was and what it was like, or the Lord's Army bookstore.'[116]

With Trifa seriously ill and struggling financially, in late 1930 Bălan decided to merge *Lumina satelor* with Father Ion Moța's *Libertatea*. Based in Orăștie, Moța's newspaper had been a popular voice of the Romanian national movement in Transylvania since 1893. Aimed primarily at a peasant audience, it focused much more heavily on nationalist politics than on religious topics and adopted a strong antisemitic tone from 1925 onwards in support of Moța's son who was a leader first of the antisemitic student movement and later of the fascist Legion of the Archangel Michael.[117] During the 1930s Bălan publicly sympathized with the grassroots ultranationalism represented by the Legion and Gheorghe Gogan argues that the merger of the two newspapers was an early attempt by Bălan to transfer Trifa's popularity to the Legion.[118] Moța had joined the Lord's Army in May 1930, suggesting that the collaboration between the two newspapers had been planned at least since then.[119] Moța wrote in 1935 that he had suggested the merger because *Libertatea* was struggling to sell enough copies, but complained that working with Trifa cost him too much money. He explained,

> I became horribly disillusioned within three or four months of merging the leadership of the newspapers. I hadn't known the men I was collaborating with – the Trifa brothers. One, Iosif, was the editor; the other, Constantin, was the administrator, but he did nothing without the approval of his brother. They soon showed themselves to be more materialistic than I could ever have imagined, greedy for riches at any price and by any means. The administrator proved this far too quickly for my liking. One day I woke up to find that they had confiscated my share from the 1931 calendar based on some calculations that fell from the moon and the stars. The calendar had been entirely my work; the only contribution of the administrator had been to sell it and take the money. They gave me nothing from the 60,000 or 70,000 lei that should have been my

---

[116] Gogan, 'Viața și activitatea', 19; Nicolae Marini, *Oastea Domnului: Istoria jertfei în mărturisirile Pr. Iosif Trifa*. Available online: http://roboam.com/Ortodoxie/oastea_domnului.htm (accessed 9 October 2019).

[117] Moța, *42 de ani de gazetărie*, 78.

[118] Gogan, 'Viața și activitatea', 20. Ionuț Biliuță suggests that Bălan's support for ultranationalist parties dated from 1927 but did not become overt until several years later. Biliuță, 'The Ultranationalist Newsroom', 191. Among other things, Bălan intervened to secure the release of imprisoned legionaries in 1933 and he gave an impassioned speech in support of the Legion following the deaths of the legionaries Ion Moța and Vasile Marin in 1937. Nicu Iancu, *Sub steagul lui Codreanu: Momente din trecutul legionar* (Madrid: Editura Dacia, 1973), 73–4; Nicolae Bălan, 'Fă Doamne să rodeasca jertfa robilor tai Ioan si Vasile, pe pământul țării noastre ...', *Lumina satelor*, 21 February 1937, 1.

[119] '"Oastea Domnului" și la Orăștie', *Libertatea*, 22 May 1930, 3.

share! They still have it. He still had to pay the interest on the precious press he had bought. And he found it hard to part with the money. They used it all to pay for the machine they had 'poetically' baptized 'the bride of the wind' ... It took the wind out of me to see my money going through the wheels of that machine as well.[120]

The police produced a similar account in 1949, when the Lord's Army had become an illegal underground movement. They wrote that, by the late 1920s,

> The soldiers began to focus more on the priest Trifa than on the bishop. The priest Trifa began having beneficial business meetings with the Army at home and he bought a printing press, opened a bookstore – separate, in Sibiu – and began travelling abroad. He amassed quite a fortune through his business dealings with the Army, which he did not want to give to the Church. Feeling that the end was approaching he passed the Army press on to his son. Seeing this Metropolitan Bălan sued Trifa on the grounds that he had claimed church property as his own. He defrocked Trifa and put the leadership of the newspaper *Lumina satelor* in the hands of other priests.[121]

Bălan officially removed Trifa from the leadership of the Lord's Army after the conflict over the ownership of Trifa's printing press, but the metropolitan had already effectively taken control of the movement in 1932. Trifa remained the official editor of *Lumina satelor* but no longer signed any of the articles. At no time did Bălan publically question Trifa's theology, but as soon as it became clear that Trifa no longer had Bălan's support newspapers from Bucharest – including *Curentul* (*The Times*), *Universul* (*The Universe*) and *Duminica ortodoxă* (*The Orthodox Sunday*) – quickly declared the Lord's Army a perilous sect.[122]

Under Bălan's leadership the Lord's Army began holding mass meetings at which tens of thousands of people came to celebrate the movement. They were originally based at Sibiu and then in other locations around the country.[123] These meetings increasingly resembled the gatherings of cultural associations and political parties, with regional groups carrying their own flags and participants benefiting from discounted train tickets. Now, instead of individual self-examination entire crowds were subject to an 'exam' led by the metropolitan. He inspected their ranks and members displayed their convictions through group

---

[120] Moța, *42 de ani de gazetărie*, 67.
[121] 'Istoric', ACNSAS, Fond Documentar, Dosar 10727, vol. 3, f. 1.
[122] Teodor N. Manolache, 'Biserica Ortodoxă Română amenințată de o nouă sectă: Oastea Domnului', *Duminica ortodoxă*, 6–13 January 1935, 4–7, and 20–7 January 1935, 4–6.
[123] Șoima, 'Cele două feluri de adunări'.

cheers.[124] The newspaper also sympathized more openly with ultranationalist causes, defending Nichifor Crianic's ultranationalist newspaper *Calendarul* (*The Calendar*), which had been temporarily shut down by the government for its extremist views.[125] The Lord's Army also now formed close ties with the Romanian Orthodox Brotherhood (Frația Ortodoxă Română, FOR) and enjoyed the patronage of leading ultranationalist political figures such as Octavian Goga, ensuring, as Bălan said, that it remained 'closely tied' to the ROC.[126] Much to Trifa's dismay, his son Viorel became a leader of the antisemitic student movement and joined the Legion of the Archangel Michael while studying theology in Chișinău. He was arrested and tried for street violence at a student congress in 1937 and later became a controversial archbishop of the Romanian Orthodox Church in America before being deported because of his involvement in the Holocaust.[127] Despite his failing health, Trifa continued publishing *Oastea Domnului* and left the running of *Lumina satelor* to Bălan.

The conflict came to a head in October 1934, when Trifa attempted to move his printing press to Bucharest. Bălan argued that the press actually belonged to the ROC because the money Trifa used to buy it had been earned while he was in the employ of the Church. Trifa was defrocked and *Lumina satelor* placed under the control of a committee.[128] Without giving Trifa the right of reply, *Lumina satelor* now published one article after another by Trifa's former supporters. They accused him of failing to respect the Church's authority and called on him to repent.[129] Ion Moța, the editor of *Libertatea*, was now given a regular column in *Lumina satelor* and he contributed with a particularly

---

[124] 'Chemare către ostașii Domnului din întreagă țară', *Lumina satelor*, 28 May 1933, 1; 'În legatură cu marea adunăre a OD', *Lumina satelor*, 4 June 1933, 1; G. Benescu, 'Examenul Oștii Domnului', *Lumina satelor*, 11 June 1933, 1; Gh. Șecaș, 'Înalțătoarea sfințire de steag din Zarnești: Țară Bârsei s'a mai cutremurat odată de suflarea cerească', *Lumina satelor*, 25 February 1934, 1.

[125] 'Sugrumarea Presei: Ziarul Calendarul, neînfricatul luptător pentru ieftinirea traiului, împedecat ca să mai apară', *Lumina satelor*, 15 May 1932, 1–2. On *Calendarul*, see Roland Clark, 'Nationalism and Orthodoxy: Nichifor Crainic and the Political Culture of the Extreme Right in 1930s Romania', *Nationalities Papers* 40, no. 1 (2012): 111–13.

[126] 'Chemare', *Lumina satelor*, 28 October 1934, 1; Gh. Șecaș, 'Serbările religioase dela Sibiu', *Lumina satelor*, 4 November 1934, 1.

[127] Viorel Trifa, 'Ție, sfântă suferință', *Cuvântul studențesc*, 10 February 1935, 12; 'Procesul studenților implicați în dezordinele dela Târgu Mureș', *Ardealul*, 16 May 1937, 1–2; '"Procesul dela Tg. Mures" se va judeca la Brașov', *Ardealul*, 11 July 1937, 1; Valerian Trifa, *Marginal Notes on a Court Case* (Jackson, MI: Valerian D. Trifa Romanian-American Heritage Center, 1988).

[128] 'Marturișiri ce se impun: Lămuriri pentru frații ostași și pentru cetitorii gazetelor "Lumina Satelor" și "Oastea Domnului"', *Lumina satelor*, 20 January 1935, 1–2; Nicolae Bălan, '*Oastea Domnului' și Biserica* (Sibiu: Tiparul Tipografiei Archdiecezane, 1935). For Trifa's side of the story, see Marini, *Învățătorul Ioan Marini*, 18–21.

[129] 'Să se facă lumină!' *Lumina satelor*, 27 January 1935, 1–4; Policarp Moruşca, 'Cuvinte de durere', *Lumina satelor*, 3 February 1935, 1–2; Constantin Trifa, 'Un cuvânt de lămurire', *Lumina satelor*, 24 February 1935, 5.

scathing parable about a farmer who worked some land then claimed that it was his when in fact the land belonged to God.[130] The parallels with Trifa's story could not have been clearer. Trifa's supporters complained that 'some priests began to write [new] statues for the Lord's Army, organizing it with leaders, bookkeepers, presidents, etc. ... so as to raise money with receipts, invoices, etc.'. Some left the movement altogether and joined Brethren communities.[131] From this point on there were effectively two movements calling themselves the Lord's Army – one under Bălan's authority and enjoying state support, the other a grassroots movement loyal to Trifa, now with a second newspaper called *Isus Biruitorul (Jesus the Conqueror)*.[132] With limited resources and battling ill health, Trifa's writings during the late 1930s focused on patiently suffering the blows of fortune like a sheep being led to the slaughter.[133] Trifa died in 1938, but Ioan Marini and Traian Dorz took over his leadership role and maintained the movement along the lines established by Trifa until it was banned by the Romanian Communist Party in 1949.[134] The communists arrested anyone who continued holding meetings, but despite heavy persecution the movement outlived state socialism and continues today as a parachurch movement affiliated with the ROC.[135]

Trifa's experiences shed a great deal of light on the religious changes taking place during the 1920s. In particular, they suggest that it was not Repenters who were 'corrupting' Orthodoxy, but that Orthodox leaders themselves were transforming their church by drawing on spiritual practices they had discovered in the West. Even though strong currents within the Lord's Army had drawn close to Repenter denominations by the end of the 1930s, Trifa originally conceived of the movement as an *anti*-Repenter endeavour that resonated with the approaches championed by anti-sectarian missionaries and preachers. The initial impetus for the Lord's Army came from Bălan, who had been trained in Germany and who hoped to use grassroots organizing to strengthen the influence of his metropolitanate within the ROC. Trifa's emphasis on temperance was also grounded in mainstream Orthodox preaching going back several decades, even if

---

[130] Ioan Moța, 'Poveste pentru zilele noastre', *Lumina satelor*, 10 February 1935, 3. Note the similarities of Moța's story with Jesus's parable of the bad tenants in Matthew 21:33–46.
[131] ACNSAS, Fond Penal, Dosar 1882, ff. 8–9.
[132] ACNSAS, Fond Documentar, Dosar 9486, vol. 1, ff. 317–18; Marini, *Învățătorul Ioan Marini*, 20–8.
[133] Iosif Trifa, *Ca o oaie fără de glas* (Sibiu: Editura Oastea Domnului, 2001).
[134] Marini, *Învățătorul Ioan Marini*, 26–104; Traian Dorz, *Hristos: Mărturia mea* (Sibiu: Editura Oastea Domnului, 2005).
[135] Gheorghe Precupescu, *Traian Dorz și vânturile potrivnice Oastea Domnului* (Sibiu: Editura Oastea Domnului, 2004); Sergiu Grossu, *Un vânt de primăvară religioasă: Rânduiala luptei spirituale în mișcarea ortodoxă Oastea Domnului* (Sibiu: Editura Oastea Domnului, 2005).

those preachers imitated Western temperance movements in both their language and tactics. It is not clear exactly where Trifa found most of his material, but the evidence suggests that he was not in conversation with Romanian Repenters. Rather, Trifa read Catholic, Anglican and Evangelical Protestant writings, taking what he found useful and ignoring the rest. Theologians such as Iuliu Scriban and Irineu Mihălcescu also read foreign works, but whereas they had the institutional authority to dictate what could and could not be adapted, Trifa was successful only so long as he had Bălan's support. Scriban, Mihălcescu and others also only took edifying illustrations and scholarly research from foreign texts, whereas Trifa eventually imported the doctrine of justification by faith wholesale from Protestant writers. In shifting the emphasis of his faith away from the church and its rituals to a message of personal conversion, Trifa exposed himself to accusations that he was no longer Orthodox and was therefore an easy target for anyone who wanted to take ownership of his printing press.

9

The Stork's Nest

One of the most disputed renewal movements of the 1920s took place at St Stefan's Church in Bucharest, known as the Stork's Nest. The parish priest there was Teodor Popescu. The Stork's Nest had been his father-in-law's church and Popescu became parish priest after the latter's death. His sermons attracted large numbers of people who flocked to hear him preach. Popescu's preaching emphasized the urgency of personal conversion and the idea of justification by faith. Popescu's pamphlet *How to Bring Souls to Christ* (1924) explained that human suffering is a result of sin's impact on the world, and that every one of his readers was a sinner. But sinners need not despair, he wrote, because Jesus Christ died for our sins. 'And so the question is: how will you face the end? Saved or unsaved? Regardless, the Saviour could come again today or tomorrow. Find out. He asks nothing of you except to believe and you'll be saved through grace.'[1] Few other Orthodox preachers of the day talked about a one-time conversion in this way and few insisted that people decide to follow Jesus lest an unexpected death might send them to hell. In fact, Orthodox writers taught that there are two judgements of the dead: one, temporary judgement immediately after death to beatitude or punishment while awaiting the resurrection, and a second, eternal one at the time of Christ's Second Coming.[2]

Popescu's message found an enthusiastic audience. Among his listeners one evening was the Minister of Denominations, Octavian Goga, who wrote that when he visited the church,

---

[1] Teodor Popescu, *Cum aducem sufletele la Hristos sau planul de mântuire* (Bucharest: Tip. 'Cultura Neamului Românesc', 1924), 27.
[2] Gherontie Nicolau, *Starea sufletelor după moarte: Scurtă privire asupra învățăturii Sf. Biserici Ortodoxe de Răsărit despre judecata particulară și răsplata temporală a sufletelor celor adormiți și folosul rugăciunilor bisericii pentru ele* (Chișinău: Imprimeria Statului, 1923); Ioan Mihălcescu, *Catehismul creștinului ortodox* (Cernica: Tipografia Bisericească din Sfânta Mânăstire Cernica, 1924), 25.

To my great surprise, the inside of the holy building was crammed with people from the beginning, a strange assembly made up of people from every walk of life ... The priest's whole body trembled, caught up in the magic of his words. Screwing up his pale, ascetic forehead, his face came back to life, filled with nervous fluid, and two drops of an unusual light shone deep in his eyes like the canvases of [Jusepe de] Ribera. The devoted crowd listened carefully to his analyses and followed the rhythm of his logic with a lively discomposure, leaving the critical spectator with a profound conviction and an incontestable spiritual message.[3]

Popescu had studied first at the seminary in Curtea de Argeș then at the Central Seminary in Bucharest which was directed by Constantin Nazarie, the author of numerous books attacking Seventh-Day Adventism.[4] He graduated in 1907 before enrolling in a theology degree at the University of Bucharest. Popescu later wrote that his early sermons focused on 'the law, morals; I would choose a vice such as drunkenness or licentiousness as an example and I would examine it from every angle. People listened and said: "Yes, yes, that's right!" Or I would take a virtue: goodness, love, generosity. "Yes, yes, that's right", people would say, happy to see these things scrutinized in an interesting way.'[5] Most collections of printed sermons from Orthodox preachers took a similar approach.[6]

Translating religion

It was Popescu's cantor, Dumitru Cornilescu, who changed his theology and preaching. Cornilescu was also a graduate of Bucharest's Central Seminary, studying there while it was directed by Iuliu Scriban.[7] Cornilescu was a devoted disciple of Scriban, who introduced his students to various Western authors, including Frank Thomas and William James.[8] 'I was amazed', Cornilescu later

---

[3] Octavian Goga, 'Răzvrățirea de la "Cuibul cu Barză"', *Țara noastră*, 24 January 1923, reprinted in Iosif Țon, *Credința adevărată* (Wheaton, IL: Societatea Misionară Română, 1988), 137–40.
[4] Nazarie, *Duminica, botezul și ierarhia bisericească*; Constantin Nazarie, *Cinstirea sfintelor icoane și adventiștii* (Bucharest: Tipografia Cărților Bisericești, 1911); Constantin Nazarie, *Combaterea principalelor învățături adventiste* (Bucharest: Tipografia Cărților Bisericești, 1913).
[5] Teodor Popescu, quoted in Horia Azimioră, *Din viața și lucrarea lui Teodor Popescu* (n.p.: n.p., 1988), 11.
[6] For example, Cristea, *Colecțiune de predici populare*; Codreanu, *Sămânța de lângă cale*; Iuliu Scriban, *50 de predici populare* (Slobozia: Editura Episcopiei Sloboziei și Călărașilor, 2014).
[7] Emanuel Conțac, *Cornilescu: Din culisele publicării celei mai citite traduceri a Sfintei Scripturi* (Cluj-Napoca: Logos, 2014), 48.
[8] Crainic, *Zile albe*, 54.

wrote, 'when I saw so many Christian books, because at the time there were very few in Romania'.⁹ As Gala Galaction commented in 1921, 'in Romania books about religious and Christian topics are as unusual and rare as rain in Egypt'.¹⁰ Cornilescu published his first translation, taken from the writings of Frank Thomas, in *Păstorul ortodox* (*The Orthodox Shepherd*) in 1910. Thomas was a charismatic preacher based in Switzerland, whose writings emphasized evangelism, piety and personal conversion.¹¹ Cornilescu continued translating Thomas's work along with those of the controversial writer and former Russian Orthodox priest Grigorii Spiridonovich Petrov, serializing them in *Revista teologică* (*The Theological Magazine*) during 1912 and 1913.¹² Cornilescu was well respected within the Romanian Orthodox Church (ROC), and even had some of his translations published in the Church's official magazine.¹³ The fact that Scriban encouraged his students to engage with an American psychologist (James), a Swiss Protestant pastor (Thomas) and a defrocked socialist priest (Petrov) shows how varied the influences on early twentieth-century Romanian Orthodoxy were.¹⁴

In 1915, while a student in theology at the University of Bucharest, he collaborated with another student Vasile Radu, who later became a celebrated Orientalist, on translating a massive tome entitled *The Orthodox Church and Canon Law* (1890) by the Serbian bishop and canon lawyer Nikodim Milaš.¹⁵ The translation was overseen by one of Cornilescu's teachers, Irineu Mihălcescu, who also wrote the preface for Cornilescu's translation of Otto Quast's attack on the theory of evolution.¹⁶ Cornilescu also collaborated with Olga Gologan in 1915, an erudite young nun two years his senior who had just established an orphanage that would soon become a flourishing school, in translating a

---

⁹ Dumitru Cornilescu, *Cum m-am întors la Dumnezeu* (Bucharest: Biserica Evanghelică Română, 2014), 5.
¹⁰ Gala Galaction, 'E bine și așa', *Luptătorul*, 21 July 1921, 1.
¹¹ Luc Weibel, *Croire à Genève: La Salle de la Réformation (XIX–XXᵉ siècle)* (Geneva: Labor et Fides, 2006), 136.
¹² Conțac, *Cornilescu*, 50; Dim. I. Cornilescu după Petrow, 'Principiile fundamentale ale civilizației', *Revista teologică* 6, no. 4-5 (1912): 131-7; Dim I. Cornilescu după F. Thomas, 'Chestiuni vitale', *Revista teologică* 7, no. 1 (1913): 17-27.
¹³ T. P. Păcescu, 'Cine propagă ce este și unde duce teoria despre un Mântuitor personal', *Noua revistă bisericească*, 1 May 1922, 34.
¹⁴ Despite his rupture with the Russian Orthodox Church, Petrov's work was actually quite popular in Romania. No less an authority than Nicodim Munteanu translated three of Petrov's books between 1908 and 1918, all of which went through multiple editions. 'Patriarhul Nicodim Munteanu', *Patriarhii României*. Available online: http://www.patriarh.ro/Nicodim/actpublicistica.php (accessed 12 August 2019).
¹⁵ Conțac, *Cornilescu*, 50-1, 60 n. 52.
¹⁶ Otto Quast, *Teoria lui Haeckel despre lume*, trans. Dumitru Cornilescu (Craiova: Ramura, n.d.).

devotional calendar containing daily meditations by Frank Thomas.[17] The calendar was praised by Nicolae Bălan and found its way into the hand of Ralu Callimachi, who immediately contacted him about translating the Bible into Romanian.[18] A noblewoman in an unhappy marriage, Ralu Callimachi was a devoted Christian who had become a Baptist while visiting Paris roughly twenty years earlier. She had personal experience translating and distributing the Bible and was known for loaning books from her extensive library of Protestant literature to enthusiastic young priests. Callimachi provided Cornilescu with room and board while he worked. He took his monastic vows during the summer of 1916 – presumably to avoid being conscripted into the army – but he continued to live at Callimachi's mansion at Stâncești at least until he had finished translating the New Testament in 1919.[19]

According to Cornilescu's later writings, he yearned for the 'new life' that he had read about in foreign books and was confused that the authors he was reading were so fascinated with the Bible. 'I didn't like the Bible', he wrote, 'I had a translation in front of me that was so bad that I couldn't understand it ... But when I started to read it in another language, I understood it and liked it'.[20] Despite his years of theological training, Cornilescu claimed that it was while he was translating the Bible that he first understood universal sinfulness, the idea that sin must be destroyed by hellfire and that Christ died on the cross for the forgiveness of sins. He prayed: 'Lord, I know only this book. You said that it is your Word. I read in it that Christ died for me; I accept forgiveness for myself and if you judge me it won't be my fault because I have believed what it says in your Word.'[21] Newly converted, Cornilescu began his translation again from scratch, telling himself that 'up until now the translation has been done by *my old self*. I am a *new person* and must have a new translation done by my new self.'[22]

There were, of course, other Romanian translations of the Bible available. The most common was the 'Iași Bible' (1874), which was the first to use the Latin alphabet adopted in the early 1860s. Nicolae Nițulescu revised the Iași Bible during the 1890s and the British Bible Society published several editions

---

[17] Dumitru Cornilescu and Olga Gologan (trans.), *Îndrăsniți! Cetiri biblice și meditațiuni pentru fiecare zi a anului, după F. Thomas* (Bucharest: Tip. Gutenberg, 1915); cited in Conțac, *Cornilescu*, 53 n. 29.
[18] Conțac, *Cornilescu*, 53.
[19] Ibid., 53–61; P. Chirică, 'Adevăratul scop al "Adevărului creștin"', *Noua revistă bisericească*, 1 January 1924, 248.
[20] Cornilescu, *Cum m-am întors*, 6.
[21] Ibid., 11.
[22] Ibid., 13.

of Nițulescu's translation between 1906 and 1921, trying to keep up with various changes in orthography.[23] In 1911 the Bible Society commissioned Iuliu Scriban and Nicodim Munteanu to produce a new translation, but both men were increasingly busy with their official functions and were unable to complete the project.[24] Munteanu continued working on his translation – mostly from Russian – after retiring to a monastery in 1923. He published a new version of the New Testament (1924) and Psalms (1927), as well as being responsible for twenty-four of the books of the Old Testament that appeared in the Synod Bible of 1936.[25] Gala Galaction began his own, more literary, translation in 1921, eventually inviting Vasile Radu to join as his collaborator. Galaction began doing readings of his Bible on the radio in 1923 and published his New Testament in 1927, but the complete translation was not finished until 1937.[26]

Cornilescu's translation was based on a revised version of Louis Segond's French Bible from 1910.[27] Relying entirely on Callimachi's financial support, Cornilescu established the Romanian Evangelical Society under whose auspices he published his New Testament (1920), Psalms (1920) and Old Testament (1921).[28] His translation met with a deafening silence from most critics.[29] Those who did comment on it were critical but generally positive. Though he later described it as 'tendentious and heretical', Galaction's initial impression was that 'this is and will remain a commendable work, providing worthwhile reading for everyone'.[30] The newspaper *Dacia* wrote that 'Cornilescu's New Testament is far superior to any previous translation in Romanian. It has a suppleness and fluency which the others lack entirely ... The language of Cornilescu's translation flows out of the heart of our people.'[31] His old teacher, Iuliu Scriban, thought it 'very

---

[23] Conțac, *Cornilescu*, 38; *Sfânta Scriptură a Vechiului și a Noului Testament* (Bucharest: Societatea de Biblie Britanică, 1921).
[24] Conțac, *Cornilescu*, 37–9.
[25] Ibid., 99; 'Patriarhul Nicodim Munteanu'.
[26] Galaction, *Jurnal*, vol. 3, 112, 301, 309; 'Citiri din Biblia nouă', *Biserica Ortodoxă Română* 41, no. 5 (1923): 394; Atanasie Mironescu, 'Noul Testament', *Biserica Ortodoxă Română* 46, no. 2 (1928): 169–85.
[27] *La Sainte Bible*, trans. Louis Segond (Paris: Alliance Biblique Universelle, 1910); Emanuel Conțac, 'Influența versiunii Segond asupra versiunii Cornilescu 1921', in *Receptarea Sfintei Scripturi. Între filologie, hermeneutică și traductologie*, ed. Eugen Munteanu (Iași: EUAIC, 2011), 122–45.
[28] Cornilescu, 'Ce este cu "Adevărul Creștin"', 99–100; *Noul Testament*, trans. D. Cornilescu (Bucharest: Societatea Evanghelică Română, 1920); *Cartea Psalmilor sau Psaltirea*, trans. D. Cornilescu (Bucharest: Societatea Evanghelică Română, 1920); *Biblia sau Sfînta Scriptură*, trans. D. Cornilescu (Bucharest: Societatea Evanghelică Română, 1921).
[29] *Noua revistă bisericească* 3, no. 1–2 (1921): 269, quoted in Conțac, *Cornilescu*, 72–3.
[30] Galaction, *Piatra din capul unghiului*, 83; Galaction, 'E bine și așa', 1.
[31] Quoted in a letter, J. W. Wiles to J. H. Ritson, 27 November 1920, in Conțac, *Cornilescu*, 118.

colloquial'.[32] In contrast, the Greek Catholic priest and scholar Victor Macaveiu noted that, although Cornilescu's translation was 'very original', it lacked 'that archaic, old hue of the word of God, it is missing what on bronze statues we would call *tarnish* – that which increases the value of the statue'.[33] The popular reception of Cornilescu's Bible was overwhelmingly enthusiastic. It sold out almost immediately and representatives of the British Bible Society who were trying to decide whether to publish Cornilescu's translation themselves heard it praised everywhere they went.[34]

The only genuinely hostile reviews came from the priests D. Mangâru and Petru Chirică, who attacked Cornilescu's translation on the grounds that his choice of words in describing 'a Sabbath rest' (*o odihnă de Sabat*) in Hebrews 4:9 supported the Seventh-Day Adventist position that Christians should worship on Saturdays.[35] In addition to attacking his opponents' knowledge of Greek, Cornilescu's response was that the Adventists erred 'in their twisted interpretation of the text, not in the meaning of the text, which should be preserved as it is and not changed for the sake of it or out of fear of one teaching or another'.[36] Possibly anticipating this criticism, in 1920 Cornilescu had already serialized his translations of two pamphlets by English and American authors attacking Adventist doctrines.[37] His Bible was popular with Repenters, who began recommending Cornilescu's translation almost immediately.[38] Despite various concerns about the precision of Cornilescu's language and over his translation of the Greek word *dikaiosynē* (righteousness) as *neprihănire* (sinlessness) instead of *dreptate* (rectitude), the British Bible Society adopted it as their official Romanian version and released a revised edition in 1924.[39]

---

[32] Letter, R. Kligor to J. W. Wiles, 21 January 1921, in Conțac, *Cornilescu*, 121.

[33] Victor Macaveiu, 'Spre o nouă ediție a Scripturii românești', *Cultura creștină* (1921), quoted in Conțac, *Cornilescu*, 72.

[34] Conțac, *Cornilescu*, 118, 126, 128, 145.

[35] D. Mangâru, 'Odihna creștinismului (Contra Adventismului)', *Noua revistă bisericească*, 1 July 1921, 123–45; D. Mangâru, 'Adaos la "Odihna creștinismului și răspuns la Domnului D. Cornilescu"', *Noua revistă bisericească*, 15 February 1922, 404–5; Petru Chirică, 'Condițiuni la studiul de combatere al adventismului', *Biserica Ortodoxă Română* 41, no. 2 (1922): 114–16. All three articles are quoted in Conțac, *Cornilescu*, 73.

[36] Dumitru Cornilescu, 'Odihna creștinismului', *Noua revistă bisericească*, 1 December 1921, 292. Cf. Dumitru Cornilescu, 'Câteva lămuriri în chestiuni de traducere a Bibliei', *Biserica Ortodoxă Română* 41, no. 8 (1923): 567–70.

[37] R. A. Torrey, 'Trebue să țină creștinii sabatul?' trans. D. Cornilescu, *Noua revistă bisericească*, January 1920, 146–8; A. J. Pollock, 'Adventismul în fața Scripturii', *Noua revistă bisericească*, June 1920, 40–2. Both are cited in Conțac, *Cornilescu*, 74–5 n. 93.

[38] 'Citiți Noul Testament', *Buna vestire*, January 1921, 8.

[39] Conțac, *Cornilescu*, 79–85.

Preaching revival

After having been 'born again' while translating the Bible, Cornilescu began holding Bible studies with young soldiers who were about to be sent to the front and who wanted to know if they would go to heaven when they died. The group met regularly and Cornilescu taught them Christian songs he had translated. He wrote that the lives of these young men were profoundly changed and that, when they were persecuted for their beliefs by a group of schoolboys throwing rocks, they began to pray and converted their persecutors through prayer.[40]

After finishing the first edition of his Bible, Cornilescu returned to St Stefan's Church in Bucharest. Excited by the power of Cornilescu's message about 'turning to God', Popescu began to preach it until he too was convicted of his sins and 'born again'.[41] 'Like any believer, I would have been ready to say that Jesus died for his ideas', Popescu wrote. 'Never, absolutely never, had I noticed the words in the creed: "And he was crucified for us". Had I noticed I would have thought that the word "us" applied to anyone else just not to me.'[42] Together they began holding evening Bible studies for men in the parish, postponing teaching women until eventually a group of women occupied the church and demanded to participate in these studies as well.[43] Meetings at the Stork's Nest became more and more popular and in 1921 Iuliu Scriban began encouraging his students to visit the church to hear Popescu preach.[44]

When he published his collected sermons Popescu received positive reviews from other renewal-oriented Orthodox publications such as Iosif Trifa's *Lumina satelor*, Vartolomeu Stănescu's *Solidaritatea* and *Renașterea*, and Teodor Păcescu's *Noua revistă bisericească*.[45] Spiritual change can only come about by the indwelling of the Holy Spirit, Cornilescu asserted, quoting sermons by Bălan and Stănescu to support his case.[46] Cornilescu established

---

[40] Cornilescu, *Cum m-am întors*, 13–20.
[41] Ibid., 22–3; Teodor Popescu, 'O mărturisire care poate fi unora de folos', *Noua revistă bisericească*, 1 August 1923, 124–30. Note that in his account, Popescu does not credit Cornilescu with having taught him the doctrine of justification by faith but claims that he arrived at this conviction on his own through the working of the Holy Spirit.
[42] Tudor Popescu, *Isus vă chiamă* (Bucharest: n.p., 1939), 19.
[43] Dumitru Cornilescu, 'Ceva despre activitatea evanghelizatoare dela "Cuibul cu barză"', *Noua revistă bisericească*, 1 June 1923, 91–2.
[44] Azimioră, *Din viața și lucrarea*, 23.
[45] C. Diaconescu, 'Iisus va chieamă!' *Noua revistă bisericească*, 1 June 1923, 112–13; Azimioră, *Din viața și lucrarea*, 24–5; Manea S. Popescu, 'O recapitulare a discuțiunilor polemice provocate de învățăturile propoveduite la biserica Cuibul cu Barză și o concluzie', *Noua revistă bisericească*, 1 June 1923, 103.
[46] Cornilescu, 'Ce este cu "Adevărul Creștin"', 95, 97.

a regular magazine known as *Adevărul creștin* (*The Christian Truth*), which aroused suspicion among some of his colleagues once Adventist and Brethren preachers began buying and distributing it on the grounds that Cornilescu had 'come over to our side'.[47] The opening editorial of *Adevărul creștin* outlined its mission statement as:

> [The magazine] knows that humans do not naturally have this life, which is a gift of God obtained through faith in a personal Saviour, whose death atones for our sins, calling us to live in close connection to the One who gave His life for us. Second, it is aimed at the children of God who have passed from death to life, have been born again, and who live bound up with their personal Saviour.[48]

Although he appreciated *Adevărul creștin* and collaborated closely with Cornilescu, Teodor Popescu never published in its pages and claimed to have no connection with Cornilescu's Romanian Evangelical Society.[49] Iosif Trifa from the Lord's Army, on the other hand, actively promoted one of Cornilescu's books, *The Human Heart: God's Sanctuary or the Devil's Workshop* (1922), saying that 'there are few books in Romanian which can do more for Christ and for the salvation of the souls of our people than this one'.[50]

During the early 1920s Cornilescu also began publishing his own translations of a variety of Protestant books, such as John Bunyan's *Pilgrim's Progress*, a seventeenth-century Baptist work that pictured the spiritual life as a pilgrimage to heaven that involves sticking to the straight and narrow path while avoiding temptations and false teachings.[51] Other British authors he translated include works by the Brethren preachers Charles Henry Machintosh and George Müller, as well as Charles Challand's biography of Müller.[52] Both Machintosh and Müller emphasized that regular study of the Bible needed to be central to the Christian life and both were committed to making the Gospel as accessible as possible by explaining Christian theology in simple language. Cornilescu published translations of books by several American authors associated with the Moody Bible Institute and the YMCA, including James Henry McConkey, Reuben

---

[47] Ibid., 99 n. 2; P. Chirică, 'Adevăratul scop al "Adevărul creștin"', *Noua revistă bisericească*, 1 January 1924, 248–9.
[48] Quoted in Păcescu, 'Cine propagă', 36.
[49] T. Popescu, 'O scrisoare a părintelui Teodor Popescu', *Noua revistă bisericească*, 1 May 1922, 63.
[50] Iosif Trifa, 'O carte de mare folos sufletesc', *Lumina satelor*, 11 February 1923, 5.
[51] John Bunyan, *Călătoria creștinului sau calea spre fericirea de veci*, trans. Dumitru Cornilescu (Bucharest: Editura Societății de Cărți Religioase, 1923).
[52] Charles Challand, *O minune din vremurile noastre: viața și lucrarea lui George Müller*, trans. Dumitru Cornilescu (Bucharest: Societatea Evanghelică Romînă, 1922); Alexandru Măianu, *Viața și lucrarea lui Dumitru Cornilescu* (Bucharest: Editura Stephanus, 1995), 73.

Archer Torrey and Samuel Dickey Gordon.[53] All were committed preachers and evangelists who emphasized giving up control of one's life into God's hands and cultivating holiness. McConkey helped establish the Africa Inland Mission, Torrey worked closely with Dwight L. Moody and was one of the three editors of the essays collected in *The Fundamentals*, which became the foundational text of American fundamentalism, and Gordon's series of 'Quiet Talks' contained detailed instructions about holy living. Cornilescu also translated works by the Swiss apologist Frédéric Bettex, who argued that the Bible was in agreement with modern science, and the Lutheran theologian Gerhard Hilbert, who encouraged local churches to commit themselves to missionary work in their communities.[54]

Cornilescu collected and translated Protestant hymns as well as books, providing ways for believers at the Stork's Nest to express their faith through song. Most Orthodox songbooks of the period included slow, reflective pieces emphasizing God's might and holiness, humanity's need for mercy, and honouring the Virgin Mary. In a 1928 collection assembled by Gheorghe Cucu, for example, one finds titles such as 'God is with us, understand you peoples and worship', 'Blessed be, Christ our God' and 'You are truly worthy of our praise, Mother of God'.[55] The songs in Cornilescu's collection were more upbeat and the musical score was written for piano, in comparison with Cucu's songbook, which was arranged for choral singing. Cornilescu's hymns focused on the idea that Jesus saves and requires an individual response from believers as well as on the joy and security to be found in God. His first songbook included hymns such as Charlotte Elliott's 'Just as I am, without one plea, / But that Thy blood was shed for me' (1835), William Doane's 'Safe in the Arms of Jesus' (1868), or Philip Doddridge's 'O happy day that fixed my choice / On Thee, my Saviour and my God!' (1755). In Cornilescu's hands Doddridge's Reformed Calvinism became clearly Arminian: 'Happy day, when I took Jesus as my Saviour! / O how good it seems to me now that I chose Him then'.[56] Any sense that one's salvation was determined ('fixed') by God beforehand is missing in Cornilescu's translation, being replaced by an overwhelming emphasis on an individual's choice to believe. As is all church music, Cornilescu's hymns were dogmatic confessions

---

[53] James Henry McConkey, *Ce înseamnă viața predată în slujba Domnului*, trans. Dumitru Cornilescu (n.p.: n.p., n.d.); Măianu, *Viața și lucrarea*, 73.
[54] Gerhard Hilbert, *Exista spirit?* (Bucharest: Libraria Max Kendler, n.d.); Măianu, *Viața și lucrarea*, 73.
[55] 'Cu noi este Dumnezeu', 'Bine ești cuvântat' and 'Vrednică ești' in Cucu, *Zece cântece religioase*, 8–10, 14–15, 28–31.
[56] 'Ferice zi …', in Dumitru Cornilescu, *47 cîntări creștinești cu note muzicale* (Bucharest: Societatea Evanghelică Romînă, 1922), 14.

that people would reflect on every time they sang them. Cornilescu asked to be allowed to renounce his monastic vows in July 1923, and the Church was only too happy to release him.[57]

Heresy charges

Other priests who had been preaching revival wanted to know why the Stork's Nest was flourishing while they were preaching to empty churches.[58] The answer, they said, was that Popescu and Cornilescu were importing foreign ideas. Nae Ionescu accused Popescu and Cornilescu of threatening the security of the Romanian state by promoting English Protestantism and of subordinating Orthodoxy to the Anglican Church through their (alleged) association with the YMCA.[59] The two preachers vehemently denied these accusations, claiming that 'ours is a purely Romanian movement and has no other goal than the moral regeneration of our people in the only way possible, today and for all time: by disinterestedly preaching the Gospel of Christ'.[60] Both sides in this dispute claimed that they were working for the salvation of their country. The highest praise that anyone gave Cornilescu's translation was that it was 'pure Romanian', and reflected the language of the people instead of the wooden language of the Church.[61] Popescu's supporters responded by questioning whether Orthodox priests were truly serving the nation. They accused priests of corruption and of exploiting the poor for their own financial gain: 'What do Christ's shepherds do when confronted with this odious spectacle [of politicianism]?', Dimitrie Nanu wrote. 'Even though the Saviour told them clearly: you cannot serve both God and money, still there are some – many, in fact – who do not wear a cross on their neck or its commands in their hearts, but instead carry the heavy steel key from the bank or cooperative.'[62] An accomplished poet and translator, Dimitrie Nanu was an outspoken supporter of the Stork's Nest and was also a patron of the Christian Youth Association (ACT) while it was affiliated with the YMCA during the 1920s.[63]

---

[57] ANIC, Fond MCA, Dosar 109/1923, f. 3.
[58] On Manea Popescu's attempts at evangelism, see 'Evanghelizare ortodoxă', *Noua revistă bisericească*, 1 May 1923, 116.
[59] Un Ortodox (probably N. Ionescu), 'Pentru apărarea ortodoxiei', *Ideea europeană* 4, no. 111 (1923): 2.
[60] T. Popescu and D. Cornilescu, 'Domnule Director', *Ideea europeană* 4, no. 113 (1923): 2.
[61] Letter, J. W. Wiles to J. H. Ritson, 27 November 1920, in Conțac, *Cornilescu*, 118.
[62] Nanu, *Iisus vă cheamă*, 6.
[63] Ciornea, *Sandu Tudor*, 281.

Both sides also accused each other of being in league with Jews. In 1922 Teodor Păcescu wrote that 'the propaganda of these Protestant sects is a product of World Judaism, which uses any means to provoke diversions and confessional conflicts so that the economic and political dominance of Judaism might be followed by religious dominance'.[64] Similarly, in 1924 seven members of the Stork's Nest attacked Gala Galaction for his philosemitism: 'He is alone among Romanian writers to have given himself body and soul to the Jews and their interests. He has written the most perverse articles, both before and after he became a priest, confusing the Romanian spirit and sustaining the interests of Masonic Judaism.'[65]

The issue came to a head in December 1923 after Galaction convinced the metropolitan to appoint a couple of other priests to serve alongside Teodor Popescu at St Ştefan's Church. It soon became apparent that Popescu was altering the liturgy, removing prayers asking the Virgin Mary and the saints to 'have mercy on us!' and emphasizing instead that it was Christ alone who has mercy and saves us.[66] Galaction caused arguments at the Stork's Nest when he invited himself to preach there in December and then finally persuaded the metropolitan to charge Popescu with heresy.[67] In Orthodox Christianity the liturgy defines how believers relate to God. It binds together everything from the veneration of the saints to the interpretation of Scripture and beliefs about salvation. As the archpriest of Arad, Florea Codreanu wrote in his explanation of the liturgy in 1940, 'Christ the Lord comes to us through the Holy Liturgy, it makes peace between us and God, and it creates bonds of brotherhood among us'.[68] Irineu Mihălcescu taught that the Church's liturgy evolved directly out of Jesus's breaking of the bread at the Last Supper.[69]

Moreover, the concrete action of changing the liturgy was one of the few ways that Popescu's opponents could clearly prove his heterodoxy. The words of the liturgy were widely available in prayer books and how it should be performed

---

[64] T. P. Păcescu, 'Biserica in pragul anului 1922', *Noua revistă bisericească*, 1 January 1922, 324.
[65] Dincescu Bolintin et al., *Lupta între Dumnezeu şi Mamonă: Între predicarea Evangheliei şi acatist* (Bucharest: Tipografiile Române Unite, 1924), 6. The signatories of this pamphlet were V. Dincescu Bolintin, F. Demetrescu Mirea, Th. C. Tomescu, Dumitru M. Pherekyde, Niculae Flipescu, Gh. Ceauşescu and Christian Theodora.
[66] Galaction, *Jurnal*, vol. 3, 151–2.
[67] Ibid., 153–6; [Gala Galaction], 'Cuvinte de lămurire', *Biserica Ortodoxă Română* 41, no. 15 (1923): 1131.
[68] Codreanu, *Cunoştinţe liturgice*, 39.
[69] Mihălcescu, *Explicarea Sfintei Liturghii*, 7–9; Ioan Mihălcescu, *Rânduiala şi tâlcuirea pe scurt a Sfintei Liturghii* (Râmnicul Vâlcea: Tipografia Episcopul Vartolomeiu, 1935), 5–6.

was clearly spelt out by the Church.[70] Trapping heretics is difficult, Păcescu noted, because 'sectarians do not attack the teachings of the Orthodox Church directly, but throw themselves over the religious identity (*conștiința religioasă*) of our people and try to subdue them'.[71] What was really at stake, Păcescu claimed, was the national identity of the Romanian people, but what could be proven was that Popescu had changed the liturgy.

Manea S. Popescu, who had gone to the same school as Teodor Popescu, published an open letter to him in March 1922 in the pages of *Noua revistă bisericească* asking him to answer five questions:

1) Whether he considers that we owe our salvation to Christ the Savior alone, and that we can obtain it only through faith – our only contribution.
2) If he has eliminated the veneration of the Virgin Mary.
3) If he permits the veneration of the saints.
4) If prayers for the dead are useless.
5) Why, after he has renounced several Orthodox beliefs, he remains in the Church and benefits from its wealth.[72]

The two priests debated these questions in *Noua revistă bisericească* for the next two years. Manea Popescu's questions and Teodor Popescu's responses are instructive because they represent a candid attempt at clarifying the boundaries of Romanian Orthodoxy during a period of institutional and theological renewal.

The disputing parties disagreed on where authority in the Church lay. Dumitru Cornliescu said of himself that 'the whole time I was reading their books, some of which were very good, I was as blind as any blind man'. Păcescu retorted: 'A blind man with a degree in Orthodox theology! … It appears that Deacon Cornliescu became a monk as a hobby'.[73] One thing that the opponents of the Stork's Nest would not allow was the idea that their education was worthless. Manea Popescu attacked Teodor Popescu by demonstrating that Irineu Mihălcescu, who had taught them both, disagreed with the latter's definition of salvation.[74] Quoting Mihălcescu when confronted with the Bible, Teodor Popescu said, was like a man who 'when attacked by a machine gun defended himself with a pistol'.[75]

---

[70] Dimitrie Lungulescu, *Manual de practică liturgică* (Bucharest: Tipografiile Române Unite, 1926); Gherontie Nicolau, *Îndrumătorul liturgic* (Bucharest: Tipografia Cărților Bisericești, 1939).
[71] Teodor P. Păcescu, 'Propaganda neo-protestantă', *Noua revistă bisericească*, 1 January 1924, 241.
[72] Manea S. Popescu, *Noua revistă bisericească*, 15 February 1922.
[73] Cornliescu, 'Ce este cu "Adevărul Creștin"', 91–101.
[74] Manea S. Popescu, 'Problema mântuirii', *Noua revistă bisericească*, 1 October 1923, 160.
[75] T. Popescu, 'Răspuns la răspunsul Părintelui Manea Popescu', *Noua revistă bisericească*, 1 May 1922, 65.

When Teodor Popescu refused to discuss the veneration of the saints until he had studied the Bible more closely, Manea Popescu responded, 'Why are you a still a priest and still accredited then? Doesn't it strike you that your answer insults our Faculty of Theology which gave you your accreditation?'[76] 'In matters of God's truths', Teodor Popescu wrote back, 'I accept only arguments made with Holy Scripture, which is the Word of God, the Word that promises to be eternal'.[77]

Teodor Popescu maintained that when Christians spoke of 'the church' in the sense of Tradition, they meant 'certain people within the church who wrote about certain things and whose writings were accepted by the majority and retained'. Furthermore, 'these people [were] obliged to take note of the Gospel', so, obviously, their writings did not replace the Bible. 'Whoever invokes the authority of the church independent of the authority of the Gospel', Teodor Popescu claimed, 'bases history on the history books; and whoever invokes the authority of the Gospel bases history on the documents'.[78] 'The Bible is not Protestant', Cornilescu added, so why accuse people who quote it of being Protestants?[79]

Manea Popescu appears to have accepted the idea of citing Scripture to support one's argument because his next contribution was suddenly full of quotes from the Bible.[80] Gala Galaction, on the other hand, complained that Popescu and Cornilescu's readings of the Bible were naive and simplistic. Galaction was quite happy to use the Church Fathers, ecumenical councils and the Holy Liturgy as authorities alongside the Bible, and to use them to interpret it. 'Most of the time when people wander from the truth it is because of the interpretation of Holy Scripture', Galaction explained, but 'in the church of the Saviour, dogmatic teachings and decisions are in the hands of the episcopal college, that is to say, in the hands of the gathering of the hierarchs. The episcopal college is the treasurer of the knowledge of the church and guards our whole lives in Christ.'[81]

Another of their major disagreements lay in their different understandings of salvation. Salvation is 'a gift', according to Teodor Popescu. A Christian draws near to God by reading the Bible and can be assured that 'he has forgiveness and peace with God through the blood of Jesus; based *only and exclusively* on

---

[76] Manea Popescu, 'Un ultim răspuns și câteva lămuriri Preotului Teodor Popescu', *Noua revistă bisericească*, 1 March 1922, 13.
[77] Teodor Popescu, 'Poate cineva să spună că e mântuit?' *Noua revistă bisericească*, 1 May 1923, 44.
[78] Ibid., 44.
[79] Dumitru Cornilescu, 'Tot cu privire la foaia "Adevărul creștin"', *Noua revistă bisericească*, 1 October 1923, 163.
[80] Popescu, 'Problema mântuirii', 159–62.
[81] Galaction, *Piatra din capul unghiului*, 44.

what the Lord has done and continues to do for him, saying "Thanks to him I am saved".⁸² 'That's not the way things are', responded Manea Popescu. Rather, Christians are united with God only through 'the pouring of the invisible grace of God into the soul through the seven holy mysteries instituted by the Saviour himself'. Moreover, Manea Popescu maintained, 'salvation is a divine-human act and ... reading the New Testament is a great thing but it is not sufficient for the salvation of one's soul'.⁸³ Only Protestants believed that 'the Lord's chosen, those He has called, are saved *"through grace"*, without any personal merit or contribution', he said, concluding that therefore the preachers at the Stork's Nest must be Protestants.⁸⁴ In a book written soon after the Stork's Nest scandal, Irineu Mihălcescu argued that although humans had fallen from grace the possibility of goodness had not completely died in the human soul. Humanity's separation from God made it impossible for them to return to their prelapsarian state by themselves – 'either man must rise to God or God must come down to man'. Like Manea Popescu, Mihălcescu asserted that sanctification requires God's grace *and* man's contribution of faith and good works.⁸⁵

Later, Manea Popescu outlined another reason why he did not believe in the idea of a personal Saviour. He wrote,

> On the basis of the Gospel and the writings of the holy apostles, our Orthodox Church teaches that the Saviour is the Saviour of everyone and thus of each individual person. It also teaches, again on the basis of the New Testament, that every soul can share in the salvation perfected at Golgotha and in the sanctification that the Holy Spirit brings through the church which Jesus established. He gave the means of salvation to the church (baptism = redemption from original sin) and sanctification through the seven mysteries administered by the hierarchy. The Protestant theory of a personal Saviour does away with these intermediaries and makes the personal Saviour into a direct Saviour.⁸⁶

The doctrine of justification by faith marginalized the role of the Church. If Christ alone saves us, then why do we need priests? 'This explanation of the problem of salvation is a great danger', Păcescu concluded, 'because it does away with all the institutions of Orthodoxy, in particular the hierarchy,

---

[82] Teodor Popescu, *Iisus vă cheamă*, quoted in Manea S. Popescu, 'Din învățăturile celor dela Cuibu cu Barză', *Noua revistă bisericească*, 1 May 1923, 52.
[83] Ibid., 52.
[84] Popescu, 'Problema mântuirii', 159.
[85] Vicovan, *Ioan Irineu Mihălcescu* 141–2.
[86] Manea Popescu, 'Cuibul cu Barză', *Biserica Ortodoxă Română* 42, no. 4 (1924): 212.

which is the *mediator* of salvation'.⁸⁷ The Church and its priests are crucial to Christianity, Păcescu insisted, because 'if the problem of salvation forms the basis of Christianity, the purpose of the church is none other than the realization of salvation, and the priest is the one who realizes salvation by means of grace and through the teachings available to him, applied through Christian pedagogy'.⁸⁸ Gala Galaction wrote that 'whoever does not believe in the church of Jesus Christ – "I believe in one, holy, catholic and apostolic church" – does not believe in the Holy Spirit which guides it and thus does not believe in the promises and the power of the Saviour either'.⁸⁹ The Stork's Nest 'is Christian, it is based on the Gospel', Petru Chirică wrote, 'but it does not support the Orthodox Church'.⁹⁰

As Manea Popescu mentioned in his opening letter, rumours had spread that Popescu was teaching people at the Stork's Nest not to venerate the saints. Popescu defended himself by claiming that

> regarding the worship of the Holy Virgin Mary and the saints, I remain within the general Orthodox formula, which is: worship God and venerate the saints. Unlike the Catholics, who canonize saints so often and present them to the world as beings that one can do business with and bow down to – and the Protestants, who ignore them entirely – the Orthodox Church has arrived at the happy formula I quoted above.⁹¹

No one was convinced. Moreover, Cornilescu appeared to have replaced the Orthodox saints with another pantheon of heroes. In a letter to *Noua revistă bisericească*, Petru Chirică asked,

> What use to me are examples of missionaries in China who – according to D. Cornilescu – died for Christ, when everyone knows that they were Protestants, Adventists, or Catholics, when in the riches of my Orthodoxy I have so many missionaries at hand (John Chrysostom, Basil and Great, Gregory of Nazianzus, St George, St Dumitru, St Nicholas, St Peter and Paul, who also died for Christ).⁹²

---

⁸⁷ Teodor Păcescu, 'Mișcarea dela biserica Cuibu cu Barză din București', *Noua revistă bisericească*, 1 January 1924, 264.
⁸⁸ Ibid., 245.
⁸⁹ Galaction, *Piatra din capul unghiului*, 26.
⁹⁰ Chirica, 'Adevăratul scop', 249.
⁹¹ Tudor Popescu, *Spulberarea Învinuirilor* (Bucharest: Tipografiile Române Unite, 1924), 10–11.
⁹² Petru Chirică, 'Scrisoare părinților Teodor Popescu și Manea Popescu', *Noua revistă bisericească*, 1 May 1923, 88.

Defrocked

The committee of priests appointed to judge Popescu's case tells us something about how close to ecclesiastical centres of power his opponents were. The ten-person committee included Iuliu Scriban, Irineu Mihălcescu, Gala Galaction and Constantin Nazarie, all of whom had been teachers and/or opponents of Popescu and Cornilescu. Other members included P. S. Platon, Atanasie Popescu, D. Georgescu, the dogmatician and canon lawyer Dimitrie Boroianu, the historian Niculae Popescu and George Gibescu, who had written his undergraduate thesis on the importance of hierarchy in the Church. The committee concluded that 'it is as clear as day that the priest Teodor Popescu does not confess our Orthodox faith'.[93]

Popescu's reputation by this stage and the state's attitude toward him was clearly summed up in a report by a policeman named 'Agent 1040' from 15 December 1923, which uncritically reproduced all of the accusations against him:

> The priest Theodor Popescu, the parish priest of 'The Stork's Nest' church, is a follower of the Protestant religion. The 'British Religious Society' from London (England) has been established for the purpose of preaching these beliefs and conducting religious propaganda. This society has followers in every country and with their help seeks to universalise the Protestant religion. The first follower and fanatical preacher of this religion in Romania was the priest Cornilescu, who had to leave the country because of his preaching and found refuge in Switzerland, where he has settled and taken up citizenship. The second follower is the priest Theodor Popescu, the parish priest of 'The Stork's Nest' church, who has preached the Protestant religion for more than two years, ignoring the existence of the saints, the Holy Virgin Mary, the icons, and the church, believing only in God and Jesus Christ. Moreover, he preaches living a life conformed with Holy Scripture, which is to say that he shows his followers how to live perfect lives.
>
> Thus, his beliefs are very similar to those of the Baptists and in part to those of the Adventists, only that he recognises Sunday as the Christian holy day. In this short time the priest Th. Popescu has won the souls of many believers and has become a saviour to them – as he indeed claims to be – preaching sermons in church. He held public meetings in the Stork's Nest school with the aim

---

[93] A.[rhimandrit Iuliu] S.[criban], 'Chestiunea de la biserica Cuibul cu Barză', *Biserica Ortodoxă Română* 41, no. 15 (1923): 1129–30.

of spreading his religious cult, later moving to 5 Sebastopol Street, where he continues to preach his message.

This conversion of large numbers of believers scandalized public opinion and on being made aware of what was taking place at this church, the metropolitan-primate ordered that Th. Popescu be replaced by the priest from the 'Dușumea' church. An incident took place during his first service, however, provoked by the followers of the priest Th. Popescu, for which reason the church was definitively shut down.

In addition, the priest Th. Popescu receives money from the Anglican society, which is clearly demonstrated by the following cases: During one discussion, the priest Th. Popescu stated that he would seek refuge in Switzerland if the authorities suppressed his activities; his only escape being the priest Cornilescu, whom I have shown has close ties with the Anglican society. The priest Th. Popescu printed a number of pamphlets for spreading his beliefs, which he distributes to his followers and which are read in church during services. In addition, he helps any poor person who asks for his help. Some time ago two Belgians who had come to Bucharest became victims of theft. Not having a penny they went to the Anglican school and asked for help from the English women there. When they heard what had happened they sent him to their priest, Th. Popescu, who without hesitating gave them the sum of 3,000 lei, which greatly impressed public opinion. It is therefore quite clear that the above-mentioned priest receives money from the Anglican society for spreading the Protestant religion because his philanthropy could not come from his own modest material situation.[94]

After Teodor Popescu had been defrocked, a number of priests continued to attack the Stork's Nest on the front page of major cosmopolitan newspapers such as *Adevărul* (*The Truth*) and *Dimineața* (*The Morning*), accompanied by occasional polemical replies from Popescu and his supporters.[95] These newspapers were particularly interested in whether or not Popescu was a 'heretic', a label which Scriban, at the very least, refused to give him, focusing instead on the fact that Popescu's ideas were 'intolerable' to the Orthodox

---

[94] ACNSAS, Fond Documentar, Dosar 105254, f. 2.
[95] Contributions supporting Popescu included D. Nanu, 'Conflictul de la biserica Sf. Ștefan', *Dimineața*, 6 January 1924, 13; Marieta G. Vasilescu, 'Incidentul dela biserica Sf. Ștefan', *Dimineața*, 21 January 1924, 1; Tudor Popescu, 'Mișcarea dela "Cuibul cu Barză"', *Dimineața*, 27 January 1924, 1; Tudor Popescu, 'Mișcarea dela "Cuibul cu Barză"', *Dimineața*, 28 January 1924, 1.

Church.[96] One contributor after another told the newspapers how sorry they were for Popescu, who had been their friend. They gave him public advice about where he went wrong and how he could mend his ways.[97] The danger of Cornilescu's brand of Christianity, Păcescu later wrote, is that 'he managed to mask the new Protestant garments in which he had dressed his Orthodox soul and to present himself to his colleagues, refugee theologians from Moldavia, even military chaplains, as Orthodox, as someone who wanted to deepen our Orthodox Christianity'.[98] Păcescu's observation that Cornilescu's initial success happened in the east is significant, because it came at a time when civil servants from Bucharest – including priests – saw it as their duty to 'civilize' the eastern provinces, dominating them through the imposition of a centralized bureaucracy and by appointing people from Bucharest to positions of influence.[99]

Galaction wrote a lengthy book aimed at Orthodox priests who were confused about where Popescu had erred, and Mihălcescu published a series of articles outlining the Orthodox Church's position on the veneration of the saints.[100] They did not want others to follow Popescu's example. Greek Catholic writers repeated earlier claims that Popescu had connections with the Anglican Church, something that his Orthodox opponents now bitterly denied because of their own increasingly frequent meetings with Anglicans. In turn, the Orthodox polemicists claimed that they knew Anglican priests who were disgusted with Popescu's behaviour.[101] Popescu's supporters responded in kind, claiming that he had been defrocked only because the other priests were jealous of his popularity.[102] They published several pamphlets defending Popescu and defaming his detractors.[103]

---

[96] Lorin, 'Conflictul de la biserica Sf. Ștefan: Ce ne spune archim. Scriban', *Dimineața*, 3 January 1924, 1; Arhim. Scriban, 'Răfuială pe chestiunea Cuibul cu Barză', *Dimineața*, 24 January 1924, 1. Cf. I.T., 'O încercare de schismă', *Dimineața*, 4 January 1924, 1; Aida Vrioni, 'Incidentul dela biserica Sft. Ștefan', *Dimineața*, 12 January 1924, 1; Vasile Dinescu-Bolintin, 'Incidentul dela biserica "Cuibul cu Barză"', *Dimineața*, 17 January 1924, 1; 'Procesul preotului dela biserica Sf. Ștefan', *Dimineața*, 18 January 1924, 1; N. Batzaria, 'Ereziile', *Adevărul*, 19 January 1924, 1–2.

[97] Lorin, 'Conflictul de la biserica Cuibul cu Barză: Ce ne spune d. Vasile Dincescu-Bolintin', *Dimineața*, 4 January 1924, 5; Lorin, 'Conflictul de la biserica Sf. Ștefan: Părerile părintelui I. Popescu-Mălăești', *Dimineața*, 5 January 1924, 1; 'Chemarea clerului!' *Dimineața*, 19 January 1924, 1–2; Gala Galaction, 'Gala Galaction are cuvântul!' *Dimineața*, 30 January 1924, 1; G. Galaction, 'Cazul dela biserica "Cuibul cu Barză"', *Dimineața*, 31 January 1924, 1.

[98] Păcescu, 'Uitându-ne înapoi', 1.

[99] Livezeanu, *Cultural Politics*.

[100] Galaction, *Piatra din capul unghiului*; Irineu Mihălcescu, 'Clasicitatea creștină și cultul sfinților', *Biserica Ortodoxă Română* 42, no. 3 (1924): 145–53; Irineu Mihălcescu, 'Cultul sfinților în fața descoperirii Dumnezești', *Biserica Ortodoxă Română* 42, no. 4 (1924): 195–201; Irineu Mihălcescu, 'Învățătura bisericii despre cultul sfinților', *Biserica Ortodoxă Română* 42, no. 5 (1924): 290–5.

[101] 'Cuibul cu Barză și anglicanismul', *Biserica Ortodoxă Română* 42, no. 2 (1924): 122.

[102] [Gala Galaction], 'Cuvinte de lămurire', *Biserica Ortodoxă Română* 41, no. 15 (1923): 1130.

[103] Nanu, *Iisus vă cheamă*; D. Nanu, *Lupta între Evanghelie și tipic, între logică și sofism* (Bucharest: Atelierele 'Adevărul', 1924); Popescu, *Spulberarea Învinuirilor*; Dincescu Bolintin et al., *Lupta între Dumnezeu și Mamonă*.

Though he himself did not attend the Stork's Nest, Cornilescu's former classmate Nichifor Crainic defended Popescu in *Gândirea*, an avant-garde literary magazine he edited. Crainic wrote that Popescu's

> preaching addresses a society whose moral conscience long been fast asleep and in which the triumph of sin has become normal. This preacher whips us as one would whip a horse, and his blows are felt in society ... This exceptional willingness to identify his personal life with the doctrine that he preaches is powerful, as is his moral beauty, which raises him above the rest of us and especially above those who are leading his persecution.[104]

According to the secret police, Popescu and Crainic remained friends and in 1928 they collaborated on a petition to prevent the singer Josephine Baker from performing in Romania.[105]

These exchanges soon degenerated into personal attacks. Manea Popescu claimed that the nationalist and antisemitic Crainic sided with Popescu simply because Galaction was a Marxist and a philosemite. He asserted that Crainic was too stupid to understand theology and too fat to look in the mirror.[106] Galaction claimed that he had been approached by a father whose daughter had been converted by Cornilescu and was planning to marry him. When challenged on this by his superiors, Galaction said that Cornilescu fled to Germany, leaving the girl behind.[107] Cornilescu's biographer, Alexandru Măianu, writes that shortly before leaving the country Cornilescu 'had a conflict with General Rusescu, whose sister frequented Christian meetings. General Rusescu felt insulted by Cornilescu, who told him that he was a sinner because he was not a believer, and the general challenged him to a duel.'[108] Whatever his motives, Cornilescu left the country for Germany several months before Popescu's trial, apparently at the urging of Miron Cristea. Supported first by Ralu Callimachi and then by gifts from congregations he spoke at, he spent time as an itinerant preacher and Bible teacher in England, France, Germany and Switzerland, before finally settling in Switzerland in 1929.[109] Following a request by *Duminica ortodoxă*, in

---

[104] Nichifor Crainic, 'Cuibul cu Barză', *Gândirea* 3, no. 11 (1924): 259.
[105] ACNSAS, Fond Penal, Dosar 13206, vol. 2, f. 336.
[106] Manea Popescu, 'Cuibul cu Barză', 211–15.
[107] [Galaction], 'Cuvinte de lămurire', 1130.
[108] Alexandru Măianu, *Viaţa şi lucrarea lui Dumitru Cornilescu* (Bucharest: Editura Stephanus, 1995), 84.
[109] Ibid., 84–104; Schweizerisches Bundesarchiv BAR, E 4264 Bundesamt für Polizei, Dosar 1989/146, vol. 266, f. K 10651, Dumitru Cornilescu, 1933–49. I am grateful to Emanuel Conţac for providing me with Cornilescu's Swiss naturalization documents.

June 1924 the Holy Synod recommended that priests no longer use Cornilescu's Bible on the grounds that 'it does not correspond to the normative canonical text of the Orthodox Church ... [and] is done tendentiously, in a spirit that encourages the reader to arrive at interpretations that are completely opposed to the doctrines of the Orthodox Church'.[110] Nonetheless, publications by the Lord's Army continued using it long after Cornilescu had fallen out of favour with the rest of the ROC.[111]

Popescu's place as parish priest at St Ştefan's Church was taken by Father Marin C. Ionescu, who was an occasional contributor to *Noua revistă bisericească*.[112] A promising young priest who obtained his doctorate on the topic of 'The Priest and the Harmonizing of Social Classes' (1925), Ionescu became a prominent defender of Romanian nationalism and of Orthodoxy as a Romanian religion.[113] Few prominent churchmen of the inter-war period avoided scandal at one time or another, and in 1933 the Stork's Nest was again upset following accusations by the cantor that Ionescu was mishandling parish funds and was promoting political causes. Parishioners quickly came to his defence and Ionescu remained in his post.[114]

Tudorists

Popescu's followers continued meeting in private homes and distributed pamphlets and tracts teaching Popescu's message.[115] Originally known as the 'Born Agains' (*Noii Renăscuți*), Popescu's movement soon spread to the nearby city of Ploieşti, where the parish priest complained to the police that they held meetings at night time 'when everyone needs peace and quiet'.[116] It was not always easy to organize their gatherings, and in February 1925 two priests

---

[110] 'Cronica Bisericească Internă', *Biserica Ortodoxă Română* 43, no. 4 (1925): 232; quoted in Conţac, *Cornilescu*, 77.

[111] Conţac, *Cornilescu*, 77 n. 108.

[112] Marin C. Ionescu, 'Moş Toader si Adventismul', *Noua revistă bisericească*, 1 May 1921, 67–9.

[113] ACNSAS, Fond Documentar, Dosar 12413, f. 1; Marin C. Ionescu, 'Unii cu Anglicanii! Alţii cu Papistaşii! Niciunul cu ortodocsii?!' *Glasul Monahilor*, 12 July 1936, 1–2; Mircea Păcurariu, 'Ionescu, Marin', in *Dicţionarul teologilor români*. Available online: http://biserica.org/WhosWho/DTR/I/MarinIonescu.html (accessed 7 August 2017).

[114] Epitropii, Consilierii, şi Enoriaşii bisericii Sf. Ştefan, 'Cuibu cu Barză', *Mi-e milă de popor: Spulberarea unei calomnii* (Bucharest: Tipografia Astoria, 1933).

[115] ANIC, Fond MCA, Dosar 16/1924, ff. 49, 57, and Dosar 167/1925, f. 6; Amzioară, *Din viaţa şi lucrarea*, 40–51.

[116] ANIC, Fond MCA, 167/1925, f. 3.

from Bucharest attacked one of their meetings accompanied by forty to fifty people. The police report stated that the building would have been destroyed had the authorities not intervened.[117] In November 1925 Popescu admitted to a representative of the British Bible Society that he was still unsure what he meant his community to be. He would not return to the Orthodox Church, he did not feel attracted to any of the major Protestant or Repenter churches, nor did he particularly want to start his own church.[118] Popescu's indecision meant that congregations of his followers formed organically, often without any deliberate attempt by Popescu to establish them. Soon communities of 'Tudorists' (Tudoriști) or 'Christians According to the Scriptures' (Creștini după Scriptură), as they were increasingly called, appeared in towns and villages throughout the counties of Ilfov, Ploiești, Brașov, Argeș, Ialomița, Constanța and Tutova. Without trained pastors, these communities depended entirely on lay leadership and on books and songs supplied by Popescu.[119] Women originally prayed in Tudorist gatherings, but on Cornilescu's advice Popescu demanded that they remain silent during the church services.[120] Tudorists also ceased making the sign of the cross or greeting each other with the phrase 'Christ has risen!' at Easter time, signalling their separation from Orthodox forms of piety.[121]

As did Repenters, Tudorists referred to each other as 'brother' and 'sister', and usually spread their beliefs through one-on-one conversations. They also began publishing a magazine entitled *Cuvântul Adevărului* (*The Word of the Truth*), which contained short sermons, devotional readings and commentaries on passages of the Bible.[122] Although it was highly illegal, some Tudorists posted tracts to non-believers through the mail or handed them to passers-by on the streets. Individuals caught doing so were promptly arrested.[123]

By 1936 Tudorist meetings in Bucharest were standing-room only, with hundreds of people in attendance, but the movement still lacked any official recognition.[124] In one pamphlet from 1937 the Tudorists described themselves thus:

---

[117] Ibid., ff. 10–11.
[118] Memo by Bishop J. H. Greig for Archbishop Davidson, 16 November 1925. Lambeth Palace Library, Douglas 88, ff. 245–9. I am grateful to Emanuel Conțac for sharing these documents with me.
[119] Amzioară, *Din viața și lucrarea*, 47, 60.
[120] Ibid., 44.
[121] ACNSAS, Fond Informativ, Dosar 189663, f. 118.
[122] Two issues of *Cuvântul Adevărului* from 1937 can be found in ACNSAS, Fond Documentar, Dosar 13408, vol. 5, ff. 135–47.
[123] ACNSAS, Fond Informativ, Dosar 189663, ff. 13, 35–46, 53–75.
[124] Ibid., Dosar 189663, ff. 1–2.

We are Christians. That is what we are called. But because the authorities ask us for a name to differentiate ourselves from other churches and directions, we call ourselves 'Christians According to the Scriptures'. Our goal is to strengthen believers spiritually through sharing the Gospel and through evangelism to bring the Lord Jesus to those who do not know him and who are not born again ... Towards the Orthodox Church and towards the other denominations, according to the instructions of Scripture (Romans 12:18), our attitude is one of peace and of non-interference in their business.[125]

Neither prohibited nor sanctioned by law, Tudorists had trouble with the police throughout the inter-war period. They had their authorization to meet approved or rescinded every few years without warning.[126] They had to request permission from the Ministry of Denominations to establish meeting houses (*case de rugăciune*) on a case-by-case basis. Approval in one village did not guarantee approval in the next. Preaching without authorization led to the immediate closure of Tudorist meeting houses.[127] Local policemen remained confused about whether 'Tudorists' and 'Christians According to the Scriptures' were one and the same thing, and wrote to their superiors that Tudorist preachers 'seek to break apart our ancestral religious beliefs, weakening the unity of the state in the process'.[128] A lay Orthodox movement known as the 'Patriarch Miron Association' lobbied to have the Tudorists banned entirely in 1937, but without success.[129]

In 1939 the government decided to close Tudorist meeting houses entirely so Popescu agreed to merge his Church with the Brethren in Romania.[130] By this stage the only serious difference between the two groups was that Brethren only baptized adults whereas Tudorists continued baptizing infants as the Orthodox Church did.[131] The Tudorists did not gain much breathing room, however, as when Ion Antonescu took power in 1940 he severely limited religious freedom and the Brethren, together with other Repenter groups, faced the threat of deportation to Transnistria during the Holocaust.[132] After the Romanian Communist Party came to power, Popescu and other Tudorist preachers such

---

[125] *Memoriu cuprinzând arătarea pe scurt a învățăturii și organizației 'Bisericei Creștinilor după Scriptură'* in ACNSAS, Fond Documentar, Dosar 13408, vol. 5, f. 123.
[126] ACNSAS, Fond Informativ, Dosar 189663, ff. 110–13.
[127] Ibid., Dosar 189663, ff. 77–8; ANIC, Fond MCA, Dosar 149/1936, ff. 2, 6, 28, 38, 40, 48.
[128] ANIC, Fond MCA, Dosar 149/1936, f. 4. Cf. ACNSAS, Fond Informativ, Dosar 189663, f. 85.
[129] ACNSAS, Fond Informativ, Dosar 189663, ff. 4–5, 9.
[130] Ibid., f. 10; Amzioară, *Din viața și lucrarea*, 66–7.
[131] ACNSAS, Fond Documentar, Dosar 13408, vol. 5, f. 122.
[132] Amzioară, *Din viața și lucrarea*, 70–4; Viorel Achim (ed.), *Politica regimului Antonescu față de cultele neoprotestante: Documente* (Iași: Polirom, 2013).

as Gheorghe Cornilescu and Emil Constantinescu frequently disparaged the Romanian Communist Party in their sermons. They encouraged their followers to have as little as possible to do with the state, including rejecting socialist literature, theatre and cinema.[133] The secret police kept these men under strict surveillance, but Tudorist gatherings in Bucharest still regularly attracted crowds of between 1,000 and 1,500 people in 1953.[134] Popescu's failing health made him less of a threat to the authorities, who preferred to limit the freedom of activity available to Repenters than to close them down entirely.

---

[133] ACNSAS, Fond Informativ, Dosar 259045, vol. 1, ff. 1–2, 5–7.
[134] Ibid., ff. 92, 105.

Conclusion

A variety of different currents shaped Romanian Orthodoxy during the 1920s. Working together with the National Liberal Party, Miron Cristea expanded the Romanian Orthodox Church (ROC) into the Banat, Maramureș, Transylvania, Bukovina, Bessarabia and Dobruja. He imposed a centralized system of church governance by suppressing autonomous tendencies that were emerging in Transylvania and Bessarabia. Cristea placed the Church at the centre of Romanian nation-building, insisting that the ROC was the *only* church that should be associated with the nation-state. He and others used arguments about 'Tradition' when framing their demands, though they were well aware that in practice over the past 500 years Tradition had been about reconciling the competing claims of Church and state by making the best out of unsatisfactory circumstances. Given Orthodoxy's potential as an ideology of social cohesion, its long tradition of supporting state authority and the fact that many of the other churches were associated with ethnic minorities, the government acquiesced to the ROC's demands for dominant status. The vast majority of police and gendarmes were ethnically Romanian and religiously Orthodox. They too were enthusiastic about wielding power over religious minorities given that their forebears had had to submit to Ottoman, Russian or Austro-Hungarian rule for so long.

Cristea did not establish the new patriarchate alone. He was surrounded – and frequently challenged – by a handful of talented leaders, almost all of whom had been trained abroad and were appointed soon after the end of the First World War. Nicolae Bălan, Gurie Grosu, Vartolomeu Stănescu and Visarion Puiu used their positions to reinforce Romanian Orthodox privilege within the regions under their control. These men did their utmost to transform ordinary Romanians into enthusiastic Christians. They introduced an unprecedented number of initiatives that encouraged priests and lay Christians to work together to cultivate their spirituality. The Lord's Army, the Rebirth society, the Take and

Read circle and the Federation of Christian Students Associations in Romania all successfully communicated church messages about temperance, morality and Bible reading to audiences which had hitherto not expressed a great deal of interest in church activities. A new generation of talented teachers helped to shape young priests into successful evangelists and preachers. Irineu Mihălcescu, Constantin Nazarie, Iuliu Scriban, Gala Galaction, Ioan Popescu-Mălăești, Grigore Cristescu and others inspired their students with what they had learned during their studies abroad. Reforming priests such as Iosif Trifa, Teodor Popescu, Dumitru Cornilescu, Grigore Comșa, Manea S. Popescu and Teodor Păcescu grew up intellectually and spiritually under their tutelage. Preaching, Bible reading, temperance, swearing and church attendance now became the standards by which Orthodox spirituality was judged.

Not all of the reform efforts of the 1920s strengthened church unity. The calendar reform of 1924 alienated large sections of the population in Moldavia and Bessarabia, giving birth to Old Calendarism. The preaching of Popescu and Cornilescu at the Stork's Nest turned out to be too Protestant for the taste of many and eventually created a new Repenter denomination. Similarly, Trifa's articles and books taught about individual piety and a personal Saviour with almost no reference to saints, icons, priests or liturgy. Bălan tried to sideline Trifa, but many members of the Lord's Army insisted on following Trifa out of the more institutionalized and nationalist movement Bălan hoped for. When university students associated with the FASCR began sharing God's love through good works their elders had to step in to redirect their energies towards nationalist politics.

The changes inside 1920s Orthodoxy all took place before a backdrop of Repenter Christianity. Despite their small numbers, the spectre of Repenters dominated Orthodox discussions about religion in Romania. In a 1937 book entitled *The Prophetic Spirit*, the deacon Vasile Ionescu wrote that 'the religious problem of our Orthodoxy today has two main aspects: one involves crushing unbelief and eliminating everything that belongs to sectarian teachings; the other is the strengthening of the faithful through their clergy, raising their religious-moral lives to a higher level'.[1] Most Orthodox writers would have agreed, seeing combating sectarianism and teaching the laity as two sides of the same coin. Almost every attempt to create a new Orthodox initiative was justified in terms of anti-sectarianism. Apart from the fact that they ignored national chauvinism and failed to respect the church hierarchy, Repenters excelled at the sort of

---

[1] Vasile Ionescu, *Duhul profetic* (Pitești: Tipografia 'Artistica' P. Mitu, 1937), 3.

religious practices reforming priests most valued. They cherished their Bibles and read them avidly, they did not drink, smoke or swear, they prayed regularly and were determined to share their faith regardless of the cost. Even anti-sectarian missionaries had little choice but to imitate the strategies and practices of Repenters if they hoped to combat them. Repenters were also associated with the sorts of foreign influences that Orthodox leaders felt powerless to stop. It is telling that anti-sectarian writers blamed Repenters for the rise of atheism, evolutionary theory and immorality. Even if Repenters taught none of those things, their religion came from the same countries as jazz music and the theory of evolution so the two became connected in the minds of anti-sectarian writers.

The relationship between Repenters and changing Orthodox practices was more complex in Romania than scholars have suggested it was elsewhere. Bojan Aleksov and Ksenija Končarević argue that in Serbia the Nazarenes taught God Worshippers and other Orthodox Christians to read their Bibles and to seek to live holier lives. They suggest that the increase in devotional literature, new translations of the Bible, vernacular liturgies and the spread of grassroots holiness movements in Serbian Orthodoxy were a direct result of Nazarene influences.[2] In Romania, on the other hand, the sorts of changes associated with Repenter religion transformed Orthodoxy at the same time that Repenter communities grew and spread. Bible reading increased as a natural consequence of the rise of literacy levels and the number of religious newspapers and grassroots associations increased because the number of *all* newspapers and associations was growing exponentially during this period. Orthodox leaders used the threat that Repenters would take over the country to promote their new initiatives, but those initiatives were not conscious imitations of Repenter practices. Nor did Repenter beliefs and parachurch movements develop organically out of Orthodoxy, as Sergei Zhuk argues happened in the Ukraine.[3] Repenters explicitly acknowledged American, British, German, Swiss and French influences, distributing foreign literature and occasionally receiving money or diplomatic support from abroad.

Despite what Orthodox writers claimed, Repenters were not the major conduit through which Romanians learned about Western Christianity. For the

---

[2] Bojan Aleksov, 'The Nazarenes Among the Serbs: Proselytism and/or Dissent?' and Ksenija J. Končarević, 'The Influence of the God Worshipper Movement on the Language Policy and Religious Service of the Serbian Orthodox Church', in *Orthodox Christian Renewal Movements in Eastern Europe*, ed. Aleksandra Djurić Milovanović and Radmila Radić (Cham: Palgrave Macmillan, 2017), 105–89.

[3] Zhuk, *Russia's Lost Reformation*, 3.

most part, Orthodox leaders discovered Western Christianity for themselves, without Repenter influence. When priests such as Iosif Trifa or Dumitru Cornilescu wanted edifying literature to give their followers there was simply too little written by Romanian Orthodox Christians. They thus had little choice but to turn to Catholic and Protestant devotional writings which contained doctrines such as justification by faith and *sola scriptura* alongside messages about temperance and morality. Similarly, so many of the bishops, archbishops and metropolitans in inter-war Romania had been educated abroad because the standards available in Romanian theological faculties before the First World War were too low. Social Christianity, modern Biblical hermeneutics, lay activism and revivalism had all developed within Western Christianity, as had the idea of temperance leagues, self-help associations and religious newspapers. Regardless of the impact of missionaries and organizations such as the YMCA, during the 1920s Christians of all persuasions had unprecedented levels of access to and contact with the West thanks to new travel and communication networks connecting the globe.

Over the centuries Eastern Orthodoxy has had a long tradition of developing through interaction with Western Christianity, sometimes incorporating Western ideas and practices and sometimes creatively rejecting them.[4] Yet chauvinistic nationalism was so entrenched during the early twentieth century that the idea that Romanian Orthodoxy might benefit from foreign ideas was incomprehensible to many people. Manea Popescu concluded that 'if we have to establish our evangelism on a foreign basis, it would be better for us to stay where we are and be happy with preserving what we have inherited'.[5] As Nicholas Doumanis has demonstrated through his study of religious change in Anatolia, there was nothing in the popular practice of early twentieth-century Orthodoxy that precluded an active and intimate cohabitation with neighbours from other religious traditions. It was, rather, the institutional cultures of church-building and nationalism coming on the back of centuries of humiliating exploitation by imperial powers that instrumentalized Orthodoxy as a xenophobic, intolerant religion.[6] Frustration at state attempts to control the ROC and a growing appreciation of the power that grassroots religiosity could give Church leaders in

---

[4] Alexander Schmemann, *The Historical Road of Eastern Orthodoxy* (Crestwood, NY: St Vladimir's Seminary Press, 1963); Georges Florovsky, *Ways of Russian Theology* (Vaduz: Büchervertriebsanst, 1979).

[5] Manea Popescu, 'Un ultim răspuns și câteva lămuriri Preotului Teodor Popescu', *Noua revistă bisericească*, 1 April 1922, 13.

[6] Nicholas Doumanis, *Before the Nation: Muslim-Christian Coexistence and Its Destruction in Late Ottoman Anatolia* (Oxford: Oxford University Press, 2012).

a democratic nation-state further encouraged metropolitans, bishops and parish priests to embrace antisemitic and fascist politics as a means of producing social change when legal means failed.

Aristotle Papanikolaou and George Demacopoulos have recently asked whether the resurgence of Orthodox(ist) 'traditionalism', which posits that there is one, authentic and traditional form of Orthodoxy and other, less orthodox strands, is a form of Orthodox fundamentalism that is seeking to find a way of maintaining an Orthodox identity in a secular world.[7] In inter-war Romania, talking about Tradition was both about establishing the limits of Orthodoxy and about reaffirming the dominance of one Church and one way of life in the face of the rapid changes that came with modernity and state-building. Although they occasionally gave lip service to the idea of Tradition as a creative force, most Romanian writers of the 1920s saw it primarily in terms of its conservative nature. Irineu Mihălcescu defined Tradition as 'those teachings given by the holy apostles ... [that were] written down by the Church Fathers and thus preserved unchanged until today in their writings and in the books of the church'.[8] As Pantelis Kalaitzidis notes, this is only one way of thinking about Tradition. 'If tradition is something that emanates only from the past', he writes, 'if its only reference points are those bequeathed and handed down to us, then any change, modification or reform is *perforce* a betrayal of the original, authentic truth. Conversely, if tradition comes to us from the future – the future of God's Kingdom, of the eschatological Christ himself – then anything is possible, everything is open, and nothing is set in stone.'[9] However much Romanian Church leaders might have hoped for a creative renewal of their faith, whether it be through Social Christianity or paligenetic ultra-nationalism, they were terrified that they would be losing something in the process. The spectre of Repenter Christianity constantly reminded them that Orthodoxy did have its limits and that these limits must be respected lest, in the words of Teodor Păcescu, 'we pass beyond Orthodox dogma in our desire to evangelize and unexpectedly find ourselves in the camp of the sectarians'.[10]

---

[7] Aristotle Papanikolaou and George E. Demacopoulos, 'Introduction: Being as Tradition', in *Fundamentalism or Tradition: Christianity after Secularism*, ed. Aristotle Papanikolaou and George E. Demacopoulos (New York: Fordham University Press, 2019), 7–9.
[8] Mihălcescu, *Catehismul creștin ortodox*, 7.
[9] Pantelis Kalaitzidis, 'Challenges of Renewal and Reformation Facing the Church', *The Ecumenical Review* 61, no. 2 (2009): 149–50.
[10] Teodor P. Păcescu, 'Biserica in pragul anului 1922', *Noua revistă bisericească*, 1 January 1922, 321.

Bibliography

Archives

Central University Library, University of Bucharest
    Litere
Lambeth Palace Archives
    Douglas 88
    R. T. Davidson Papers
National Council for the Study of the Securitate Archives (ACNSAS)
    Fond Documentar
    Fond Informativ
    Fond Penal
Romanian National Archives (ANIC)
    Fond Direcția Generală a Poliției (DGP)
    Fond Ministerul Cultelor și Artelor (MCA)
    Fond Ministerul Instrucțiunii
    Fond Ministerul Propagandei Naționale
    Fond Miron Cristea
Romanian National Archives – Brașov County (ANIC – Brașov)
    Fond Chestura de Poliție Brașov, Serv. Siguranței.
    Fond Personal Gyurgyevich
Romanian National Archives – Craiova County (ANIC – Craiova)
    Fond Parohia Bisericii Obedeanu Craiova
    Fond Societatea Preoțească Renașterea
Romanian National Archives – Iași County (ANIC – Iași)
    Fond Universitatea A. I. Cuza, Rectoratul
Swiss Federal Archives
    BAR, E 4264 Bundesamt für Polizei

Periodicals

Adevărul (1888–1951)
Apărarea națională (1922–7)
Ardealul (1920–43)
Biserica Ortodoxă Română (1874–present)
Biserica și școala (1877–1948)

Buna vestire (1937–8, 1940–1)
Calendarul (1932–3)
Credința ortodoxă (1932–40)
Crucea (1923–4)
Cultura creștină (1911–26)
Curierul creștin (1922–44)
Cuvântul (1924–38, 1940–1)
Cuvântul Adevărului (1927–40)
Cuvântul studențesc (1923–40)
Dimineața (1904–38)
Duminca ortodoxă (1918–37)
Farul mântuirei (1919–32)
Foaia diecezană (1886–1949)
Gazeta Transilvaniei (1838–1989)
Gândirea (1921–45)
Ideea europeană (1919–28)
Ideea românească (1935–6)
Libertatea (1902–41)
Lumina satelor (1922–52)
Luminătorul (1923–44)
Luptătorul (1920–2)
Misionarul (1929–38)
Monitorul oficial (1832–present)
Noua revistă bisericească (1919–30)
Oastea Domnului (1930)
Ogorul nostru (1923–6)
Predania (1937)
Renașterea (Cluj) (1923–50)
Revista culturală (1910–11)
Revista teologică (1907–47)
Telegraful român (1904–present)
Țara noastră (1932–8)
Unirea (1891–1945)
Unirea poporului (1919–48)
Viața literară (1925–38)
Zion's Watch Tower (1879–present)

Published primary sources

Actele Adunării Eparhiale Ordinare a Eparhiei Vadului, Feleacului și Clujului ținută la Cluj în anul 1930. Cluj: Tiparul Tipografiei Eparh. Ort. Rom., 1930.
Anuarul Episcopiei Chișinăului și Hotinului (Basarabia). n.p.: n.p., 1922.

Asociația Misionară a Studenților Creștini Ortodocși. Zece ani de activitate (1926–1936). Bucharest, 1936.

Biblia sau Sfînta Scriptură, translated by D. Cornilescu. Bucharest: Societatea Evanghelică Română, 1921.

Cartea Psalmilor sau Psaltirea, translated by D. Cornilescu. Bucharest: Societatea Evanghelică Română, 1920.

Datoriile preoților, translated by C. Mavrula. Bucharest: Editura Bizantină, 2011.

Fassiunea credinței și (întocmirea iei): Pentru adunările creștine, cari de comun pórtă numirea de adunări baptiste, translated by Georgiu Slăvŭ.. 2nd edn. n.p.: n.p., 1905.

La Sainte Bible, translated by Louis Segond. Paris: Alliance Biblique Universelle, 1910.

Noul Testament, translated by D. Cornilescu. Bucharest: Societatea Evanghelică Română, 1920.

Rugăciunile sfinților părinți sau Apanthisma. Bucharest: Cartea Ortodoxă, 2007.

Scurtă expunere a principiilor de credință a "Bisericii lui Dumnezeu Apostolice" (Penticostale) din România. Arad: Editura Vestitorul Evangheliei, 1947.

Sfânta Scriptură a Vechiului și a Noului Testament. Bucharest: Societatea de Biblie Britanică, 1921.

Bălan, Nicolae. *Problema religiósă în timpul de azi*. Sibiu: Tiparul Tipografiei Arhidiecezane, 1906.

Bălan, Nicolae. *Chestiunea bisericească din România și autonomia bisericii noastre*. Sibiu: Tiparul Tipografiei Arhidiecezane, 1910.

Bălan, Nicolae. *Un congres românesc biblic*. Sibiu: Tiparul Tipografiei Arhidiecezane, 1912.

Bălan, Nicolae. *În chestia 'micii Biblii'*. Sibiu: Tiparul Tipografiei Arhidiecezane, 1914.

Bălan, Nicolae. *Cuvântări rostite cu ocazia alegerii, sfințirii și investiturii*. Sibiu: Tiparul Tipografiei Arhidiecezane, 1921.

Bălan, Nicolae. *Biserica împotriva concordatului*. Sibiu: Tiparul Tipografiei Arhidiecezane, 1929.

Bălan, Nicolae. *"Oastea Domnului' și Biserica*. Sibiu: Tiparul Tipografiei Archdiecezane, 1935.

Beldie, Const. P. *Cultul sfintelor icoane*. Bârlad: Tipografia N. Chiriac, 1937.

Bunyan, John. *Călătoria creștinului sau calea spre fericirea de veci*, translated by Dumitru Cornilescu. Bucharest: Editura Societății de Cărți Religioase, 1923.

Caesarius of Arles. *The Fathers of the Church: St. Caesarius of Arles, Sermons*, vol. 2. Translated by Mary Magdeline Mueller. Washington, D.C.: The Catholic University of America Press, 1963.

Călinescu, Ștefan. *Dialog între Moș Dragne și Logofătul Stoîca Călinénu explicând întregul organism liturgic*. Bucharest: Tipografia Gutenberg, 1904.

Călinescu, Ștefan. *Povățuitor în activitatea pastorală a preotului*. Bucharest: Tipografia Gutenberg, 1908.

Cernăianu, C. *Răspuns adversarilor mei spre eterna lor osândă*. Bucharest: Tipografia Capitalei, 1934.

Challand, Charles. *O minune din vremurile noastre: viaţa şi lucrarea lui George Müller*, translated by Dumitru Cornilescu. Bucharest: Societatea Evanghelică Romînă, 1922.

Chirică, Const. Gr. *Lupi răpitori în piei de oi*. Galaţi: Institutul de Arte Grafice 'Energia', n.d.

Chiricuţă, Toma, Gh. Comana, Marin C. Ionescu and Manea S. Popescu. *Chemări de departe: predici la radio*. Bucharest: Editura Librariei Pavel Suru, 1929.

Chiriţescu, Gheorghe. *Otrava vieţii*. Târgu Neamţ: Tipografia Monastirii Neamţu, 1924.

Ciauşanu, G. F., G. Fira and C. M. Popescu. *Culegere de folclor din jud. Vâlcea şi împrejurimi*. Bucharest: Cultura Naţională, 1928.

Coculescu, N. *Chestiunea calendarului*. Bucharest: Tipografia Corpului Didactic C. Ispăsescu & G. Brătănescu, 1898.

Codreanu, Florea. *Sămânţa de lângă cale*. Arad: Tiparul Tipografiei Diecezane, 1929.

Codreanu, Florea. *Cunoştinţe liturgice*. Arad: Editura Diecezană, 1945.

Comşa, Grigorie. *Predici pentru toate duminicile de peste an şi alte ocaziuni*. Arad: Tiparul Tipografiei Diecezane, 1918.

Comşa, Grigorie. *Istoria predicei la români*. Bucharest: Tipografia Cărţilor Bisericeşti, 1921.

Comşa, Grigorie. *Pentru neam şi lege: Patruzeci cuvântări de învăţătură împotriva adventiştilor şi baptiştilor*. Caransebeş: Editura 'Librăriei Decezane', 1923.

Comşa, Grigorie. *Combaterea catehismului baptiştilor*. Arad: Tiparul Tipografiei Diecezane, 1926.

Comşa, Grigorie. *Pedepsirea păcătoşilor şi scoaterea din adunările Baptiste*. Arad: Tiparul Tipografiei Diecezane, 1929.

Comşa, Grigorie. *Cheia sectelor religioase din România*. Arad: Tiparul Tipografiei Diecezane, 1930.

Comşa, Grigorie. *Zece ani de luptă împotriva baptiştilor*. Arad: Tiparul Tipografiei Diecezane, 1930.

Comşa, Grigorie. *Glasul pietrelor: Principii călăuzitoare pentru ortodoxia activă*. Chişinău: Tipografia Eparhială 'Cartea Românească', 1931.

Comşa, Grigorie. *Fiinţa şi necesitatea misionarismului*. Arad: Tiparul Tipografiei Diecezane, 1932.

Comşa, Grigorie. *Scrisori creştineşti*. Arad: Tiparul Tipografiei Diecezane, 1934.

Comşa, Grigorie. *Cultura satelor noastre*. Arad: Tiparul Tipografiei Diecezane, 1935.

Cornilescu, Dumitru. *47 cîntări creştineşti cu note muzicale*. Bucharest: Societatea Evanghelică Romînă, 1922.

Cornilescu, Dumitru. *Cum m-am întors la Dumnezeu*. Bucharest: Biserica Evanghelică Română, 2014.

Cosma, Aurel. *Cosmogonia poporului român*. Bucharest: Tipografia Ziarului Universul, 1942.

Cotârlă, Ioan. *Sf. Cruce, Sf. Icoane, luminările şi tămâia*. Arad: Tiparul Tipografiei Diecezane, 1929.

Crainic, Nichifor. *Zile albe – zile negre: memorii*. Bucharest: Casa Editorială Gândirea, 1991.

Crainic, Nichifor. *Puncte cardinale în haos*. Iași: Editura Timpul, 1996.

Cristea, A. *Colecțiune de predici populare*. Bucharest: Tipografia 'Speranța', 1907.

Cristea, Elie Miron. *Note ascunse: Însemnări personale (1895–1937)*. Cluj-Napoca: Editura Dacia, 1999.

Cristescu, D. *Viața și înfăptuirile Prea Sfințitului Episcop Vartolomeiu până la împlinirea vârstei de 60 ani*. Râmnicul-Vâlcea: Tipografia Episcopul Vartolomeiu, 1936.

Cristescu, Grigore. *Isus în viață modernă*. Sibiu: Tiparul Tipografiei Arhidiecezane, 1927.

Cucu, Aristide C. *Carte de religie pentru clasa IV-a primară*. n.p.: Editura Autorului, 1938.

Cucu, G. ed. *Zece cântece religioase*. Bucharest: Editura Proprie, 1928.

Dăvărescu, I. N. *Feriți-vă de adventiști și de toți rătăciții vremurilor noastre!* Arad: Tiparul Tipografiei Diecezane, 1930.

Demetrescu, Ștefan. *Ce credem noi adventiștii: Răspuns calomniilor debitate despre noi de către cei interesați*. Bucharest: Atelierele grafice SOCEC, 1915.

Dincescu, Bolintin et al. *Lupta între Dumnezeu și Mamona: Între predicarea Evangheliei și acatist*. Bucharest: Tipografiile Române Unite, 1924.

Direcția Generală a Statisticei. *Anuarul statistic al României 1922*. Bucharest: Tipografia Curții Regale, 1923.

Dolinescu, V. *Lupta contra sectelor religioase*. Bârlad: Atelierele Grafice N. Peiu, 1939.

Dorz, Traian. *Din lupta Domnului. Popasuri în 'istoria unei jertfe'. Poezii religioase. Cartea III*. Oradea: Grafica, 1939.

Dorz, Traian. *Hristos: Mărturia mea*. Sibiu: Editura Oastea Domnului, 2005.

Douglas, J. A. 'Prospects of Union between the Eastern and Anglican Churches'. *The Christian East* 1, no. 1 (1920): 36–46.

Epitropii, Consilierii și Enoriașii bisericii Sf. Ștefan, 'Cuibu cu Barză'. *Mi-e milă de popor: Spulberarea unei calomnii*. Bucharest: Tipografia Astoria, 1933.

Felea, Ilarion V. *Critica ereziei baptiste*. Sibiu: n.p., 1937.

Galaction, Gala. *O lume nouă*. Bucharest: Editura Cugetarea, 1919.

Galaction, Gala. *Piatra din capul unghiului: Scrisori teologice*. Bucharest: Tipografiile Române Unite, 1926.

Galaction, Gala. *Roxana*. Bucharest: Editura Națională S. Ciornei, 1930.

Galaction, Gala. *Jurnal*. Bucharest: Editura Albatros, 1999.

Gârboviceanu, Petru. *Biserica Ortodoxă și cultele străine din regatul român*. Bucharest: Institutul de Arte Grafice, 1904.

Gașpar, Mina. *Legea lui Moise, sâmbăta evreilor, și duminica creștinilor*. Arad: Tiparul Tipografiei Diecezane, 1929.

Georgescu, Ion V. *Actualitatea profeților*. Bucharest: Tiparul Academic, 1934.

Gheorghiu, Vasile. *Despre botezul 'cu Spirit Sfânt și cu foc' și darurile harismatice*. Arad: Tiparul Tipografiei Diecezane, 1929.

Gherasimescu, Toma. *Propaganda religioasă prin cinematograf: Cum se poate face ea cu o cheltuială foarte mică*. Roman: Editura Autorului, 1930.
Grofşorean, Iuliu. *Scrieri pentru popor*. Arad: Tiparul Tipografiei diecezane Gr-Or. Rom., 1906.
Grossu, Sergiu. *Un vânt de primăvară religioasă: Rânduiala luptei spirituale în mişcarea ortodoxă Oastea Domnului*. Sibiu: Editura Oastea Domnului, 2005.
Grosu, Gurie. *I – Cinstirea Duminicei şi a serbătorilor, II – Păcatul sudălmilor şi vorbilor urâte*. Chişinău: Tipografia Eparhială, 1923.
Grosu, Gurie. *I. Păcatul dela umblarea la iarmaroce în zilele de Dumineci. II. Păcatul fumatului de tutun*. Chişinău: Tipografia Eparhială, 1924.
Gusti, Dimitrie ed., *Enciclopedia României*. Bucharest: Imprimeria Naţională, 1938.
Hilbert, Gerhard. *Există spirit?* Bucharest: Libraria Max Kendler, n.d.
Iancu, Nicu. *Sub steagul lui Codreanu: Momente din trecutul legionar*. Madrid: Editura Dacia, 1973.
Iliescu, Marin. *Poligamiea în America: Secta mormonilor: Doctrina, obieceiurile şi istoria lor*. Alexandria: Tipografia Alecsandri, 1932.
Imbrescu, Ilie I. *Misionarul eparhial al Tomisului: Gânduri după un an de încercări*. Bazargic: Tip. 'Gutenberg' Hristo Radilof, 1935.
Ionescu, Nae. *Roza vânturilor*. Bucharest: Editura Roza Vânturilor, 1990.
Ionescu, Petru. *Observări critice la opul 'Metropolia românilor ortodoxi din Ungaria şi Transilvania' etc. şi observări la răspunsul prea cuvioşiei sale Dlui Arhimandrit Dr Ilarion Puşcariu*. Caransebeş: Tiparul Tipografiei Diecesane, 1901.
Ionescu, Vasile. *Duhul profetic*. Piteşti: Tipografia 'Artistică' P. Mitu, 1937.
Ionică, Ion I. *Drăguş: Un sat din ţara Oltului (Făgăraş)*. Bucharest: Institutul de Ştiinţe Sociale al României, 1944.
Iorga, Nicolae. *Istoria bisericii româneşti şi a vieţii religioase a românilor*. 2nd edn. Bucharest: Saeculum, 2011.
Ispir, Vasile Gh. *Bibliografia subiectelor tratate în Seminarul de Sectologie de sub direcţiunea d-lui Profesor Dr. V. Gh. Ispir, în anii 1932/33, 1933/34 şi 1934/35*. Bucharest: Tipografia Ziarului, 1936.
Ispir, Vasile Gh. *Curs de sectologie*. Bucharest: Facultatea de Teologie din Bucureşti, 1938.
Ispir, Vasile Gh. *Sectele religioase. Un pericol naţional şi social*. Bucharest: Tipografia 'Cărţilor Bisericeşti', 1942.
Loichiţa, Vasile. *Chiliasmul (Milenarismul): Expunere şi critică dogmatică*. Cernăuţi: Editura Autorului, 1926.
Lungulescu, Dimitrie. *Manual de practică liturgică*. Bucharest: Tipografiile Române Unite, 1926.
Luţcan, Antonie. *Cuvinte de îndrumare*. Jud. Soroca: Editura Monăstirei Dobruşa, 1926.
Magieru, Andrei. *Acatistul Domnului nostru Iisus Hristos şi Paraclisul Născătoarei de Dumnezeu*. Arad: Diecezană, 1940.
Mai mulţi ortodoxi. *La 'Ierarchia Românilor din Ardeal şi Ungaria'*. Sibiu: Tiparul Tipografiei Archidiecesane, 1905.

Manuilă, Sabin. *Recensământul general al populației României din decemvrie 1930.* Bucharest: Institutul Central de Statistică, 1938.

Marini, Ioan and Traian Dorz. *Să cântăm Domnului: Carte de cântări religioase.* Oradea: Grafica, 1940.

Mateiu, I. *Valoarea Concordatului încheiat cu Vaticanul.* Sibiu: Tiparul Tipografiei Arhidiecezane, 1929.

McConkey, James Henry. *Ce înseamnă viața predată în slujba Domnului*, translated by Dumitru Cornilescu. n.p.: n.p., n.d.

Mehedinți, Simion. *Pentru biserica noastră.* Bucharest: Tipografia Gutenberg, 1911.

Mihălcescu, Irineu. *Cauzele necredinței contimporane și mijloacele de a-o combate.* Bucharest: Tipografia Cărților Bisericești, 1915.

Mihălcescu, Irineu. *Explicarea Sfintei Liturghii.* Bucharest: Institutul de Arte Grafice Carol Göbl, 1917.

Mihălcescu, Irineu. *Catehismul creștinului ortodox.* Cernica: Tipografia Bisericească din Sfânta Mânăstire Cernica, 1924.

Mihălcescu, Irineu. *Rânduiala și tâlcuirea pe scurt a sfintei liturghii.* Râmnicul Vâlcea: Tipografia Episcopul Vartolomeiu, 1935.

Mihălcescu, Irineu, and Petru Barbu. *Carte de religie pentru clasa III-a primară.* n.p.: Editura Librăriei Pavel Suru, n.d.

Ministerul Industriei și Comerțului, *Anuarul statistic al României: 1922.* Bucharest: Tipografia Curții Regale, 1923.

Moisescu, Epiharia. *O chestie de interes moral.* Bucharest: Minerva, 1910.

Moldovan, Valer. *Biserica în serviciul maghiarizării.* Brașov: Tipografia A. Mureșeanu, 1913.

Moldovan, Valer. *Biserica Ortodoxă Română și problema unificări: Studiu de drept bisericesc.* Cluj: Ardealul Institut de Arte Grafice, 1921.

Moța, Ioan. *42 de ani de gazetărie.* Orăștie: Tipografia Astra, 1935.

Munteanu, Nicodim. *Ce să crezi și cum să trăești? Adică schema credinței și moralei creștine.* Bucharest: Albert Baer, 1905.

Nanu, D. *Iisus vă cheamă.* Bucharest: Atelierele Adevărul, 1923.

Nanu, D. *Lupta între Evanghelie și tipic, între logică și sofism.* Bucharest: Atelierele 'Adeverul', 1924.

Nazarie, Constantin. *Călăuza predicatorului.* Bucharest: Tipografia Cărților Bisericești, 1902.

Nazarie, Constantin. *Duminica, botezul și ierarhia bisericească după adventiști.* Bucharest: Tipografia 'Cărților Bisericești', 1910.

Nazarie, Constantin. *Cinstirea sfintelor icoane și adventiștii.* Bucharest: Tipografia Cărților Bisericești, 1911.

Nazarie, Constantin. *Combaterea principalelor învățături adventiste.* Bucharest: Tipografia Cărților Bisericești, 1913.

Nicolau, Gherontie. *Starea sufletelor după moarte: Scurtă privire asupra învățăturii Sf. Biserici Ortodoxe de Răsărit despre judecata particulară și răsplata temporală a sufletelor celor adormiți și folosul rugăciunilor bisericii pentru ele.* Chișinău: Imprimeria Statului, 1923.

Nicolau, Gherontie. *Îndrumătorul liturgic*. Bucharest: Tipografia Cărților Bisericești, 1939.

Păcescu, Teodor P. *Inspirația cărților Sfintei Scripturi: Teză pentru licență*. Bucharest: Tipografia Speranța, 1907.

Pâclișanu, Zenovie. *Biserica și românismul*. Târgu-Lăpuș: Galaxia Gutenberg, 2005.

Pârvulescu, Sebastian. *Biserica noastră națională în raport cu celelalte confesiuni*. Vălenii de Munte: Tipografia Neamul Românesc, 1911.

Pocitan, Vasile. *Biserica românească din Basarabia*. Bucharest: Tipografia Albert Baer, 1914.

Pocitan, Vasile *Patriarhatele Bisericii Ortodoxe*. Bucharest: Tipografiile Române Unite, 1926.

Popescu, Teodor. *Cum aducem sufletele la Hristos sau planul de mântuire*. Bucharest: Tip. 'Cultura Neamului Românesc', 1924.

Popescu, Teodor. *Spulberarea Învinuirilor*. Bucharest: Tip. Romane Unite, 1924.

Popescu, Teodor. *Isus vă chiamă*. Bucharest: n.p., 1939.

Popescu, Tudor. *Concordatul cu Papa*. Bucharest: Institutul de Arte Grafice Răsăritul, 1927.

Popescu-Cernica, Alexandru. *Catechismul religiunei creștine ortodoxe conform cu programa analitică în us și însoțit de povestirĭ și istorióre morale și evangelice pentru usul clasei IV urbană și V rurală*. Bucharest: Lito-Tipografia Motzatzeanu și Lambru, 1896.

Popescu-Cernica, Alexandru. *Predica și foloasele ei*. Bucharest: 1911.

Puiu, Visarion. *Glas în pustie: Îmbunătățiri bisericești întârziate*. Chișinău: Tipografia Eparhială 'Cartea Românească', 1931.

Puiu, Visarion. *Monahismul ortodox din România de astăzi*. Chișinău: Tipografia Uniunii Clericilor Ortodocși din Basarabia, 1936.

Quast, Otto. *Teoria lui Haeckel despre lume*, translated by Dumitru Cornilescu. Craiova: Ramura, n.d.

Săndulescu, Al. *Mergerea la biserică*. Buzău: Tipografia M. Mracek, 1941.

Savin, Ioan G. *Iconoclaști și apostați contemporani*. Bucharest: Editura Anastasia, 1995.

Schifirneț, Constantin ed., *Biserica noastră și cultele minoritare: Marea discuție parlamentară în jurul legea cultelor*. Bucharest: Editura Albatros, 2000.

Scriban, Iuliu. *Manual de ermeneutică biblică pentru învățătura clasei VII a seminariilor teologice*. 2nd edn. Bucharest: Editura Casei Școalelor, 1922.

Scriban, Iuliu. *Studiul pastoralei în biserica românească*. Sibiu: Tiparul Tipografiei Arhidiecezane, 1924.

Scriban, Iuliu. *50 de predici populare*. Slobozia: Editura Episcopiei Sloboziei și Călărașilor, 2014.

Scriban, Neofit. *Apologia Prea Sfințitului Arhiereŭ D. D. Neofit Scriban, față cu clevetitori Sĕĭ din Iașĭ și Bucureștĭ: Saŭ respunsŭ acelora ce fac Apoteosa nenorocituluĭ de dînșiĭ Cuza-vodă, pentru falșa independință a Bisericeĭ Române*. Bucharest: Theodorescu, 1867.

Singh, Sadhu Sundar. *La picioarele stăpânului meu*. Sibiu: Tiparul Tipografiei Arhidiecezane, 1928.

Stănescu, Vartolomeu. *O lămurire în legătură cu eparhia locală*. Râmnicul Vâlcea: Tipografia Episcopul Vartolomei, 1938.

Stănescu, Vartolomeu. *În lumina cuvântului*. Râmnicu Vâlcea: Editura Sfântul Antim Ivireanul, 2013.

Stănescu, Vartolomeu. *Puterile sociale ale creștinismului: Opere alese*. Cluj-Napoca: Eikon, 2014.

Stănoiu, Damian. *Cum se vizitează o mănăstire*. Bucharest: Tip. Convorbiri Literare, 1923.

Suciu, Iustin. *Ermeneutica biblică sau știința interpretării Sfintei Scripturi*. Arad: Editura Autorului, 1933.

Toma, Moise. *Catehism pentru învățământul religiunei dreptcredincioase-răsăritene în școalele primare*. Nagyszeben: Tiparul Tipografiei Arhidecezane, 1912.

Trifa, Iosif. *Spre Canaan ... 15 predici în legătură cu răsboiul și vremile noastre*. Arad: Tipografia Diecezană, 1919.

Trifa, Iosif. *Cetiri și tâlcuiri din Biblie*. Sibiu: Editura Archdiecezană, 1924.

Trifa, Iosif. *Oglinda inimii omului*. Sibiu: Tiparul Tipografiei Arhidiecezane, 1927.

Trifa, Iosif. *Pe urmele Mântuitorului: Însemnări din călătoria la Ierusalim*. Sibiu: Tiparul Institutului de Arte Grafice, 1928.

Trifa, Iosif. *Ce este Oastea Domnului?* 5th edn. Sibiu: Editura Oastea Domnului, 1934.

Trifa, Iosif. *Spre Canaan*. Sibiu: n.p., 1936.

Trifa, Iosif. *Ca o oaie fără de glas*. Sibiu: Editura Oastea Domnului, 2001.

Trifa, Iosif. *Munca și lenea văzute în lumina evangheliei*. n.p.: n.p., n.d.

Trifa, Valerian. *Marginal Notes on a Court Case*. Jackson, MI: Valerian D. Trifa Romanian-American Heritage Center, 1988.

Un preot de mir. *Chestiuni de discutat*. Pitești: Tipografia Transilvania, 1909.

Underhill, Evelyn. *Mysticism: A Study in the Nature and Development of Man's Spiritual Consciousness*. New York: E. P. Dutton & Company, 1911.

Vasilache, Vasile. *Biblia în ortodoxie*. Neamț: Tipografia Sfintei Mănăstiri Neamțu, 1939.

Vasilescu, Coman. *Datoria preotului de a predica învățătura creștină*. Bucharest: 1900.

Velimirovich, Nicholai D. *The Universe as Symbols and Signs: As Essay on Mysticism in the Eastern Church*. Libertyville, IL: St Sava Monastery, 1950.

Voniga, D. *Presa bisericească: Importanța ei și mijloace de întreținere*. Timișoara: Tipografia Huniadi, 1925.

Secondary sources

Achim, Viorel. *Politica regimului Antonescu față de cultele neoprotestante: Documente*. Iași: Polirom, 2013.

Aleksov, Bojan. *Religious Dissent between the Modern and the National: Nazarenes in Hungary and Serbia 1850–1914*. Wiesbaden: Harrassowitz Verlag, 2006.

Aleksov, Bojan. 'The Nazarenes Among the Serbs: Proselytism and/or Dissent?' In *Orthodox Christian Renewal Movements in Eastern Europe*, edited by Aleksandra Djurić Milovanović and Radmila Radić, 105–36. Cham: Palgrave Macmillan, 2017.

Anderson, Allan Heaton. *An Introduction to Pentecostalism*. Cambridge: Cambridge University Press, 2014.

Aurel, Teleanu Bogdan. *Metaforă și misiune: Valorificarea literaturii laice în predica românească*. Iași: Doxologia, 2007.

Azimioră, Horia. *Din viața și lucrarea lui Teodor Popescu*. n.p.: n.p., 1988.

Bălăban, Ciprian. *Istoria Bisericii Penticostale din România (1922–1989): Instituție și harisme*. Oradea: Editura Scriptum: 2016.

Bălan, Ioanichie. *Sfintele moaște din România*. Roman: Editura Episcopiei Romanului, 1999.

Baran, Emily B. *Dissent on the Margins: How Soviet Jehovah's Witnesses Defied Communism and Lived to Preach about It*. Oxford: Oxford University Press, 2014.

Basciani, Alberto. *La Difficile Unione: La Bessarabia e La Grande Romania, 1918–1940*. Rome: Aracne, 2007.

Bejan, Cristina A. *Intellectuals and Fascism in Interwar Romania: The Criterion Association*. New York: Palgrave Macmillan, 2019.

Besier, Gerhard and Katarzyna Stoklosa eds, *Jehovas Zeugen in Europa – Geschichte und Gegenwart: Band 1. Belgien, Frankreich, Griechenland, Italien, Luxemburg, Niederlande, Portugal und Spanien*. Münster: Lit Verlag, 2013.

Biliuță, Ionuț. 'Periphery as Center? The Fate of the Transylvanian Orthodox Church in the Romanian Patriarchy'. In *Discourse and Counter-Discourse in Cultural and Intellectual History*, edited by Carmen Andraș and Cornel Sigmirean, 378–93. Sibiu: Astra Museum, 2014.

Biliuță, Ionuț. 'Arianizarea studiilor biblice în perioada interbelică: O polemică în studiile biblice românești'. In *Interpretarea Biblică între Biserică și Universitate: perspective interconfesionale*, edited by Alexandru Ioniță, 9–31. Sibiu: Andreiană, 2016.

Biliuță, Ionuț. 'Sowing the Seeds of Hate: The Antisemitism of the Orthodox Church in the Interwar Period', *S:I.M.O.N.* 3 (2016): 20–33.

Biliuță, Ionuț. 'Un fascism regional? Cazul Academiei Teologice Andreiene din Sibiu (1930–1941)'. In *Cler, Biserică și Societate în Transilvania, sec. XVIII–XX*, edited by Cornel Sigmirean and Corina Teodor, 404–24. Cluj-Napoca: Argonaut, 2016.

Biliuță, Ionuț. '"Agenții schimbării": Clerul ortodox din Principatele Române de la regimul feudal la statul național'. In '*Ne trebuie oameni!': Elite intelectuale și transformări istorice în România modernă și contemporană*, edited by Cristian Vasile, 27–64. Târgoviște: Editura Cetatea de Scaun, 2017.

Biliuță, Ionuț. 'Rejuvenating Orthodox Missionarism among the Laymen: The Romanian Orthodox Fellowship in Transylvania'. *Studia Universitatis Babes-Bolyai. Theologia Orthodoxa* 62, no. 2 (2017): 21–38.

Biliuță, Ionuț. 'The Ultranationalist Newsroom: Orthodox "Ecumenism" in the Legionary Ecclesiastical Newspapers'. *Review of Ecumenical Studies* 10, no. 2 (2018): 186–212.

Binder, Ludwig. *Die Kirche der Siebenbürger Sachsen*. Erlangen: Martin Luther Verlag, 1982.

Bocșan, Nicolae. 'Nation et confession en Transylvanie au XIXe siècle. Le cas de la Métropolie roumaine'. In *Ethnie et confession en Transylvanie (du XIIIe au XIXe siècles)*, edited by Nicolae Bocșan, Ioan Lumperdean and Ioan-Aurel Pop, 93–181. Cluj-Napoca: Centrul de Studii Transilvane, Fundația Culturală Română, 1996.

Boldișor, Veronica. *File din viața unei biserici și a unui mitropolit*. Chișinău: Pontos, 2014.

Brackney, William H. *Baptists in North America: A Historical Perspective*. Malden: Blackwell, 2006.

Brewster, Paul G. 'The Foundation Sacrifice Motif in Legend, Folksong, Game, and Dance'. In *The Walled-Up Wife: A Casebook*, edited by Alan Dundes, 42–6. University of Wisconsin Press, Madison, 1996.

Brown, Candy Gunther. *The Word in the World: Evangelical Writing, Publishing, and Reading in America, 1789–1880*. Chapel Hill: University of North Carolina Press, 2004.

Brusanowski, Paul. *Învățământul confesional ortodox din Transilvania între anii 1848–1918: Între exigențele statului centralizat și principiile autonomiei bisericești*. Cluj-Napoca: Presa Universitară Clujeană, 2005.

Brusanowski, Paul. *Autonomia și constituționalismul în dezbaterile privind unificarea Bisericii Ortodoxe Române (1919–1925)*. Cluj-Napoca: Presa Universitară Clujeană, 2007.

Brusanowski, Paul. *Reforma constituțională din Biserica Ortodoxă a Transilvaniei între 1850–1925*. Cluj-Napoca: Presa Universitară Clujeană, 2007.

Brusanowski, Paul. *Stat și Biserică în Vechea Românie între 1821–1925*. Cluj-Napoca: Presa Universitară Clujeană, 2010.

Brusanowski, Paul, Ulrich A. Wien and Karl W. Schwarz eds, *Rumänisch-orthodoxe Kirchenordnungen 1786–2008: Siebenbürgen – Bukowina – Rumänien*. Köln: Böhlau, 2011.

Buchiu, Ștefan and Cristinel Ioja. 'The Development of Dogmatic Studies'. In *Orthodox Theology in the 20th Century and Early 21st Century: A Romanian Orthodox Perspective*, edited by Viorel Ioniță, 395–464. Bucharest: Basilica, 2013.

Bucur, Maria. *Heroes and Victims: Remembering War in Twentieth-Century Romania*. Bloomington: Indiana University Press, 2009.

Butoi, Ionuț. *Mircea Vulcănescu: O microistorie a interbelicului românesc*. Bucharest: Editura Eikon, 2015.

Buzilă, Boris. 'Patriarhie pentru țara întregită, Mitropolie pentru provincia revenită la sînul Țării'. In *Mitropolitul Gurie: Misiunea de credință și cultură*, edited by Silvia Grossu, 18–26. Chișinău: Epigraf, 2007.

Chamedes, Giuliana. *A Twentieth-Century Crusade: The Vatican's Battle to Remake Christian Europe*. Cambridge, MA: Harvard University Press, 2019.

Cherciu, Ion. *Spiritualitate tradițională românească în epoca interbelică*. Bucharest: Muzeul Național al Satului 'Dimitrie Gusti', 2010.

Ciornea, Carmen. *Sandu Tudor și asociațiile studențești creștine din România interbelică*. Bucharest: Eikon, 2017.

Clark, Roland. 'Nationalism and Orthodoxy: Nichifor Crainic and the Political Culture of the Extreme Right in 1930s Romania'. *Nationalities Papers* 40, no. 1 (2012): 107–26.

Clark, Roland. 'Orthodoxy and Nation-Building: Nichifor Crainic and Religious Nationalism in 1920s Romania'. *Nationalities Papers* 40, no. 4 (2012): 525–43.

Clark, Roland. *Holy Legionary Youth: Fascist Activism in Interwar Romania*. Ithaca: Cornell University Press, 2015.

Clay, J. Eugene. 'Orthodox Missionaries and "Orthodox Heretics" in Russia, 1886–1917'. In *Of Religion and Empire: Missions, Conversion, and Tolerance in Tsarist Russia*, edited by Robert P. Geraci and Michael Khodarkovsky, 38–69. Ithaca: Cornell University Press, 2001.

Coleman, Heather. 'Becoming a Russian Baptist: Conversion Narratives and Social Experience'. *Russian Review* 61, no. 1 (2002): 94–112.

Coleman, Heather. 'Defining Heresy: The Fourth Missionary Congress and the Problem of Cultural Power after 1905 in Russia'. *Jahrbücher für Geschichte Osteuropas* 52, no. 1 (2004): 70–91.

Coleman, Heather. *Russian Baptists and Spiritual Revolution, 1905–1929*. Bloomington: Indiana University Press, 2005.

Coleman, Heather. 'Theology on the Ground: Dmitrii Bogoliubov, the Orthodox Anti-Sectarian Mission, and the Russian Soul'. In *Thinking Orthodox in Modern Russia: Culture, History, Context*, edited by Patrick Lally Michelson and Judith Deutsch Kornblatt, 64–84. Madison, WI: University of Wisconsin Press, 2014.

Conțac, Emanuel. 'Influența versiunii Segond asupra versiunii Cornilescu 1921'. In *Receptarea Sfintei Scripturi. Între filologie, hermeneutică și traductologie*, edited by Eugen Munteanu, 122–45. Iași: EUAIC, 2011.

Conțac, Emanuel. *Cornilescu: Din culisele publicării celei mai citite traduceri a Sfintei Scripturi*. Cluj-Napoca: Logos, 2014.

Curelaru, Mihai. 'Convertirea religioasă în comunitățile evanghelice – o abordare psihologică'. In *Omul evanghelic: O explorare a comunităților protestante românești*, edited by Dorin Dobrincu and Dănuț Mănăstireanu, 602–40. Iași: Polirom, 2018.

Dăncilă-Ineoan, Andreea, Marius Eppel and Ovidiu-Emil Iudean. *Voices of the Churches, Voices of the Nationalities: Competing Loyalties in the Upper House of the Hungarian Parliament (1867–1918)*. Berlin: Peter Lang, 2019.

Davis, R. Chris. *Hungarian Religion, Romanian Blood: A Minority's Struggle for National Belonging, 1920–1945*. Madison: University of Wisconsin Press, 2018.

Demacopoulos, George E. and Aristotle Papanikolaou. 'Orthodox Naming of the Other: A Postcolonial Approach'. In *Orthodox Constructions of the West*, edited by George E. Demacopoulos and Aristotle Papanikolaou, 1–22. New York: Fordham University Press, 2013.

Dimanopoulou, Pandora. 'L'oeuvre de la propagation de la foi et de la morale chrétienne dans la société grecque: L'action de la Confrérie Zôè en Grèce, 1907–1938'. *Revue d'Histoire Ecclésiastique* 105, no. 1 (2010): 121–46.

Djurić-Milovanić, Aleksandra. '"Our Father is Good, but Strict": The Transformation of the Apostolic Christian Church-Nazarene in North America'. *Journal of Amish and Plain Anabaptist Studies* 6, no. 1 (2018): 61–72.

Dobrincu, Dorin. 'Sub puterea Cezarului. O istorie politică a evanghelicilor din România (a doua jumătate a secolului al XIX-lea-1989)'. In *Omul evanghelic: O explorare a comunităților protestante românești*, edited by Dorin Dobrincu and Dănuț Mănăstireanu, 37–243. Iași: Polirom, 2018.

Doumanis, Nicholas. *Before the Nation: Muslim-Christian Coexistence and Its Destruction in Late Ottoman Anatolia*. Oxford: Oxford University Press, 2012.

Eliade, Mircea. *Zalmoxis, The Vanishing God: Comparative Studies in the Religions and Folklore of Dacia and Eastern Europe*. Chicago: University of Chicago Press, 1972.

Enache, George. 'Biserică – societate – națiune – stat în România interbelică: I. Explorări în orizont liberal'. *Revista teologică* 2 (2010): 166–202.

Evans, R. J. W. *The Making of the Habsburg Monarchy, 1550–1700*. Oxford: Clarendon Press, 1979.

Florovsky, Georges. *Ways of Russian Theology*. Vaduz: Büchervertriebsanst, 1979.

Franzén, Ruth. *Ruth Rouse Among Students: Global, Missiological and Ecumenical Perspectives*. Uppsala: Uppsala University, 2008.

Geantă, Nicolae. 'Dinamica teritorială a bisericilor evanghelice din România'. In *Omul evanghelic: O explorare a comunităților protestante românești*, edited by Dorin Dobrincu and Dănuț Mănăstireanu, 532–72. Iași: Polirom, 2018.

Geffert, Bryn. *Eastern Orthodox and Anglicans: Diplomacy, Theology, and the Politics of Interwar Ecumenism*. Notre Dame: University of Notre Dame Press, 2009.

Ghișa, Ciprian. 'Întărind vechi alterități, ridicând noi frontiere: Concordatul dintre România și Vatican – 1929'. *Studia Universitatis Babeș Bolyai – Theologia Catholica* 55, no. 4 (2010): 43–56.

Ghișa, Ciprian. 'The Greek-Catholic Discourse of Identity in the Inter-War Period: The Relation between the Nation and People's Religious Confession'. *Studia Universitatis Babeș-Bolyai Historia* 57, no. 2 (2012): 54–82.

Ghișa, Ciprian. 'The Image of the Roman Catholic Church in the Orthodox Press of Romania, 1918–1940'. In *Eastern Orthodox Encounters of Identity and Otherness: Values, Self-Reflection, Dialogue*, edited by Adreeii Krawchuk and Thomas Bremer, 109–23. New York: Palgrave Macmillan, 2014.

Gogan, Gheorghe. 'Viața și activitatea predicatorială a preotului Iosif Trifa'. MA diss., Universitatea 'Aurel Vlaicu', Arad, 2003.

Goncharova, Galina. 'The Bulgarian Orthodox Charity Network and the Movement for Practical Christianity After World War I'. In *Orthodox Christian Renewal Movements in Eastern Europe*, edited by Aleksandra Djurić Milovanović and Radmila Radić, 303–22. Cham: Palgrave Macmillan, 2017.

Gordon, Vasile and Silviu Tudose. 'The Development of Pastoral Studies: Homiletics, Catechetics and Pastoral Theology'. In *Orthodox Theology in the 20th Century and Early 21st Century: A Romanian Orthodox Perspective*, edited by Viorel Ioniță, 771–842. Bucharest: Basilica, 2013.

Green, Bernard. *Tomorrow's Man: A Biography of James Henry Rushbrooke*. Didcot: The Baptist Historical Society, 1997.

Grossu, Silvia. 'Impactul social al problemei modificării calendarului creștin'. In *Mitropolitul Gurie: Misiunea de credință și cultură*, edited by Silvia Grossu, 147–61. Chișinău: Epigraf, 2007.

Hanebrink, Paul. *In Defense of Christian Hungary: Religion, Nationalism, and Antisemitism, 1890–1944*. Ithaca: Cornell University Press, 2006.

Hausleitner, Mariana. *Die Rumänisierung der Bukowina: Die Durchsetzung des nationalstaatlichen Anspruchs Grossrumäniens 1918–1944*. Munich: R. Oldenbourg Verlag, 2001.

Heo, Angie. 'Imagining Holy Personhood: Anthropological Thresholds of the Icon'. In *Praying with the Senses: Contemporary Orthodox Christian Spirituality in Practice*, edited by Sonja Luehrmann, 83–102. Bloomington, IN: Indiana University Press, 2018.

Herrlinger, Page. 'Orthodoxy and the Politics of Emotion in the Case of "Brother Ioann" Churikov and His Followers, 1910–1914'. In *Orthodox Paradoxes: Heterogeneities and Complexities in Contemporary Russian Orthodoxy*, edited by Katya Tolstaya, 193–212. Leiden: Brill, 2014.

Himka, Jean-Paul. *Last Judgement Iconography in the Carpathians*. Toronto: University of Toronto Press, 2009.

Hitchins, Keith. 'Samuel Clain and the Rumanian Enlightenment in Transylvania', *Slavic Review* 23, no. 4 (1964): 660–75.

Hitchins, Keith. *Orthodoxy and Nationality: Andreiu Șaguna and the Rumanians of Transylvania, 1846–1873*. Cambridge, MA: Harvard University Press, 1977.

Hitchins, Keith. 'Religion and Rumanian National Consciousness in Eighteenth-Century Transylvania'. *The Slavonic and East European Review* 57, no. 2 (1979): 214–39.

Hitchins, Keith. *A Nation Affirmed: The Romanian National Movement in Transylvania 1860/1914*. Bucharest: The Encyclopaedic Publishing House, 1999.

Hitchins, Keith. *A Nation Discovered: Romanian Intellectuals in Transylvania and the Idea of Nation, 1700–1848*. Bucharest: The Encyclopaedic Publishing House, 1999.

Hitchins, Keith. *Rumania, 1866–1947*. Oxford: Oxford University Press, 2007.

Hitchins, Keith. *A Concise History of Romania*. Cambridge: Cambridge University Press, 2014.

Holmes, Janice. *Religious Revivals in Britain and Ireland, 1859–1905*. Dublin: Irish Academic Press, 2000.

Introvigne, Massimo. *The Plymouth Brethren*. Oxford: Oxford University Press, 2018.

Ionașcu, Stelian. 'Chanting in the Romanian Orthodox Church in a Pan-Orthodox Context'. In *Orthodox Theology in the 20th Century and Early 21st Century: A Romanian Orthodox Perspective*, edited by Viorel Ioniță, 859–67. Bucharest: Basilica, 2013.

Ioniță, Viorel. 'Orthodox Institutions of Theological Education: Key Factors in Promoting Orthodox Theology'. In *Orthodox Theology in the 20th Century and Early 21st Century: A Romanian Orthodox Perspective*, edited by Viorel Ioniță, 151–78. Bucharest: Basilica, 2013.

Iordachi, Constantin. 'From Imperial Entanglements to National Disentanglement: The "Greek Question" in Moldavia and Wallachia, 1611–1863'. In *Entangled Histories of the Balkans. Vol. 1: National Ideologies and Language Policies*, edited by Roumen Dontchev Daskalov and Tchavdar Marinov, 67–148. Leiden: Brill, 2013.

Isar, Nicolae. *Biserică-stat-societate în România modernă (1821–1914): Sinteză și culegere de documente*. Bucharest: Editura Universitară, 2014.

Kalaitzidis, Pantelis. 'Challenges of Renewal and Reformation Facing the Church'. *The Ecumenical Review* 61, no. 2 (2009): 136–64.

Kann, Robert. *A History of the Habsburg Empire 1526–1918*. Berkeley: University of California Press, 1977.

Kapaló, James A. *Inochentism and Orthodox Christianity: Religious Dissent in the Russian and Romanian Borderlands*. London: Routledge, 2019.

Kis-Juhász, Vilmos and Iulian Teodorescu. 'Bazele închinării evanghelice – Cazul evanghelicilor din România'. In *Omul evanghelic: O explorare a comunităților protestante românești*, edited by Dorin Dobrincu and Dănuț Mănăstireanu, 720–50. Iași: Polirom, 2018.

Klopfenstein, Perry. *Marching to Zion: A History of the Apostolic Christian Church of America*. 2nd edn. Eureka, IL: Apostolic Christian Church of America, 2008.

Končarević, Ksenija J. 'The Influence of the God Worshipper Movement on the Language Policy and Religious Service of the Serbian Orthodox Church'. In *Orthodox Christian Renewal Movements in Eastern Europe*, edited by Aleksandra Djurić Milovanović and Radmila Radić, 173–89. Cham: Palgrave Macmillan, 2017.

Krasniqi, Driton. 'The Development of Pentecostalism in South-Eastern European Nations: Albania, Bosnia and Herzegovina, Greece, Macedonia, Montenegro, Kosovo, Serbia'. In *European Pentecostalism*, edited by William K. Kay and Anne E. Dyer, 205–24. Leiden: Brill, 2011.

Kührer-Wielach, Florian. *Siebenbürgen ohne Siebenbürger?: Zentralstaatliche Integration und politischer Regionalismus nach dem Ersten Weltkrieg*. Munich: De Gruyter Oldenbourg, 2014.

Kührer-Wielach, Florian. 'Orthodoxer Jesuitismus, katholischer Mystizismus: Konfessionalismus in Rumänien nach dem Ersten Weltkrieg'. In *Orthodoxa*

Confessio?: Konfessionsbildung, Konfessionalisierung und ihre Folgen in der östlichen Christenheit, edited by Mihai-D. Grigore and Florian Kührer-Wielach, 305–48. Göttingen: Vandenhoeck & Ruprecht, 2018.

Ladouceur, Paul. '"In My Father's House There are Many Mansions" (Jn 14:2): New Institutions in Modern Orthodox Spirituality'. *St Vladimir's Theological Quarterly* 55, no. 4 (2011): 439–83.

Land, Gary. *Historical Dictionary of Seventh-Day Adventists*. Lanham, MA: Scarecrow Press, 2005.

Leustean, Lucian N. 'The Political Control of Orthodoxy in the Construction of the Romanian State, 1869–1914'. *European History Quarterly* 37, no. 1 (2007): 61–80.

Leustean, Lucian N. *Orthodoxy in the Cold War: Religion and Political Power in Romania, 1947–65*. Houndmills: Palgrave Macmillan, 2009.

Leustean, Lucian N. 'The Romanian Orthodox Church'. In *Orthodox Christianity and Nationalism in Nineteenth-Century Southeastern Europe*, edited by Lucian N. Leustean, 101–63. New York: Fordham University Press, 2014.

Livezeanu, Irina. *Cultural Politics in Greater Romania: Regionalism, Nation Building, and Ethnic Struggle, 1918–1930*. Ithaca: Cornell University Press, 1995.

Logotheti, Amaryllis. 'The Brotherhood of Theologians: Zoe and Its Influence on Twentieth-Century Greece'. In *Orthodox Christian Renewal Movements in Eastern Europe*, edited by Aleksandra Djurić Milovanović and Radmila Radić, 285–302. Cham: Palgrave Macmillan, 2017.

Maner, Hans-Christian. *Multikonfessionalität und neue Staatlichkeit: Orthodoxe, griechisch-katholische und römisch-katholische Kirche in Siebenbürgen und Altrumänien zwischen den Weltkriegen (1918–1940)*. Stuttgart: Franz Steiner Verlag, 2008.

Marian-Bălașa, Marin. 'Muzica în cadrul bisericilor minore: Funcții, identități și roluri socioculturale'. In *Omul evanghelic: O explorare a comunităților protestante românești*, edited by Dorin Dobrincu and Dănuț Mănăstireanu, 705–19. Iași: Polirom, 2018.

Marinescu, Adrian. 'Patrology and Related Studies in Orthodoxy in the 20th Century and Early 21st Century: Schools and Research Directions'. In *Orthodox Theology in the 20th Century and Early 21st Century: A Romanian Orthodox Perspective*, edited by Viorel Ioniță, 327–94. Bucharest: Basilica, 2013.

Marini, Nicolae. *Învățătorul Ioan Marini: O viață de apostol*. Sibiu: Editura Oastea Domnului, 2002.

Marini, Nicolae. *Oastea Domnului: Istoria jertfei în mărturisirile Pr. Iosif Trifa*. Available online: http://roboam.com/Ortodoxie/oastea_domnului.htm. Accessed 9 October 2019.

Matei, Eugen. 'Teologia evanghelicilor români: Rădăcini și perspective'. In *Omul evanghelic: O explorare a comunităților protestante românești*, edited by Dorin Dobrincu and Dănuț Mănăstireanu, 421–57. Iași: Polirom, 2018.

Măianu, Alexandru. *Viața și lucrarea lui Dumitru Cornilescu*. Bucharest: Editura Stephanus, 1995.

Mănăstireanu, Dănuț. 'Identitatea evanghelicilor români: rădăcini, actualitate, perspective'. In *Omul evanghelic: O explorare a comunităților protestante românești*, edited by Dorin Dobrincu and Dănuț Mănăstireanu, 244–96. Iași: Polirom, 2018.

Mercea, Lucian Ionel. 'The Concept of Sect in the Interwar Period'. In *The Holistic Society: Multi-Disciplinary Perspectives*, edited by Ioan-Gheorghe Rotaru and Denise Elaine Burrill, 192–205. Beltsville, MD: Scientia Moralitas Research Institute, 2017.

Meyendorff, John. *Byzantine Theology: Historical Trends and Doctrinal Themes*. 2nd edn. New York: Fordham University Press, 1983.

Michelson, Paul E. 'The History of Romanian Evangelicals 1918–1989: A Bibliographical Excursus'. *Arhiva Moladviae* 9 (2017): 191–234.

Mihoc, Vasile. 'The Development of the Biblical Studies'. In *Orthodox Theology in the 20th Century and Early 21st Century: A Romanian Orthodox Perspective*, edited by Viorel Ioniță, 179–242. Bucharest: Basilica, 2013.

Miller, Matthew Lee. *The American YMCA and Russian Culture: The Preservation and Expansion of Orthodox Christianity, 1900–1940*. Lanham, MD: Lexington Books, 2012.

Mitu, Sorin. *National Identity of Romanians in Transylvania*. Budapest: Central European University Press, 2001.

Moraru, Simion. 'Organizarea slujbelor și a cîntării bisericești în timpul Mitropolitului Gurie al Basarabiei'. In *Mitropolitul Gurie: Misiunea de credință și cultură*, edited by Silvia Grossu, 95–7. Chișinău: Epigraf, 2007.

Mureșan, Radu Petre. *Stilismul în România (1924–2011)*. Sibiu: Agnos, 2012.

Murgescu, Bogdan. *România și Europa: Acumularea decalajelor economice (1500–2010)*. Iași: Polirom, 2010.

Naumescu, Vlad. 'Becoming Orthodox: The Mystery and Mastery of a Christian Tradition'. In *Praying with the Senses: Contemporary Orthodox Christian Spirituality in Practice*, edited by Sonja Luehrmann, 29–54. Bloomington, IN: Indiana University Press, 2018.

Nicolencu, Viorica. *Extrema dreaptă în Basarabia (1923–1940)*. Chișinău: Civitas, 1999.

Oanța, Marius. 'Arhidieceza romano-catolică de București între România Mare și Republica Populară Română (1918–1948): Date statistice'. *Anuarul Institutului de Istorie George Barițiu din Cluj-Napoca*, 57 (2018): 335–44.

Oișteanu, Andrei. *Inventing the Jew: Antisemitic Stereotypes in Romanian and Other Central-East European Cultures*. Lincoln: University of Nebaska Press, 2009.

Onicov, Eugen. 'Viața monastică din Basarabia în cadrul României Mari (1918–1940)'. In *Monahismul ortodox românesc: Istorie, contribuții și repertorizare*, 867–94. Bucharest: Editura Basilica, 2014.

Papanikolaou, Aristotle, and George E. Demacopoulos, 'Introduction: Being as Tradition'. In *Fundamentalism or Tradition: Christianity after Secularism*, edited by

Aristotle Papanikolaou and George E. Demacopoulos, 1–17. New York: Fordham University Press, 2019.
Păcurariu, Mircea. *The Policy of the Hungarian State Concerning the Romanian Church in Transylvania Under the Dual Monarchy 1867–1918*. Bucharest: Bible and Mission Institute of the Romanian Orthodox Church, 1986.
Păcurariu, Mircea. *Istoria Bisericii Ortodoxe Române*. Sibiu: Patriarhul Bisericii Ortodoxe Române, 1991.
Păcurariu, Mircea. *Dicționarul teologilor români*. Available online: http://teologiromani.com/. Accessed 27 October 2019.
'Patriarhul Nicodim Munteanu', *Patriarhii României*. Available online: http://www.patriarh.ro/Nicodim/actpublicistica.php. Accessed 12 August 2019.
Petcu, Cristian Vasile. *Guvernarea Miron Cristea*. Bucharest: Editura Enciclopedică, 2009.
Petcu, Tudor, and Andy Besuden. 'The History of Jehovah's Witnesses in Hungary'. *Studia humana* 7, no. 2 (2018): 45–50.
Petreu, Marta. 'Istoria unui Plagiat: Nae Ionescu – Evelyn Underhill'. *România literară* 27, no. 49–50 (1994).
Petruescu, Andreea. 'Mișcarea stilistă în Basarabia, 1935–1936. Cauze și soluții. Perspective locale'. *Caietele CNSAS* 9, no. 1–2(17–18) (2016): 61–78.
Pfeiffer, Joseph F. 'Between Remnant and Renewal: A Historical and Comparative Study of the "Apostolic Christian Church" among Neo-Anabaptist Renewal Movements in Europe and America'. MA diss., Associated Mennonite Biblical Seminary, Elkhart, Indiana, 2010.
Plămădeală, Antonie. *Tradiție și libertate în spiritualitatea ortodoxă*. Bucharest: Sophia, 2010.
Ploscariu, Iemima. 'Pieties of the Nation: Romanian Neo-Protestants in the Interwar Struggle for Religious and National Identity'. MA diss., Central European University, Budapest, 2015.
Popa, Ion. 'Miron Cristea, the Romanian Orthodox Patriarch: His Political and Religious Influence in Deciding the Fate of the Romanian Jews (February 1938–March 1939)'. *Yad Vashem Studies* 40, no. 2 (2012): 11–34.
Pope, Earl A. 'Protestantism in Romania'. In *Protestantism and Politics in Eastern Europe and Russia: The Communist and Postcommunist Eras*, edited by Sabrina Petra Ramet, 157–208. Durham: Duke University Press, 1992.
Popovici, Alexa. *Istoria baptiștilor din România*. Oradea: Făclia, 2007.
Precupescu, Gheorghe. *Traian Dorz și vânturile potrivnice Oastei Domnului*. Sibiu: Editura Oastea Domnului, 2004.
Prenton, M. James. *Apocalypse Delayed: The Story of Jehovah's Witnesses*. 3rd edn. Toronto: University of Toronto Press, 2015.
Putney, Clifford. *Muscular Christianity: Manhood and Sports in Protestant America, 1880–1920*. Cambridge, MA: Harvard University Press, 2001.

Radić, Radmila and Aleksandra Djurić Milovanović. 'The God Worshipper Movement in Serbian Society in the Twentieth Century: Emergence, Development, and Structures'. In *Orthodox Christian Renewal Movements in Eastern Europe*, edited by Aleksandra Djurić Milovanović and Radmila Radić, 137–72. Cham: Palgrave Macmillan, 2017.

Raiu, Cătălin. *Democrație și statolatrie: Creștinismul social la Bartolomeu Stănescu, Episcopul Râmnicului Noului Severin (1875–1954)*. Bucharest: Editura Universității din București, 2014.

Răduț, Bogdan Emanuel. 'Comunitatea creștinilor după Evanghelie: 100 ani în Oltenia și 90 ani la Craiova'. *Oltenia: Studii, documente, cercetări* 4, no. 2 (2014): 111–21.

Renders, Helmut. 'As origens do livro emblemático *O coração do ser humano* (1812) de Johannes Evangelista Gossner: continuidade e releituras da religio cordis nos séculos 16 a 19'. *Protestantismo em Revista* 29 (2012): 65–78.

Rotar, Marius. 'Alcoholism in Transylvania in the Second Half of the Nineteenth Century and Early Twentieth Century'. *The International Journal of Regional and Local Studies* 3, no. 2 (2007): 41–64.

Rushbrooke, James Henry. *The Baptist Movement in the Continent of Europe*. London: The Carey Press, 1923.

Rusu, Ieremia. *Cine sunt Creștinii după Evanghelie? Curente teologice care au influențat doctrinele specifice ale Bisericilor Creștine după Evanghelie din România în perioada interbelică și comunistă*. Bucharest: Editura Didactică și Pedagogică, 2011.

Samson, Jim. *Music in the Balkans*. Leiden: Brill, 2013.

Săsăujan, Mihai. 'Țara Românească și Moldova'. In *Monahismul ortodox românesc: Istorie, contribuții și repertorizare*, 607–40. Bucharest: Editura Basilica, 2014.

Schmemann, Alexander. *The Historical Road of Eastern Orthodoxy*. Crestwood, NY: St Vladimir's Seminary Press, 1963.

Schneider, Johann. *Der Hermannstädter Metropolit Andrei von Șaguna: Reform und Erneuerung der orthodoxen Kirche in Siebenbürgen und Ungarn nach 1848*. Köln: Böhlau, 2005.

Serafim. *Isihasmul: Tradiție și cultură românească*. Bucharest: Editura Anastasia, 1994.

Setran, David P. *The College Y: Student Religion in the Era of Secularization*. New York: Palgrave Macmillan, 2007.

Shevzov, Vera. *Russian Orthodoxy on the Eve of Revolution*. Oxford: Oxford University Press, 2004.

Silveșan, Marius. *Bisericile creștine baptiste din România între persecuție, acomodare și rezistență (1948–1965)*. Târgoviște: Editura Cetatea de Scaun, 2012.

Silveșan, Marius, and Vasile Bel. *Rolul lui James Henry Rushbrooke în obținerea libertății religioase pentru credincioșii baptiști din România între anii 1907–1947*. Cluj-Napoca: Editura Risoprint, 2017.

Soica, Sergiu. *Biserica Greco-Catolică din Banat în perioada anilor 1920–1948*. Timișoara: Editura Eurostampa, 2011.

Sperlea, Petre. *Vartolomeu Stănescu: Episcop al Râmnicului Noului Severin (1921-1938)*. Bucharest: Basilica, 2014.

Stănciulescu-Bârda, Alexandru. *Bibliografia revistei 'Biserica Ortodoxă Română' (1874-1994)*. Bârda: Editura Cuget Românesc, 2000.

Stan, Constantin I. *Patriarhul Miron Cristea: o viață, un destin*. Bucharest: Editura Paideia, 2009.

Stanley, Brian. *The History of the Baptist Missionary Society 1792-1992*. Edinburgh: T&T Clark, 1992.

Steuer, Kenneth. *Pursuit of an 'Unparalleled Opportunity': American YMCA and Prisoner of War Diplomacy among the Central Power Nations during World War I, 1914-1923*. New York: Columbia University Press, 2009.

Streza, Laurențiu. 'Liturgical Space'. In *Orthodox Theology in the 20th Century and Early 21st Century: A Romanian Orthodox Perspective*, edited by Viorel Ioniță, 591-603. Bucharest: Basilica, 2013.

Stunt, Timothy C. F. 'John Nelson Darby: Contexts and Perceptions'. In *Protestant Millennialism, Evangelicalism, and Irish Society, 1790-2005*, edited by Crawford Gribben and Andrew R. Holmes, 83-98. Basingstoke: Palgrave Macmillan, 2006.

Stylianopoulos, Theodore G. 'Scripture and Tradition in the Church'. In *The Cambridge Companion to Orthodox Christian Theology*, edited by Mary B. Cunningham and Elizabeth Theokritoff, 21-34. Cambridge: Cambridge University Press, 2008.

Surugiu, Romina. 'Nae Ionescu on Democracy, Individuality, Leadership and Nation: Philosophical (Re)sources for a Right-Wing Ideology'. *Journal for the Study of Religions and Ideologies* 8, no. 23 (2009): 68-81.

Țon, Iosif. *Credința adevărată*. Wheaton, IL: Societatea Misionară Română, 1988.

Ursul, George R. 'From Political Freedom to Religious Independence: The Romanian Orthodox Church, 1877-1925'. In *Romania Between East and West: Historical Essays in Memory of Constantin C. Giurescu*, edited by Stephen Fischer-Galati, Radu Florescu and George Ursul, 217-44. Boulder: East European Monographs, 1982.

Vance, Laura L. 'God's Messenger: Ellen G. White'. In *Female Leaders in New Religious Movements*, edited by Inga B. Tøllefsen and Christian Giudice, 29-49. New York: Palgrave Macmillan, 2017.

Vanhaelemeersch, Philip. *A Generation 'Without Beliefs' and the Idea of Experience in Romania (1927-1934)*. Boulder, CO: East European Monographs, 2006.

Vicovan, Ion. *Ion Irineu Mihălcescu: 'Apostol al teologiei românești'*. Iași: Trinitas, 2006.

Wanner, Catherine. *Communities of the Converted: Ukrainians and Global Evangelism*. Ithaca: Cornell University Press, 2007.

Weibel, Luc. *Croire à Genève: La Salle de la Réformation (XIX-XXe siècle)*. Geneva: Labor et Fides, 2006.

Wien, Ulrich Andreas. 'Biserica Evanghelică C.A. din România începând cu anul 1918'. In *Un veac frământat. Germanii din România după 1918*, edited by Ottmar Trașcă and Remus Gabriel Anghel, 199-252. Cluj-Napoca: Institutul pentru Studierea Problemelor Minorităților Naționale, 2018.

Wilson, Robert S. 'Coming of Age: The Post-War Era and the 1920s'. In *Baptists Together in Christ, 1905–2005: A Hundred Year History of the Baptist World Alliance*, edited by Richard V. Pierard, 47–72. Birmingham, AL: Samford University Press, 2005.

Wittstock, Oskar. *Johannes Honterus, der Siebenbürger Humanist und Reformator: der Mann, das Werk, die Zeit*. Göttingen: Vandenhoeck und Ruprecht, 1970.

Wright, Stephen. *The Early English Baptists, 1603–49*. Woodbridge: Boydell, 2006.

Yannaras, Christos. *Orthodoxy and the West*. Brookline, MA: Holy Cross Orthodox Press, 2006.

Zhuk, Sergei I. *Russia's Lost Reformation: Peasants, Millenialism, and Radical Sects in Southern Russia and Ukraine, 1830–1917*. Washington, DC: Woodrow Wilson Center Press, 2004.

Index

alcohol 8, 12, 30, 103, 116, 118, 134, 148–51, 155–6, 161, 194–6
Andriene Theological Academy, Sibiu 40–1, 59
anti-sectarianism 3, 6, 8, 39–40, 125–39, 147, 154, 161, 166, 170, 179–80, 190, 194–5, 197
antisemitism 9, 40–1, 43–4, 46, 65, 80, 118, 122, 125, 132–4, 147, 150–1, 161, 163, 165, 179, 187, 197
atheism 1, 3, 133, 136, 151, 195

Bălan, Nicolae 5, 9, 33, 41, 68, 70, 94, 96, 132, 143–5, 147–8, 154, 161–6, 172, 175, 193–4, 200
baptism 7, 20–1, 23, 83, 102–3, 106, 111–12, 129, 131, 133–5, 182, 190
  of the Holy Spirit 114, 116
Bible
  authority of 30, 35, 45, 101–2, 135, 157, 180–1, 196
  hermeneutics 9, 11, 15, 24, 29–31, 47, 103, 113, 121, 136, 181, 196
  reading 8, 19–22, 24, 35–6, 40, 47, 103–6, 109, 120–1, 138, 145, 148, 152–3, 155, 161, 175–6, 181–2, 194–5
  translation 1–2, 60, 135, 137, 172–4, 178, 188, 195
Bible Students 7, 15, 119–23, 125, 136
Brătianu, Ionel 68–9, 71–3

Călinescu, Ștefan 22, 26–9, 200
Callimachi, Ralu 172–3, 187
catechization 13, 20–3, 28–9, 135, 137–8
Catholicism 4, 32–3, 38, 44, 57, 60, 87–99, 144–5, 167, 183, 196
Central Theological Seminary, Bucharest 4, 170, 180
Chiricuță, Toma 37, 201
Church
  Adventist, Seventh Day 1, 7–8, 15, 36, 116–19, 125, 130–1, 134–6, 144, 147, 156, 170, 174, 176, 183–4

Anglican 1, 3–4, 14, 38, 46, 145, 147–8, 167, 178, 185–6
Baptist 6–10, 15, 36, 47 n.67, 101–12, 114, 116, 125, 132–6, 144, 172, 176, 184
Brethren (*Creștini după Evanghelie*) 1–2, 7, 9, 15, 36, 101, 109–10, 114, 125, 166, 176, 190
Bulgarian Orthodox 13–14, 45, 88–9
Evangelical Lutheran 6, 95, 111–12, 126, 131, 144, 177
Greek Catholic 5, 15, 31, 57–9, 63, 69, 72, 87–93, 95–9, 107, 131–2, 136–7, 144–5, 154, 174, 186
Greek Orthodox 12–13, 31, 45, 51–3, 56–7
Methodist 32, 107, 116
Nazarene 7, 15, 102, 111–13, 125, 127, 156, 195
Pentecostal 7–9, 15, 102, 113–16, 125, 132, 134
Reformed 6, 8, 32, 94–5, 112, 126, 144, 177
Roman Catholic 1, 5, 15, 32, 60, 63, 67, 88–9, 93–9, 112, 116, 131, 137, 160–1, 183
Romanian Orthodox passim
Russian Orthodox 9–12, 31–2, 45, 51, 61–2, 78–9, 127–8, 133, 157, 160, 171
Serbian Orthodox 2, 9–10, 12, 23, 45, 58, 60, 112, 127, 171, 195
church–state relations 3, 15, 38–9, 51–74, 81–2, 84–5, 90–1, 93–9, 106, 109, 112–13, 115, 117–18, 122–3, 127–8, 132–3, 137–8, 145–7, 178, 184, 190–1
cinema 85, 103, 130–1, 138, 191
Colan, Nicolae 31–2
Colporteur 107, 110, 119
communism 38–9, 46, 66, 133, 147, 171, 187
Comșa, Grigorie Gh. 3, 19, 29–30, 129–38, 194, 201

concordat 15, 87, 93, 95–7, 145
Constitution of Romania 4, 54, 59, 69, 71–3, 96, 108, 138
conversion 6, 8, 47, 58, 98, 104–7, 110, 112, 114, 116, 121, 126–7, 129, 153, 156–7, 161, 169, 171–2, 175, 185, 187
Cornilescu, Dumitru 5, 170–89, 194, 196, 200–1
corruption, accusations of 2, 41, 92, 110, 134, 146, 151–2, 157, 161, 163–5, 178, 188
Crainic, Nichifor 48, 97–99, 165, 187, 202
Cristea, Miron (Ilie) 4, 9, 28, 33, 42, 46, 51, 64–73, 81, 85, 149, 187, 190, 193, 202
Cristescu, Grigore 30, 37, 41, 147, 194, 202
Cuza, A. C. 41, 151
Cuza, Alexandru Ion 53–4

Dorz, Traian 159, 166, 202, 204

Eliade, Mircea 44
end times, *see* eschatology
eschatology 77–8, 109–10, 115–16, 120–1, 123
ethnography 19–20, 22
Evangelicalism 2–5, 8–10, 45, 105, 125, 152, 161, 167, 173, 176

fascism 9, 40–1, 48, 97, 137, 153, 163, 165, 197
Federation of Christian Students' Associations in Romania (FASCR) 42–9, 194
Feodorovna, Elizabeth 11–12
France 4, 38, 44, 53, 98, 119–20, 160, 172–3, 187, 195
Frollo, Iosif 98

Galaction, Gala 31, 33, 37–9, 46–8, 130, 171, 173, 179, 181, 183–4, 186–7, 194, 202
Georgescu, Ion V. 30–1, 41, 202
Georgescu, Pimen 42, 46
Germans, ethnic, *see* Saxons
Germany 4, 6–7, 32, 81, 98, 104, 108, 110–11, 117, 120, 144, 161–2, 166, 187, 195

God worshippers 12–13
Goga, Octavian 69, 165, 169–70
Great Britain 1–3, 32, 42, 45, 60, 71, 95, 97, 102, 107–9, 113, 147, 174, 176, 178, 184–5, 187, 189, 195
Grosu, Gurie 5, 27, 33, 41, 46, 62, 70, 72, 81–3, 128–9, 149, 193, 203
Gusti, Dumitru 44

Hacman, Eugenie 61
healing, by faith 113–4
holiness 12–15, 28, 36, 40, 101, 103, 109, 113–14, 117–18, 121, 139, 148, 155–6, 177, 184, 194–5
Hossu, Iuliu 64, 96
Hungarians 6–7, 44–5, 57, 59, 63–4, 67, 87, 90–6, 101, 111–12, 120, 133–4, 146, 151

icons 21, 23–5, 36–7, 84, 103, 118, 130, 138, 161, 184, 194
Ionescu, Marin C. 30, 188, 201
Ionescu, Nae 44, 46–8, 79, 97–9, 178, 203
Ionescu, Ștefan 39
Iorga, Nicolae 3, 42, 56, 73, 88, 203
Imbrescu, Ilie 130–1, 138, 203
Inochentie of Balta 78–9
Inochentism 15, 62, 77–80, 101, 125, 128, 147
Ispir, Vasile 39, 45, 127, 203

justification by faith 102–3, 158, 167, 169, 172, 176, 179–82, 196

lay ministry 1–5, 12, 32, 47, 54, 58–62, 70, 80, 91–2, 130, 138–9, 157, 189–90, 193, 196
Legion of the Archangel Michael 9, 40–1, 60, 163, 165
Levizor, Ioan, *see* Inochentie of Balta
literacy 1, 9, 19, 24, 84, 144–5, 148, 195
liturgy 5, 19, 21, 24, 30, 33, 41, 52, 72 n.113, 77, 84, 88–9, 111, 129, 131, 179–80, 194–5
Lord's Army, the (*Oastea Domnului*) 5, 8–11, 15, 138, 143–67, 188, 193–4
Lossky, Vladimir 32
Lumina satelor (*The Light of the Villages*) 5, 143–66

magazines, *see* newspapers
Magyars, *see* Hungarians
Marini, Ioan 159, 162, 166, 204
Martha and Mary House of Mercy, the 11–12
Mary, Mother of God 21, 25, 45, 103, 118, 162, 177, 179–80, 183–4
Mehedinți, Simion 37, 42, 67
Meteș, Ștefan 32
Mețianu, Ion 62–4
Micu-Klein, Ion Inochențiu 89–90
Mihălcescu, Irineu 5, 33, 41, 131, 167, 171, 179–80, 182, 184, 186, 194, 197, 204
military chaplains 54, 186
Ministry of Denominations 45, 53, 55, 119, 126, 131, 169, 190
missionaries
    Orthodox 8, 10, 14–15, 62, 85, 88, 126–39, 154, 166, 183
    Protestant 1, 3, 7, 45–6, 48, 103–4, 107, 109–10, 116, 121, 177, 183
Mladin, Nicolae 41
Moga, Vasile 58, 61
Moldovan, Valer 69, 91
monasticism 26–7, 77–80, 84, 130, 138, 160, 172, 178
Morușca, Pomponiu 40
Moța, Ion 163–6, 204
Munteanu, Nicodim 21–2, 46, 171 n.14, 173
music, *see* singing

Nanu, Dimitrie 37, 178, 204
National Christian Defense League 9, 41, 83, 151
National Liberal Party 41, 51, 68, 73, 89, 193
National Peasantist Party 41, 68–9, 74
National Union of Christian Students in Romania (UNSCR) 43, 45–7
Nazarie, Constantin 170, 184, 194, 204
Neaga, Nicolae 40
neo-Protestants, *see* Repenters
newspapers 3–6, 9, 13–14, 27, 54, 59, 62, 79, 83, 97, 106, 110, 112, 119, 125, 128–9, 138, 143–4, 152–3, 162–4, 175, 185–6, 195–6, 198–9
Nițulescu, Nicolae 172–3
Noua revistă bisericească 35, 175, 180–3, 188

Old Calendarism (*Stilism*) 5, 15, 77, 80–5, 101, 125, 194
Orthodoxism 48, 96–7, 188

Păcescu, Teodor 31, 35–36, 179–80, 182–3, 186, 194, 197, 205
pacifism 112–13, 118, 122
Pâclișanu, Zenovie 92, 205
Pârvulescu, Sebastian 56, 88, 205
Patriarchate, Romanian Orthodox 15, 51, 73, 193
peasants 9–10, 15, 19–20, 22, 30, 57–8, 78–85, 101–23, 125–39, 141, 143–60, 190
persecution 12, 57–9, 62–3, 65, 67, 79–80, 84, 91, 93–5, 104, 108, 112, 115, 118–19, 122, 126, 132, 138–9, 145, 175, 186, 190–1
philanthropy, *see* poverty
Pișculescu, Grigorie, *see* Galaction, Gala
Plămădeală, Antonie 11
Poctian, Vasile, *see* Pocitan, Veniamin
Pocitan, Veniamin 41, 89, 205
police 8, 12, 43–4, 64, 79, 82–5, 95, 108, 110, 112–15, 117–23, 125, 132, 138, 155, 161, 164, 184, 187–91, 193
Popescu, Manea S. 180–3, 194, 201
Popescu, Teodor 5, 130, 169–70, 175–91, 194, 205
Popescu-Mălăești, Ioan 5, 40, 194
Popescu-Mozăceni, Ion 41
poverty 13, 29, 44, 55, 128, 134, 137–8, 146, 151, 185
prayer 2, 8, 21–6, 29–30, 37, 47–8, 52, 64–5, 83–4, 103, 106, 109, 114–15, 117, 126, 130, 137, 150, 154–5, 158, 172, 175, 179–80, 189, 195
preaching 9, 27–31, 37, 40, 78, 105–7, 110, 115, 117, 127, 129–30, 137, 143, 145–9, 151, 154–5, 157–8, 160, 170, 175, 178–9, 184, 186, 190, 194
priests
    and politics 40–2, 52–3, 66
    criticism of 1, 56, 59, 119, 132, 134, 136–7, 178, 188
    education of 1, 30–1, 39–40, 45, 55–6, 59–60, 63, 137, 170, 180–1, 194, 196
    role of 26–7, 30, 37–40, 52, 129–30, 143
proselytism 85, 104–7, 110, 125, 132, 134, 152–3, 155, 157, 175, 184–5, 189–90, 195

Protestantism 1, 6, 32, 35–6, 45, 47–8, 139, 147, 161–2, 167, 172, 176–8, 181–6, 194–6
Puiu, Visarion 5, 27, 30, 33, 41, 83, 139, 193, 205

Racoveanu, Gheorghe 41
Radu, Vasile 171, 173
Rebirth (*Renașterea*) movement 5, 39–40, 193
reform, religious 1, 4–5, 9–11, 14, 32, 33, 35–41, 58–9, 61–2, 81, 92, 111, 151, 194, 196
religiosity, lack of 1–3, 35–6, 136, 149
repentance 5, 8, 12, 25, 36, 78, 103, 111, 115, 151, 157–60, 165
Repenters 6–10, 14–15, 33, 36, 46, 62, 80, 99, 101–23, 125–39, 147, 151, 155–9, 161, 166–7, 174, 189–91, 193–7
Romanian Christian Students' Association (ASCR), *see* Federation of Christian Students' Associations in Romania (FASCR)
Romanul, Miron 62–3
Rouse, Ruth 1–4
Rushbrooke, James Henry 107–8
Russia 9–12, 31–2, 42–3, 45, 51, 61–2, 66, 72, 74, 78–80, 82, 84, 93, 98, 101, 104–5, 116–17, 119, 125, 127–8, 133, 157, 160–1, 171, 173, 193
Rusu, Alexandru 92

Sadoveanu, Mihail 37
Șaguna, Andrei 59–61, 64, 69
saints 23–4, 78, 80, 103, 117–18, 162, 179–80, 183–4, 194
Savin, Ioan Gheorghe 41, 133, 205
Saxons 6–7, 67, 101, 104, 109, 119, 134
schools 13, 19–22, 26, 36, 57, 59, 64, 67–8, 70, 85, 94–6, 106, 110, 117, 126–8, 133, 136–8, 144–5, 156, 162, 171, 180, 184–5
Scriban, Iuliu 4–5, 11, 24, 30–33, 81, 98, 162, 167, 170–1, 173, 175, 184, 185, 194, 205
secularization of church property 26–7, 53, 55, 93, 132
Simedrea, Tit 48, 84

singing 25, 85, 107, 117, 128, 130, 134, 138, 155–6, 158–60, 175, 177–8, 189
Social Christianity 14, 38–40, 44, 47, 49, 60, 196–7
socialism 122, 171
Solidaritatea (*Solidarity*) 5, 39, 175
soteriology 102–3, 111, 125, 135, 158, 169, 177, 180–2
Stan, Liviu 41, 60
state socialism 13, 79, 112, 133, 166, 190–1
Stănescu, Vartolomeu 5, 9, 14, 33, 38–42, 44, 60, 71, 126, 137–8, 175, 193, 206
Stăniloae, Dumitru 32
Stork's Nest, the 5, 9–11, 15, 169–91, 194
students 1, 4, 13–14, 20–1, 30–2, 40–9, 67, 127, 130, 143, 151, 163, 165, 170–1, 175, 194
Șuluțiu, Alexandru Șterca 59
Switzerland 4, 7, 95, 104, 109–11, 120, 170–1, 177, 184–5, 187, 195

Take and Read (*Ia și citește*) 5, 193
teetotaller (*trezvenniki*) movement 12
temperance, *see* alcohol
tradition 11–12, 23, 25, 47, 60, 71, 97, 146, 161, 181, 193, 196–7
Trifa, Iosif 5, 137, 143–67, 175–6, 194, 196, 206
Tudor, Sandu 47–8

United States of America 32, 42, 45–6, 48, 104–5, 107–8, 112–14, 116, 120–2, 134, 147, 152–3, 157, 165, 171, 174, 176–7, 195

Velimirović, Nikolaj 23
Vulcănescu, Mircea 44, 47–8

White Cross fraternity 13–14
Witnesses, Jehovah's, *see* Bible Students
women 3, 11–14, 38, 44, 79, 110, 114, 117, 122, 126, 134, 146, 149, 171–2, 175, 185, 189
World Christian Student Federation 1, 4

YMCA 14, 42–9, 176, 178, 196

Zoe movement 12–13

www.ingramcontent.com/pod-product-compliance
Lightning Source LLC
Chambersburg PA
CBHW072232290426
44111CB00012B/2056